IT'S THE MEDIA, STUPID!

Essays in Honour of Brian Winston

Edited by
Richard Lance Keeble

Published 2022 by Abramis academic publishing

www.abramis.co.uk

ISBN 978 1 84549 796 5

© Richard Lance Keeble 2022

All rights reserved

This book is copyright. Subject to statutory exception and to provisions of relevant collective licensing agreements, no part of this publication may be reproduced, stored in a retrieval system, or transmitted in any form or by any means, without the prior written permission of the author.

This book is sold subject to the conditions that it shall not, by way of trade or otherwise, be lent, re-sold, hired out, or otherwise circulated without the publisher's prior consent in any form of binding or cover other than that which it is published and without a similar condition including this condition being imposed on the subsequent purchaser.

Abramis is an imprint of arima publishing.

arima publishing
ASK House, Northgate Avenue
Bury St Edmunds, Suffolk IP32 6BB
t: (+44) 01284 700321

www.arimapublishing.com

About the Editor

Richard Lance Keeble is Professor of Journalism at the University of Lincoln and Honorary Professor at Liverpool Hope University. He has written and edited 44 books on a wide range of media-related topics. Chair of The Orwell Society (2013-2020), he edited *Orwell Today* (2012) and *George Orwell Now!* (2015) and he is the author of *Orwell's Moustache* (2021). In 2020, Routledge published a collection of his recent essays – on George Orwell, literary journalism, war and peace reporting, and journalists and the secret state under the title *Journalism Beyond Orwell*. He is emeritus editor of *Ethical Space: The International Journal of Communication Ethics* which he launched in 2003 and joint editor of *George Orwell Studies*. In 2011, he gained a National Teaching Fellowship, the highest award for teachers in higher education in the UK, and in 2014 he was given a Lifetime Achievement Award by the Association for Journalism Education. He is a member of Louth Male Voice Choir, Louth Film Club and (through thick and thin) Nottinghamshire County Cricket Club..

Contents

PREFACE

How Brian Winston Helped Turn Shibboleths of Traditional Universities on Their Head 1
David Chiddick

INTRODUCTION

The Search for Understanding 3
Richard Lance Keeble

SECTION 1. DOCUMENTARY, CLAIMING THE REAL AND BEYOND

Chapter 1. The Documentaries of Magnus Isacsson (1948-2012): A Case Study in the Local and the Global 27
Tom Waugh

Chapter 2. Naïve Realism: Repositioning Kracauer's Theory 39
Deane Williams

Chapter 3. Covid-19 Conspiracy Documentary: Claiming the Real in a Context of Uncertainty 52
Kate Nash

Chapter 4. The Act of Watching Documentary 65
Annette Hill

SECTION 2. FREE EXPRESSION, OFFENCE AND CRITICAL HUMAN RIGHTS

Chapter 5. Humans as Cultural Beings in Theory and Practice 77
Clifford G. Christians

Chapter 6. Doing Harm: How the UK Government Threatens to Impose Online Censorship 94
Julian Petley

Chapter 7. The Price of Ridiculing the Prophet: The *Charlie Hebdo* Affair 110
Raphael Cohen-Almagor

SECTION 3. OBJECTIONS TO OBJECTIVITY: POLITICS AND ETHICS OF THE MEDIA

Chapter 8.	Fake News, Double Spin and Strategic Lying in the Post-Truth Era *Ivor Gaber*	125
Chapter 9.	The Media of the Past Determining the Politics of the Future? *Martin Conboy*	139
Chapter 10.	Towards Restorative Narrative *Pratāp Rughani*	151

APPENDIX 1.

Beyond the Bog-Standard Grammar School 163
Richard Lance Keeble in conversation with Brian Winston

APPENDIX 2.

Professor Brian Winston: 179
The Range and Depth of his Academic Achievements

INDEX 189

Preface

How Brian Winston Helped Turn Shibboleths of Traditional Universities on Their Head

David Chiddick

A few of the academic pioneers in the formative years of the University of Lincoln were gathered in an area outside my office, waiting for their external examiner to collect his thoughts, before the end-of-year examination board. I asked who he was and then followed not only a reverential account of the examiner's academic standing but also a fulsome appreciation of his generosity in coming to this embryonic backwater of a university to help develop a new and ambitious degree programme. At the end of the board meeting Brian Winston dropped in to my office to tell me how impressed he was with the quality of the work on the degree.

Within a week, Brian had taken a bold and courageous step to take up the first senior professorial appointment at the new University of Lincoln. I cannot overstate the importance of this decision to join what many others at the time saw as a pretentious upstart of a university. I recall a government official forcefully telling me that we should focus on teaching rather than be distracted by research. She was unimpressed by the truth that universities cannot use that handle if they do not contribute to the development of the subject they teach, through research. Thank goodness for the relative independence of universities.

Brian's appointment was the first of many – a stream of some sixty world-class academics joined the university within two years – mainly, initially, because Brian Winston 'was there'.

Culturally, Brian helped turn shibboleths of traditional universities on their head. The professors would teach the first-year undergraduates and inspire all, even the most intransigent, academics to add to the body of knowledge in their discipline, in some form.

At the beginning of the week, walking through the atrium of one of just three buildings on campus at the time, I would often meet an academic member of Brian's faculty to discuss the failings of our rugby teams at the weekend. One morning he looked ashen. Brian had asked this member of his faculty if he would mind stepping in for him to give a paper at an international conference in the US. An excellent teacher, Brian's colleague had never undertaken research, let alone given a paper at the annual conference in his own discipline. On his return the blood had flowed back into his face and he was exhilarated. Five years later, by then an esteemed researcher in his own right, that academic hosted the same international conference at Lincoln. Inclusivity, not a word normally associated with academics at the time, permeated the culture at Lincoln and led to what *The Sunday Times* referred to as the 'most dramatic transformation of a university in recent times'.

It is so appropriate that Professor Brian Winston holds the unique distinction of The Lincoln Professor and that this publication celebrates his commitment to his discipline, higher education and Lincoln. He was the catalyst for the establishment of a world-class faculty, but more than that he was and is generous, inclusive, empowering and transformative.

NOTE ON THE CONTRIBUTOR

Professor David Chiddick, CBE, is the founding Vice-Chancellor of the University of Lincoln. An urban economist and town planner, David focused academically and in practice on urban regeneration in inner cities. At Lincoln, David developed with others the concept of 'enabling development frameworks' to facilitate viable investment in inner cities – a methodology now widely used in planning and development projects globally. Playing a part in the growth of Lincoln academically, whilst transforming the run-down infrastructure and economic base of the city of Lincoln, was a perfect match for David. In 2008, he chaired a £750,000 research project on 'learning landscapes' with ten universities. The project explored the paradigm shift in learning and teaching over recent decades and exemplars of responses by universities to this change. David retired in 2009, but has continued to be involved in university-led regeneration projects in Ireland, with a focus on sustainable development and social housing.

Introduction

The Search for Understanding

Richard Lance Keeble

Brian Winston has a favourite joke which he never tires of telling: every morning during his trans-Atlantic voyage, an eastern European immigrant arrives at his breakfast table to be greeted by his companion, a Frenchman, with the phrase: 'Bon appetit.' On the first morning, somewhat surprised, the immigrant replies courteously: 'Goldberg,' shakes the hand of his companion and sits down. On the third day of the voyage the mistake is pointed out to him. So on the fourth day he arrives primed. Before the Frenchman can speak, Goldberg utters a loud and cordial: 'Bon appetit' to which the Frenchman replies urbanely: 'Goldberg.'[1]

Brian tells me that most Jewish jokes are based on such misunderstandings. And in a way, Brian's career as an academic researcher, writer and teacher has sought – at root – to replace misunderstanding with understanding. Significantly, the joke appears on the very first page of his first published text, *The Image of the Media* (1973) – and after a quote from a Joni Mitchell song: 'They've paved Paradise and put up a parking lot' (his writings and talks bursting with eclectic cultural references like this). He goes on to place the plight of Goldberg and the Frenchman in broader cultural context: 'The mass of messages generated by our communication systems serve often to confuse rather than to clarify. Instead of reducing our overall uncertainties the messages that bombard us increase them. Indeed, for many the very apparatus that generates the messages is a source of confusion.' In the face of this confusion, Brian (through his vast *oeuvre*) has, then, sought to promote understanding and to bring some order to the chaos.

A CAREER TO CELEBRATE

Brian has had a glittering career – which this *festschrift* seeks to celebrate. The number of prestigious awards gained, in itself, reflects the depth, breadth, significance and originality of his work – in both the media industry and the academy. In 1985, he was the recipient of a US National Emmy for an 'outstanding individual achievement writing for an information series', namely Episode 8 of *Heritage*. The same script also gained him a US Christopher Award. In the following year, the Communications Institute at Jerusalem University gave him the Joss Award.

In 1999, his *Media Technology and Society: A History from the Telegraph to the Internet* won him the prize for the Best Book of the Year, 1998, from the American Association of History and Computing. In 2012, the British University Film and Video Council gave him the Special Jury Award for his *A Boatload of Wild Irishmen*, a 90-minute documentary about the life and film work of Robert Flaherty. Two years later, following the publication of *The Rushdie* Fatwa *and After: A Lesson to the Circumspect*, he was the recipient of a Special Prize for 'increasing understanding of human rights' from the International Press Institute (Vienna) Book Awards.

The accolades have been many. According to Betsy McLane, writing in *A New History of Documentary* (New York, Continuum, 2012: 3): 'Teachers and writers who helped shape the emergent field [of Documentary Studies] included … especially, Brian Winston in England, who succeeds both as a filmmaker and a scholar. Winston's keen, witty and adversarial writings are perhaps the most challenging and entertaining in the field.' John Kampfner, former chief executive of Index on Censorship, commented in the *British Journalism Review*: 'Brian Winston's *A Right to Offend* provides two important contributions to this fraught and often under-researched debate. He brings a welcome international scope to his inquiry, guiding the reader through the differing legal systems of, say, France and the US. But it is his frequent recourse to history that is most instructive. … A highly readable and informative compendium on freedom of expression.' Also on *A Right to Offend*, Professor Larry Gross, of the Annenberg School for Communication and Journalism, offered these words of praise: 'As usual, Brian Winston is an ideal guide to the past as well as the present and even future challenges faced by those who are devoted to preserving this most basic human right.' While the citation for the International Press Institute's Special Award in 2014 following the publication of *The Rushdie* Fatwa *and After: A Lesson to the Circumspect* read: 'This is a sensible, scholarly passionate explanation … of a crucial position that bulwarks all our human rights. It is also an immensely timely contribution to current debates.'

Brian has also occupied some major roles in the industry and academy. After studying law at Merton College, Oxford (and remaining a devoted and active alumnus ever since), he began a two-year stint as a researcher for Granada TV's *World in Action* in 1963. Then, from 1965 to 1972, he worked as a producer/director for a range of programmes including *24 Hours, Talkback, Aden: Special Report, Space Shot*s, *Shape of 68* (BBC) and *On-Site, Newsday, Octopus, Campaign* and the party conferences (Granada). Combining academic with professional work, he later served as consultant for Granada's American election coverage of 1981 and for London Weekend Television the following year. His work as a scriptwriter for *Heritage: Civilization and the Jews*, won him awards and honours (as we have seen) while he was a consultant/interviewee for Channel 4 programmes (1989-1992).

In sparkling form: Brian Winston addresses another conference

As an academic, his career started in 1971 as media course director at Alvescot College (or as the blurb for his first book reads: 'Too old at thirty for the hectic and glamorous life [of a TV producer], he retired to darkest Oxfordshire to put nearly a decade of practical experience and thought into print.'). Since then his posts have included research director of the media project in the Sociology Department, University of Glasgow. From this came the seminal texts of the Glasgow Media Group, *Bad News* (1976) and *More Bad News* (1980). In 1976, he moved to America to be Visiting Adjunct Professor at New York University. Prominent positions followed – at Pennsylvania State University, the University of Wales College of Cardiff and the University of Westminster. He was the founding chair of the British Association of Film, Television and Screen Studies and, in 1993, helped launch the Visible Evidence international conference series on documentary film (see www.visibleevidence.org). He has given keynote presentations at conferences across the globe (see Appendix 2.). Since 2002, he has taken on a number of prominent positions at the University of Lincoln and, in 2007, was awarded the university's highest academic post, being named The Lincoln Professor.

Now follows a critical overview of a selection of Brian's writings.

FROM THE START: BRILLIANCE AND ORIGINALITY

The brilliance and originality of Brian's approach is clear from his first published work, the densely argued, 108-page *The Image of the Media* (1973). Brian, in forensic detail, examines the sources and popular notions about the power and importance of films, journalism and broadcasting and shows how most sociological studies on media effects are inconclusive and obscure, merely providing ammunition for political attacks on the institutions of mass communication. In response, Brian draws on information theory and the work of Marshall ('the medium is the message') McLuhan – particularly as interpreted by his 'disciple' John Culkin. He is excited by McLuhan's stress on television as the 'coolest, most participational medium of all' (ibid: 75). He writes:

> Thus the TV image becomes audio-tactile rather than simply visual. It therefore restores the importance of sound and touch to Western man's sensorium. This restoration means in turn the possibility of a return to the group living of the tribal world. It is as if, for McLuhan, the electronic media restore the possibility of Western man achieving a state of grace which he lost when he invented print (ibid: 76).

Brian stresses the originality of McLuhan's approach to the media: 'His insights have a verve about them which contrasts sharply with the querulous quality of much culturalist work' (ibid: 72). But he is far from uncritical. Some of McLuhan's thinking he dubs either 'absurd' or 'amazing rubbish'. 'He claims typography responsible for a host of Western European advances, some of which post-date the introduction of type by four centuries. This places some little strain on all received notions of historical cause and effect, especially since he makes such assertions in vacuo without taking cognizance of many other factors' (ibid: 77).

As a foretaste of the intellectual eclecticism and polymathic knowledge[2] which is to appear throughout his later works, Brian finishes with a flourish: presenting a mathematical formula based on E. E. Shannon's celebrated *A Mathematical Theory of Communication* (1948) which allows him to conclude that information is therefore defined 'as the logarithm of a number of choices' (ibid: 109). Brian's concerns to inspire more popular understanding of the media dominate his short follow-up volume, *Hardware/Software* (1974). Here he explains the structure of the eye and the ear, delves into the complexities of modern linguistics and outlines the organisation of broadcasting companies around the world. Concluding that new developments in satellites, cables, video cassettes and other media technologies will be decided, as usual, behind closed doors, he stresses that, if the public are to have any say, 'there must be a general understanding of the technical background to the discussions on media policy and planning'.

Moving to Glasgow, Brian helped in the creation of the University's Media Group which went on to become – alongside the Birmingham School, the Toronto School and the Chicago School – one of the most important institutions for the study of the production, content and reception of public communication. *Bad News* (1976), their first text under Brian's direction, challenged head-on the commonly-held view that television news in Britain, on whatever channel, is more neutral, objective and trustworthy than press coverage. Not surprisingly, the BBC, its halo punctured, was hostile even before publication, threatening the group with the possibility of copyright action, protesting to the university's Principal and putting pressure on the Social Science Research Council to limit the freedom of the researchers.'³ In his Foreword, Richard Hoggart, then-Warden of Goldsmith's College, University of London, anticipates the heated controversy, recommending the text to anyone concerned with the making of television news but then adding:

> They should scrutinise it in the closest detail and be severe on any error, distortion, omission, bias they may find. But they should try to do so dispassionately, not in the mood of defensiveness so rancorous that they are unable to see the main drift of the argument, nor with an implicit urge to let niggles about this or that statistical point justify their resolute refusal to face the general case. The time is overdue for them to look steadily at that case.

I remember reading the first edition in the late 1970s (when I was deputy editor of *The Teacher*, the weekly newspaper of the National Union of Teachers) and being so impressed by the marriage of extraordinarily detailed quantitative research with tightly argued qualitative analysis. This is what I thought about television – finally some academics were spelling out the critical arguments. And they were doing it so succinctly, often wittily and persuasively. Here, for instance, is part of the section on 'social control':

> Without doubt, the weight of the BBC'S tradition and organizational authority weigh very heavily on employees. The pressure to conform to the BBC ethos is constantly maintained in many ways. All kinds of benefits and privileges accompany the upward path through the hierarchy. Breaches of conformity can be punished by removal to obscure managerial shuntings in the case of those thought to be dependable, or for the creative 'mavericks' a removal to Current Affairs or some more expansive department. I spoke to one or two who thought that potential nonconformists were noted by the management – 'they turn down the left-hand corner of your file' – 'and you get discreetly pushed' (ibid: 83).

More Bad News followed in 1980, developing the analytical method of the first volume through a series of case studies of television news and arguing, again, that what is presented as balanced and factual reporting is actually produced from a highly partial viewpoint. Over 482 pages, the research focuses on the coverage of the British economy in crisis and its thematic linkage with the Social Contract during the early part of 1975. The vocabulary of industrial news talk, the handling of headlines, the use of reported speech, the flow of visual presentation and the rules for opening and closing sequences are all examined in detail. Many of the findings are striking: interviewees are drawn from an extremely narrow section of the social and political spectrum; the overwhelming majority of all reported statements and references were for supporting the Social Contract; there were 289 references in favour of wage restraint and lower living standards, just 17 opposing wage restraint; while the vocabulary used is 'a tightly closed system' involving 'a peculiar and restricted use of even its own limited range of words which does not convey the open-endedness of the actual situation to which it refers' (ibid: 173).

Brian and his colleagues – including Peter Beharrell, Howard Davis, John Eldridge, John Hewitt, Jean Oddie, Grego Philo and Paul Walton – thus built the foundations on which the GUMG has continued to grow moving on to examine the coverage of the Falklands conflict, media images of developing countries and public understanding, mental health, AIDS and suicide, race, teaching journalism, the Israeli/Palestinian conflict and much more.[4]

NO REVOLUTION BUT 'BUSINESS AS USUAL'

Given the stress on 'misunderstanding' in the Goldberg joke referred to earlier, it is interesting that Brian's next book is titled *Misunderstanding Media* (1986). Here, Brian takes on the maverick role in which he so often delights, suggesting that the widely trumpeted 'information revolution' is nothing more than a rhetorical gambit, 'an expression of profound historical ignorance and a movement dedicated to purveying misunderstanding and disseminating misinformation'. He examines in great detail the complex histories of four central information technologies – telephones, television, computers and satellites – and in describing how they were created and diffused shows, controversially, that instead of revolution there is just 'business as usual'. Along with this argument and drawing on Saussurian linguistic theory, he formulates a 'law' of the suppression of radical potential suggesting that new telecommunication technologies are introduced only insofar as their disruptive potential is contained. Amidst the build-up of supportive evidence, there is the typical Winstonian wit: 'Television knows that in our culture, from mediaeval magistrates' benches and clerical pulpits on, authority hides its knees. Newscasters do the same. The rank and file are ranked and filed on unenclosed chairs. And it is a mark of the common touch for talk show hosts and hostesses to be similarly exposed' (ibid: 7).

For Brian, the most obvious proof of the existence of the 'law' of suppression is the continuation, despite the bombardments of technology, of all the institutions of our culture. Above all, the great corporation is preserved as the primary institution of society:

> The 'law' of the suppression of radical potential explains the delay of the introduction of television into the United States which lasted at least seven years, excluding the years of war. It explains the period, from around 1880 to the eve of the First World War, during which the exercise and control of the telephone (in both the US and UK) was worked out while its penetration was much reduced. It accounts for the delays holding up the long-playing record for a generation and the videocassette for more than a decade.

The Search for Understanding

The inspirational teacher: Brian Winston in dialogue with his students

ON THE 'PRIMACY OF SOCIETY'

In *Technologies of Seeing: Photography, Cinematography and Television* (1996), Brian develops his ideas relating to the 'invention' of the cinema. Drawing, in particular, on the theories of Fernand Braudel and Saussurean linguistics, he points to the need for 'thick' rather than monocausal explanations. The insight into the primacy of society as the main agent in setting technology's agenda applies:

> ... more widely than just to what we might see as the industrial revolution. What is less clearly perceived is that the sort of prefiguration Braudel points to in the industrial revolution occurs (indeed, necessarily occurs) with all innovations great or small. The state of the market, or better, of society is the crucial factor in enabling the development and diffusion of any communications technology or in hindering it. That is as true of the computer chip and the internet as it was of the telegraph and the telephone. Thus, innovations are the creatures of society in a general sense (ibid: 3).

A crucial factor in the 'invention' of cinema, then, is the emergence of the mass audience. In Britain, the slow disappearance of the street entertainer, the increasing marginalisation of the fair and the rise of the music hall all worked to turn popular theatrical experience into a collective urban experience. By 1895, 'the broad mass of the audience, addicted to naturalistic illusion and narrative, was sitting in the darkened seats of the auditorium watching highly professional entertainments created by a logistically complex, capital-intensive, if somewhat risky, industry. Both the producers and the consumers of this product were waiting for the cinema' (ibid: 31).

In one chapter, Brian examines the proposal for a new analogue television standard of 1,125-lines – about which there was much professional and popular debate in the 1980s – as a case study for the study of 'the law of the suppression of radical potential' at work. He adds: 'Strategies were deployed to push the technology but counter-strategies of those seeking to frustrate it were so effective that the system was virtually abandoned as a potential world transmission standard a little more than a decade after it was introduced in the market' (ibid: 88).

The breadth and depth of Brian's research always impresses. In *Media Technology and Society* (1998), he returns to his notions challenging the concept of the 'information revolution' taking in the complex histories of the telegraph, the telephone, radio, television, calculators, computers, microcomputers, broadcasting networks, communications satellites, cable television and the internet. The surprisingly long histories of communications technologies are highlighted: for instance, the fax was introduced in 1847, the idea of television was patented in 1884, digitalisation was demonstrated in 1938. Even the concept of the 'web' dates back to 1945. 'Take the idea of associative databanks: in July 1945, in a popular (but nevertheless quite densely argued) article Vannevar Bush envisaged a machine which, in essence, allows for the entire compendium of human knowledge to be accessed or searched in an associative manner' (ibid: 322). Brian examines why some prototypes are abandoned, why many 'inventions' are created simultaneously by innovators not aware of each other's existence – and how new industries emerge around these developments.

THE GREAT BRITISH DOCUMENTARY SCANDAL

On 15 October 1996, *The Connection*, a film about a new drug-running route from Colombia to the UK. (produced by Marc de Beaufort working for Carlton Television as a freelance) was screened to an audience of 3.7 million in the 'Network First' slot. Then in 1997, reporters at the *Guardian* began investigating the use of extensive reconstruction (actually downright fabrication) in the film which purported to show a 'mule' passing into Britain with heroin concealed in his stomach. So splashed across four pages on 6 May 1998, the *Guardian* ran the exclusive: 'Exposed: The TV drugs fake.' Not surprisingly a massive controversy erupted and, in the end, the Independent Television Commission fined Carlton £2million for 'grave breaches of the programme code'.

In *Lies, Damn Lies and Documentaries* (2000), Brian starts out by focusing on the ITC charge of 'misleading' its audience. Misleading remains undefined, 'not least since there is no test for measuring its consequences nor even a need to produce any actual misled member of the audience to attest to such a state of mind. One thing is clear: being "misled" does not involve the levels of damage the law would acknowledge to be actionable' (ibid: 15). He argues this represents a clear and worrying development since damage – direct, indirect or potential – has hitherto been essential in cases involving obscenity, sedition, incitement to racial hatred and protecting the public from the harm of false trading (ibid: 16). Moreover, Carlton's Inquiry Panel's ruling grievously limits 'the legitimate discretion' of documentarists by suggesting anything that works 'to edit reality' is incompatible with 'strict reliability' (ibid: 19). Documentary-makers claiming not 'to edit reality' need to be treated with a great deal more caution than is being envisaged here. By British documentary standards, such editing techniques were without question an essential part of 'the creative treatment of actuality', which is how the pioneer documentarist John Grierson defined the documentary in 1933 (ibid). Returning to the controversy in *Claiming the Real II: Documentary: Grierson and Beyond* (2008 [1995]: 253), he points out that *The Connection* used fake people and portrayed false actions.

> The 'drug lord' was actually a bank manager, the cocaine was not cocaine and the mule was no mule because he was not actually 'loaded'. ... The mendacity of the documentarist in such cases is uninteresting as it is straightforwardly wrong and there can be no deployment of either a consent or public interest deference. (It is another matter whether, in a free society, a fine for misleading the public where no evidence of damage of any kind was either sought or found is warrantised, however much such a sanction is disguised as a consequence of breach of contract.) (ibid).

Brian proceeds, in *Lies, Damn Lies and Documentaries*, to place the scandal in the context of the history of the documentary. The American Robert Flaherty produced the first documentary in 1921 – *Nanook of the North*. Grierson's first film, *Drifters*, appeared in 1929. Grierson was very careful to distinguish this new film-type from other sorts of factual cinema such as the newsreel, the travelogue or the scientific/nature film. Documentaries would go beyond the conventions of news reel into a world hoping to achieve the 'ordinary virtues of an art' passing 'from the plain (or fancy) descriptions of natural material to arrangements, rearrangements and creative shapings of it'. Hence the 'creative treatment of actuality' becomes a mark of documentary difference promising insights into the world, not a mechanistic reflection of it (ibid: 20). Documentary allowed 'for poetic image-making, essays, polemics, and, at the level of production, it clearly permitted the reconstruction of prior witnessed events, commentary, non-naturalistic dubbed sound, editing to produce a point of view and all manner of interventions and manipulations' (ibid).

Special Inquiry, which ran from 1952-1957, was the BBC Documentary Department's first major series. By the early 1960s a whole new style, Direct Cinema, and with it a journalistic ethic of non-intervention and strict observation, was developed. Enter 'the fly on the wall'. In the 1960s, the new Cinéma Verité showed filmmakers revealing themselves in the process of making the film. But Direct Cinema's untenable, unGriersonian claim to be able to present 'truth' in the form of films consisting only of events as they actually spontaneously occurred before the lens triumphed.

And then, provoked by the bare-faced lying in the 'fakery' scandals, even the norms of editing became suspect. ... No distinctions were being drawn between reconstructing scenes that actually happened, that could have happened and those that never happened and were thus entirely fictional. The draconian interpretation of 'reconstruction', for example, was rendering many standard practices deviant – breaches of public trust (ibid: 23).

Brian next highlights the way in which UK regulators created the notion of 'breach of public trust' to justify the sanctions imposed on mendacious broadcasters. 'Central to this regulatory development is that it invents a quasi-judicial "offence" for which legally defined damage need not be proved.' Documentaries, he suggests, do have a duty of care to those who participate in their programmes and this, not an amorphous 'truth telling' responsibility to the audience, is where their ethics should be grounded.

Moreover, Brian's affirmation of the value of documentary shines through his Introduction to *The Documentary Film Book* (2013) in which he brings together the work of 47 international scholars. With the new, post-Griersonian documentary, 'responsibility for determining documentary value is removed from the image and its maker and is passed to the audience (where, in fact, it should always have been). ... The Vertovian injunction to "show us life" remains, giving the documentary a crucial role in society, one that it is well able to play. Documentary approaches its second century with its value and validity in good order' (ibid: 26).

HOW THE RIGHT TO FREE EXPRESSION UNDERPINS ALL HUMAN RIGHTS

Brian dedicates *Messages: Free Expression, Media and the West from Gutenberg to Google* (2005) to the University of Lincoln, reflecting the profound importance of the institution's collegiality to his personal and intellectual life. It's an unusual Winstonian production, containing no in-text references – only end-of-chapter lists of sources – and the Routledge blurb advertises it as being 'essential and entertaining reading for anyone concerned about the protection of liberty of expression' (so not strictly an academic text). Brian also clearly has fun choosing the cover images. None of those drab, abstract splodges that so often adorn academic monographs here. Instead, there's a reproduction of a nude Nell Gywnne reclining as Venus with her baby son as Cupid, a still from Charlie Chaplin's *The Gold Rush* (1925) and an image of the *Radio Times* rolling off the printing presses. With typical panache, Brian covers the histories of print and stage, photography, film and broadcasting – mixing anecdotes and quotations, all the time stressing the media's importance as an essential driver of free expression which underpins all human rights. But there is also an underlying concern that free expression is 'in very deep trouble'.

He quotes a survey conducted on behalf of the American Society of Newspaper Editors revealing that, overall, those surveyed 'displayed an alarming willingness to remove legal protection from forms of free expression they merely disagreed with or found offensive' (ibid: 396). He continues:

> It is not just free expression that is 'in very deep trouble'; rights in general are being recast as 'entitlements' and then denied as nothing more than 'politically correct' – a phrase transformed in weaselly fashion by the anti-liberals into a term of abuse. ... Instead of a right, duly limited by law, newer media are being allowed, in the words of the new British Communications Act of 2003, something less – 'an *appropriate* level of freedom of expression' (emphasis added) as determined by statutory bureaucratic structures beyond the courts. ... the influence of non-print mass-communication systems is deemed so vast that they cannot be allowed to function without extra control (ibid: 397-398).

THE CREATIVE TREATMENT OF ACTUALITY – AND ASSOCIATED PROBLEMATICS

With around 600 references, Brian's massively researched study of the history of the documentary, together with an exploration of the relevant ethical and theoretical issues, *Claiming the Real II: Documentary: Grierson and Beyond* (2008 [1995]), begins in typical Winstonian light style. His opening page carries a quotation from Roland Barthes's *Mythologies*: 'Bourgeois ideology is of the scientific, or the intuitive kind, it records facts or perceives values, but refuses explanations; the order of the world can be seen as sufficient or ineffable, it is never seen as significant.' But he immediately follows that with these cryptic words from David Bordwell: 'A quotation from Barthes does not automatically carry the day.'

For Brian, John Grierson's definition of documentary as 'the creative treatment of actuality' along with the rhetoric accompanying the 'fly-on-the-wall' Direct Cinema style appear increasingly inadequate faced with new theoretical complications, ethical quagmires and the photographic image's claim on the real. The emergence of agitprop and advocacy documentaries, satire, poetry and pictorialism, docusoaps, dramadocs and documusicals, mockumentaries, rockumentaries not to mention 'reality' television add further ingredients to the post-Griersonian feast. New voices are speaking out. Feminist documentary is emphasising the autobiographical; the experiences of gays, lesbians and Afro-Americans are being explored (ibid: 278). 'Within these radical traditions also lies the renegotiation of the entire directorial function of the documentarist by working as a collective or by turning an individual media worker into a "socio-cultural animator". At its most extreme are the obviously transformative attempts that occur when the victims of the Griersonian tradition are given the camera' (ibid: 279).

Ethical issues, such as those relating to 'informed consent', are constantly raised. For instance (ibid: 248): 'The undiminishing flood of those persuaded that participation in a reality television show will bring them fame and riches suggests that the possibility of malignant outcomes continues to remain largely hidden. ... Too often when faced with ethical issues the filmmaker's first response tended to be that if the subjects consent, where is the difficulty?'

He cites the example of Dennis O'Rourke's *Cunnamulla* (1999) in which two First People girls give him a graphic interview outlining their actual (or fantasised) sexual adventures with the boys of the town. 'I felt, when I discussed the problem with him at the Sheffield International Documentary Festival, that any duty of care towards the girls that he might have been expected to have on ethical grounds was quite underwhelmed in his mind by his right of free expression and their de facto consent' (ibid: 250).

Ethical issues involved in the use of subterfuge and the associated notion of the 'public interest' also preoccupy him, tracing the controversy back to Nellie Bly's exposé of her ten days in the New York women's asylum in 1888. 'It is the filmmakers' regular, almost automatic, public interest justification for the exploitation of participants that is worrying' (ibid: 259). And on the exploitation of participants in 'reality' TV:

> Today people participate in 'reality' television precisely to have the actuality of their lives and personalities creatively treated and, indeed, transformed. One might think that this would make the ethical worries and inhibitions rather passé. Far from it. Out of the world of 'reality' television there have been successful actions for misrepresentation; people have committed suicide; divorce proceedings have been threatened; actions have been brought for harassment and injury. ... If you listen to those responsible for this programming, these concerns about outcomes – the results, palpably, of less than fully informed consent – are apparently regarded as nothing more than quaintly old-fashioned prudery. There is, the producers would have us believe, a basic human desire in some to expose themselves ... (ibid: 265).

IN THE FACE OF *FATWA*: THE RIGHT TO OFFEND

Concerns over serious threats to freedom of expression also drive his next major text, *A Right to Offend* (2012). It follows the global controversy over the declaration of a *fatwa* against Salman Rushdie's *The Satanic Verses* (1988) by the Imam Ruhollah Khomeini, Supreme Leader of the Iranian Islamic Republic, the consequent deaths of hundreds in riots across the globe, the stabbing to death of Rushdie's Japanese translator, the murder of the book's Italian translator and the shooting of its Norwegian publisher. The journalistic abuses involving ruthless privacy invasions exposed in the UK 'Hackgate' scandal (which ultimately led to the Leveson Inquiry in 2011) are also of central concern. Brian's background as a law student at Oxford is clearly evident here – as he meticulously examines in chronological order the major cases. Thus he begins with Henry VIII's *Defence of the Seven Sacraments against Martin Luther*, of 1521, and moves on to John Milton's *Areopagitica*, 'the first great plea for free media' on 25 November 1644 (ibid: 52-53). In all, he covers 38 cases, the most recent being *Sir Paul Stephenson et al. v. Alan Rusbridger and Paul Johnson* (2010-2011) in which the then-Metropolitan Police Commissioner castigated the editor of the *Guardian* and his deputy, Johnson, for 'stories they had run which suggested that the Metropolitan Police had been failing to investigate possible criminal behaviour by employees of News International'.

He notes the murder of Russian journalist Anna Stepanovna Politkovskaya whose fearless reporting of the attack on Chechnya earned her the enmity of President Vladimir Putin, and the arrest on an obscenity charge of the US comedian Lenny Bruce, in October 1961, after using the word 'cocksucker' as part of a joke. 'The right to free speech and the right within it to offend, because without it we have no free speech, must be maintained. At whatever cost' (ibid: 353).

WHEN THE RIGHT TO FREE EXPRESSION TURNS DEADLY

Brian returns to *The Satanic Verses* controversy in his concise, 173-page *The Rushdie Fatwa and After: A Lesson to the Circumspect* (2014) that also considers the murder of the Dutch film-maker Theo van Gogh and the publication of 12 cartoons depicting Mohamed in the Danish journal, *Jyllands Posten*, on 30 September 2005 that provoked global protests by offended Muslims. Between February and May 2006, some 250 people are estimated to have died in riots and at least 800 were injured. Brian acknowledges the political right's long-term hostility to the concept of rights in general. But he finds surprising that, in the *fatwa*'s aftermath, 'Western left *bien-pensants* also expressed doubts about the right to free expression: they agreed, peaceably of course, with those protesting against Rushdie that censorship was necessary, at least on occasion'. He adds:

> They did so not only in the name of maintaining social harmony but also on the emphatic basis that they 'understood' the 'pain' of those offended by this novel (ibid: viii).

Brian extends his treatment of the *fatwa* in a completely original way – examining the trends in often esoteric Islamic thinking that lie behind the declaration. Syed Abul A'ala Maududi, Hassan al-Banna, the Sufi founder in 1928 of the Muslim Brotherhood, Sayyid al-Qut'b and Taqi al-Nabhani are amongst those whose ideas he outlines. And he traces the creation of the UK Action Committee on Islamic Affairs and its attempt to mount a blasphemy case against Rushdie (ibid: 52-53). In the end, toleration must be intolerant of intolerance:

As Walt Whitman said: 'Do I contradict myself? Very well then I contradict myself. (I am large, I contain multitudes).' The complexity of human affairs requires complex responses and these, it should be acknowledged without embarrassment, might well necessarily involve some measure of inconsistency (ibid: 138).

In addition, an 'offence principle' should not be substituted for the harm principle while non-externally verifiable hurt should not be considered as worthy of redress. And he urges the circumspect to 'have the courage of their convictions and not dilute them in the name of sensitivity or glib assumptions about cultural imperialism' (ibid: 139). According to Emeritus Professor Julian Petley, of Brunel University: 'What we have here is a resounding defence of the principles of free expression, not in the debased, self-interested and ill-informed manner in which the British press habitually defends its "right" to do as it damn well pleases, but in highly sophisticated philosophical terms. This is a key contribution to the debate not only on the right to free expression, including the right to offend, but on media freedom in general in the post-Leveson era.'

THE FRUITS OF COLLABORATIVE RESEARCH: 'POLEMICAL YET LYRICAL, FORCEFUL YET INVITING'

Patricia Z. Zimmermann, Professor of Screen Studies at Ithaca College, USA, sums up the qualities of Brian's *The Act of Documenting: Documentary Film in the 21st Century* (2017): 'Fiercely argued, urgently rendered and rigorously researched, it whacks through the ethical, political, moral, evidentiary and argumentative acts undergirding documentary production and reception: it interrogates the place of documentary in the world and how it engages people and ideas in ways that truly matter. Polemical yet lyrical, forceful yet inviting, this book leaves the reader exhilarated with new ways of thinking about and through documentary.' A collaborative venture with Gail Vanstone, of York University, Toronto, and Wang Chi, a lecturer at the Communication University of China and one of Brian's doctoral students at the University of Lincoln, it sets out with an ambitious goal: to examine how documentary has changed over the first years of the twenty-first century and how changed is the world as a consequence.

One chapter looks at the dominant patriarchal tone of the story documentary tells about the world – and how digital's potential aids the spectator's escape from the constraints of narrative linearity and its patriarchal voice. Another essay acknowledges that while not all documentary has an overt political agenda, in the context of social change then the filmed/filmers' presence is highly significant, transforming filmmakers (directors) into facilitators, embedded in the co-creation of projects (ibid: 103). Elsewhere, the authors follow-up their argument over film and patriarchy (and, in particular, Brian's preoccupations with objectivity notions) suggesting that recent years have seen a new legitimation of overt displays of subjectivity. 'This leaves all the old ethical problems in place but it also neuters the traditional claim on objective, empirical truth. As subjectivity is an enemy to the patriarchal concept of scientific objectivity (and therefore in this sense also to documentary's claim on the real as it has its roots in science), arguably this is of deeper significance than are digital affordances' (ibid: 125). Considering the complex issues relating to audience reception, the authors note the essential Eurocentrism of the debate.

> Matters of the raising of consciousness or the provocation of action are entirely for the individual; but, from the global perspective, this focus might seem to be a luxury. Extrapolating from the conditions of laissez-fair control such as exist in northern polities is, obviously, Eurocentric. When these comparative freedoms do not exist – as is the case in huge swathes of the world – the whole documentary agenda changes. It does so for the filmed and the filmer, of course, but also for the spectator. Concerns about the state of the documentary in the digital era, as in the past, are transformed if soldiers or secret police are at the door (ibid: 209).

Brian achieves a remarkable ambition, collaborating with his son, Matthew, a teacher in the School of Media, Communication and Sociology at the University of Leicester, in co-editing *The Roots of Fake News: Objecting to Objectivity* (2021). As I say in my cover endorsement: 'This long overdue study by Winston father and son finally elevates the fake news debate to a completely new, high level, taking in its historical, philosophical, legalistic, scientific and ethical dimensions – and much more. Writing with panache and wit, the authors create a text for all teachers, students and members of the public seeking a reliable – and still challenging – guide through the fake news jungle.'

The authors dare the seemingly impossible – considering the epistemology of journalism. When I started at the Nottingham *Guardian Journal* as a sub-editor in 1970, I was introduced to the Who, What, Where, When and How of the typical news intro (opening section in the jargon): so Who is going to buy the next round? What is the price of a pint here? Where are we going for a drink next? When does the pub shut? And How are we going to drive home now we've all drunk far too much?

The Winstons tackle the topic impressively with the appropriate seriousness and gravitas: 'Journalism and philosophy do not initially appear to have much in common, perhaps representing, or at last being seen as representing, respectively, the practical versus the abstract, the specific versus the general, the timely versus the timeless etc. It would nevertheless seem reasonable to address the thought that if journalists are concerned with the limits of what can be confirmed, proved, known, there may be some value in considering how their approaches and understanding relate to the theories and practices of philosophy's longstanding investigation of the nature of knowledge itself and the role of truth within that' (ibid: 155). So they proceed to consider the views of Bill Kovach and Tom Rosenstiel, Bertrand Russell and G. E. Moore, Friedrich Nietzsche, Charles Peirce, Karl Marx, Emmanuel Kant, John Stuart Mill, Steve Knowlton, Bernard Williams and Michael Schudson.

In calling for an 'honest, subjective, biased foundation on which journalism may be rebuilt' (ibid: 199), they cite Schudson's six core functions of journalism: to provide information about what is not generally known, to investigate as guardians those who should be guardians of public welfare, to be a public forum for the expression of ideas and opinions, to analyse the context in which events occur, to encourage 'social empathy' better to understand 'how the other half lives', and to mobilise, in the name of partisanship, like-minded groups of the citizenry. The Winstons conclude that if there is a 'crisis' in journalism it is not around fake news, alt facts, post-truth. 'Rather, the current lack of confidence is grounded, history clearly shows, in the centuries of claims to be providing that which cannot be delivered; claims to be honoured and respected which cannot be sustained. This is what threatens the press's ability to perform its crucial roles' (ibid: 201).

And throughout his career, Brian has been an inspirational teacher, much admired by his students. A number of his texts over the years have focused on training/educational and curriculum issues such as *Working with Video* (with Julia Keydel), of 1986, and *Reporting Diversity: Curriculum Framework*, of 2003.

It's the Media, Stupid!

Brian's writings, as we have seen, cover a substantial area – the history of documentary and the communications industry in general, the ethics and techniques of documentary-making, free expression, the history and ethics of the press and television, journalism training, the politics of the media, reporting cultural diversity, the 'fake news' problematic and so on. This *festschrift* brings together essays on just a selected few of these fields.

DOCUMENTARY, CLAIMING THE REAL AND BEYOND

Tom Waugh puts the spotlight on Magnus Isacsson's twenty films and three-decades-long career which is largely unknown outside of Canada. The films offer a case study in documentary canon-formation and historiography, and in issues close to Brian Winston's heart: non-fiction media ethics and impact, and documentary practices both independent and shaped by state/corporate patronage. Working with English, French and Indigenous languages, Isacsson focuses on the strong narratives of local struggles, the people who led them and the settings in which they lived. Waugh writes: 'I hope … this personal encounter with my jogging partner Magnus, will introduce a useful dialectic into a volume celebrating the life achievement of such a prodigious and influential scholar. I hope moreover that the prolific and inspired work of Magnus Isacsson from Montreal may soon infiltrate the canons we have built up in our centres of taste-making and gatekeeping within the empires of documentary scholarship and culture.'

Deane Williams also highlights the work of someone whom he considers seriously under-valued – namely the theorist Siegfried Kracauer. In particular, the chapter aims to restore the term 'naïve realism' to the heart of documentary studies. Beginning with some notes on surrealism and photography, Williams examines the reception of documentary film in the post-World War II years and then some 'naïve' documentaries at the dawn of the digital era, such as Jia Zhangke's *In Public* (2001). For Williams, a 'thorough-going understanding of the theoretical underpinning of naïvete in relation to documentary film is needed to reposition documentary film theory and criticism in relation to cinema studies more generally'.

In my own research into the press coverage of US/UK post-1945 militarism, secret warfare and the links between mainstream journalists and the intelligence services I have had to deal head-on with all the complex issues relating to conspiracy theories. Here, Kate Nash takes a close and critical look at four Covid-19 conspiracy documentaries, examining the ways in which they might create pandemic counter-narratives. Challenging the notion that conspiracy documentary is easily dismissed as documentary's Other, the essay considers how they 'claim the real' by both co-opting and contesting expertise and official knowledge. Thus, according to Nash: 'The Covid-19 documentaries point to the complexities of claiming the real in the context of uncertainty and in an environment where the various discourses of sobriety with which documentary has claimed kinship have lost at least some of their epistemic authority.'

In *The Act of Documenting* (2016), Brian Winston and his colleagues Gail Vanstone and Wang Chi explore the connections between reception studies and production studies in docmedia. A particular focus of their critique are the highly controversial films, *The Act of Killing* (2012) and *The Look of Silence* (2014), directed by Joshua Oppenheimer. Annette Hill – through interviews with members of the audience in various countries at screenings of *The Act of Killing* – considers issues relating to engagement and impact. And she says: 'As commissioners and funders for documentary place emphasis on measurable engagement and demonstrable impact, the vexed issue of what engagement means and methodological questions of how to substantiate claims of impact will continue to challenge filmmakers and researchers.'

FREE EXPRESSION, OFFENCE AND CRITICAL HUMAN RIGHTS

Clifford Christians, one of the world leaders in communication ethics, opens the second section with an essay based on the notion that humans, as the one living species constituted by language, are therefore fundamentally cultural. According to Christians's philosophy-of-the-human, humans know themselves through their symbolic expressions. 'Communication is the creative process of building and affirming the human order though symbols, with cultures the human habitat that results. ... When humans are defined as cultural beings, human affairs are fundamentally interpretive, rather than a matter of scientific explanation presuming neutrality. Since humanity is embedded in an existing cultural world, its sense of being is necessarily historical.'

In this philosophical context, theories are not to be seen as scholastic paradigms of mathematical precision; rather, they tap into the imaginative power that gives an inside perspective on reality. From here, the essay moves on to consider Habermas and critical inquiry, the ideology of instrumentalism, Harold Innis's notion of the 'monopoly of knowledge', perspectivism, Clifford Geertz's stress on 'thick description' (replacing the thinness of statistically precise objectivism) – and much more.

Christians ends with a wonderful celebration of Brian Winston who 'exemplifies the humanities perspective of this essay. As a world class critical theorist, his hermeneutical depth on mediated symbolic systems demonstrates how interpretive scholarship ought to be done in a global era of cross-cultural complexity'.

Questions relating to harm, offence, insult, free expression, censorship, broadcasting regulation and journalistic codes of conduct are at the heart of many of Brian Winston's writings. Julian Petley, in a chapter titled 'Doing Harm: How the UK Government Threatens to Impose Online Censorship', focuses on the notion of harm, deriving from John Stuart Mill, that Brian Winston employs to indicate where the limits of freedom of expression should lie. According to Winston, claims relating to offence and insult have increasingly expanded definitions of harm and, in the process, narrowed the bounds of freedom of expression. Building on these ideas, Petley examines the regime of online regulation currently proposed by the UK government in the form of the Online Safety Bill. This 'threatens to create an unwieldy, unaccountable and unnecessary state apparatus of online censorship, operates with far too broad and vague a notion of harm, and will see material expelled from the online world which is entirely legal in the offline world'.

Next, in contrast, Raphael Cohen-Almagor challenges Brian Winston when he writes, in *A Right to Offend*, that freedom of expression 'can only be said to exist if it encompasses a right to offend. The right to offend is the right of expression's touchstone, just as the right of expression is the touchstone to human rights in general'. While Cohen-Almagor agrees that there is a right to freedom of expression, he does not think people have a 'right' to ridicule. The issues raised by the terrorist attack on the Parisian offices of the French satirical magazine, *Charlie Hebdo*, on 7 January 2015, are of central concern here – as they are in Winston's text.

But for Cohen-Almagor, if editors and authors know that certain provocations are likely to lead to violence against themselves and against innocent bystanders, 'then they responsibly need to weigh the pros and cons of the so-called "right to ridicule" versus the well-recognised right to life and make a reasonable judgement call. I leave it to the editors to decide. I do not suggest that the law should be involved. I call for prudent, responsible thinking before rushing to provocations that are likely to yield violence.' Ultimately, Cohen-Almagor does not assign ridicule the same degree of importance that is assigned to life, freedom of expression, health and education. 'Ridicule is one category of freedom of expression and, to my mind, not a very important category, certainly not an essential part of the right to free expression.'

OBJECTIONS TO OBJECTIVITY: POLITICS AND ETHICS OF THE MEDIA

Brian's most recent text, co-written with his son, Matthew, examines the 'fake news' controversy from typically original, Winstonian perspectives. It is appropriate, then, that Ivor Gaber, one of his colleagues on the editorial board of the *British Journalism Review*, should examine this controversy in an essay titled 'Fake News, Double Spin and Strategic Lying in the Post-Truth Era'. Gaber coins the term 'double-spin':

> It can be characterised as an act of political communication that has an overt, above-the-line message – a traditional spun communication. But it also has below-the-line content designed to convey a broader positive message about the sender and/or a negative message about his or her opponent. In addition, it is designed to initiate or sustain a particular news agenda or to block or divert a damaging one. This is double spin but if the message itself contains palpably false, or substantially misleading, information then this brings us to the concept of strategic lying.

For Gaber, the strategic lie is a form of double spin that aims to control the news agenda through either a straightforward lie or the distortion of factual information with the intention to mislead or deceive its audience.

The essay concentrates on two case studies: the first examines the 2016 Brexit referendum when, according to Gaber, the Leave campaign, co-ordinated by Dominic Cummings, used strategic lying and double spin. Two key slogans: 'We send the EU £350 million a week. Let's fund our NHS instead' (painted on the side of the Leave campaign bus) and 'Turkey (population 76 million) is joining the EU' were 'examples of effective campaign communications, but both were serious misrepresentations involving double spin and strategic lying'. For his second case study, Gaber looks at the 2019 General Election where he observes closely the Conservative Party's campaign strategy. This included, for instance, 'the repetition of falsehoods or seriously misleading statements despite knowing them to be so but being prepared to take any flak because in a post-truth environment little long-term electoral damage ensues'. He concludes:

> In light of the events surrounding the 2020 US election and the subsequent invasion of the Capitol in Washington in January 2021, further research is urgently required not only to investigate the extent to which strategic lying is now a central feature in the political communications culture of liberal democracies but also to evaluate its impact on voter behaviour.

In a chapter titled 'The Media of the Past Determining the Politics of the Future?', Martin Conboy conducts a detailed analysis of the images and language deployed by British national newspapers on 31 January 2020, the day Britain finally left the European Union. He compares these representations and their political implications with Ofcom statistics on readers' political preferences. And he writes: 'Newspapers have driven a hard Brexit to the extent that they have, in the main, gambled on a set of representations that flatter the prejudices of an older and more conservative generation. … independence for Britain means less the release from the burdensome weight of outside control and more a reassertion of the status of bygone days.'

Across thirty years of documentary practice in broadcast, NGO and fine art spaces, Pratāp Rughani has reported on people facing conflict, atrocity or their aftermaths. In South Africa, Rwanda, Aboriginal Australia, the UK and elsewhere he has conceived his documentary filmmaking, 'as a kind of arena in which many experiences can unfold, with enough open space for an audience to make sense of competing perceptions and experiences and settle on their own view'. In his chapter, 'Towards Restorative Narrative', Rughani calls for the creation of 'a more relational media – socially designed and biased enough to nurture the connective tissue between communities, drawing on practices from restorative justice including deep listening and searching for shades of grey'. Rughani tells of his experience shooting the documentary *Justine* (2013), about a young woman who rarely speaks and reports enthusiastically on the techniques of the pioneering Vietnamese video artist, Trinh T. Minh-ha, who describes her aspiration in moving image practice as 'restoring proximity of the subject and recognising the place of subjectivity'.

Rughani closes his essay on an important questioning note: 'Can a story production process now emerge that re-conceives media as ethically responsible "connective tissue" to configure a public space to enable storytellers, subjects and audiences to understand and relate to their diverging perspectives?'

NOTES

[1] Another joke Brian tells is this: a Jewish man goes into a restaurant owned by a friend who greets him. He sits down and orders his meal from the waiter. He's a Chinaman but speaks perfect Yiddish. He is very impressed. The waiter comes to his table and engages in small-talk, friendly conversation – all in perfect Yiddish. When he is leaving he tells his friend, the restaurant owner, how impressed he was with the meal but also with the waiter: 'He's a Chinaman but he speaks perfect Yiddish.' 'I know,' the restaurant owner says. 'He thinks we are teaching him English'

[2] I was privileged, then, to work with two polymaths at the University of Lincoln, the other being Professor John Tulloch (and with the consistent, always jovial, support of Vice-Chancellor David Chiddick). My tribute to John is published as 'John Tulloch: On the importance of mischief-making', *Ethical Space: The International Journal of Communication Ethics*, Vol 12, No. 1 pp 23-29 and republished in *Journalism Beyond Orwell*, Routledge, 2020 pp 106-117

[3] See https://romulusstudio.com/variant/7texts/Media_Group.html

[4] See http://www.glasgowmediagroup.org/images/stories/pdf/timeline.pdf. *Message Received: Glasgow Media Group Research 1993-1998* (edited by Greg Philo, Longman, 1999), for instance, contains studies of audience research, children and film/video/TV violence, media and mental illness, soaps, audiences responses to suicide, coverage of the BSE crisis, trace, migration and the media – and teaching journalism

ACKNOWLEDGEMENTS

I would like to thank all the contributors for their wonderful chapters – to Professor David Chiddick for his Preface, to Dave Miller for his front cover cartoon that captures Brian's personality so brilliantly and to Gail Vanstone for her consistent encouragement. Pete and Richard Franklin, of Abramis, deserve a special mention for their commitment to this book project from the very start. Thanks also to my colleagues and students in the Journalism School at Lincoln who helped establish such a creative, collegiate space for me since I joined the university in 2003. And, as always, thanks to my partner, Maryline, and our son, Gabriel, for their love and support.

BIBLIOGRAPHY

1973	*Dangling Conversations: The Image of the Media*, London: Davis-Poynter
1974	*Dangling Conversations: Hardware/Software*, London: Davis-Poynter
1976	*Bad News: The Structure of Television News* (with the Glasgow Media Group), London: Routledge and Kegan Paul. 2010 Reprinted, London: Routledge Revivals
1980	*More Bad News: The Structure of Television News* (with the Glasgow Media Group), London: Routledge and Kegan Paul. 2009 Reprinted, London: Routledge Revivals
1986	*Misunderstanding Media*, London: Routledge and Kegan Paul. 2017/2018 Reprinted, London: Routledge Library Editions: Cultural Studies, Vol. 4
1986	*Working with Video* (with Julia Keydel), New York: Amphoto
1995	*Claiming the Real: The Documentary Film Revisited*, London: British Film Institute (BFI)
1996	*Technologies of Seeing: Photography, Cinematography and Television*, London: BFI
1998	*Media Technology and Society: A History from the Telegraph to the Internet*, London: Routledge
1999	*Fires Were Started: BFI Film Classics*, London: BFI
2000	*Lies, Damn Lies and Documentaries*, London: BFI
2003	*Reporting Diversity: Curriculum Framework*, London and Belgrade: Media Diversity Institute and Samizdat
2005	*Messages: From Gutenberg to Google*, London: Routledge
2008	*Claiming the Real II: Documentary: Grierson and Beyond*, London: BFI
2012	*A Right to Offend*, London: Bloomsbury
2013	*The Documentary Film Book* (editor), London: BFI
2014	*Documenting and Methods* (Wang Chi and Brian Winston, editors), Beijing: China/International Broadcasting Press
2014	*The Rushdie* Fatwa *and After: A Lesson to the Circumspect,* Basingstoke: Palgrave Macmillan
2017	*The Act of Documenting: Documentary in the 21st Century* (with Gail Vanstone and Wang Chi), London and New York: Bloomsbury Academic
2021	*The Roots of Fake News: Objecting to Objective Journalism* (with Matthew Winston) London: Routledge

SECTION 1

Documentary, Claiming the Real and Beyond

Chapter 1

The Documentaries of Magnus Isacsson (1948-2012): A Case Study in the Local and the Global

Thomas Waugh

Magnus Isacsson's twenty films and three-decades-long career, largely unknown outside of Canada, offer a case study in documentary canon-formation and historiography, and in issues that have been dear to Brian Winston's heart: non-fiction media ethics and impact, and documentary practices both independent and shaped by state/corporate patronage. Based in Montreal, within Quebec and Canada's vibrant documentary scenes, Isacsson won recognition in festivals from Paris to Mumbai. Yet his rich, varied contribution risks neglect by international documentary scholars – not only because of today's volatile virtual environment. Working with English, French and Indigenous languages and subjects struggling to transform their worlds, Isacsson focused on the strong narratives of these local struggles, the exemplary characters who led them and the vivid local relations and settings in which they lived. Here, then, is an essay on a prolific artist of the here and now, a friend of the author and 'committed' documentarist, and his reach towards the global.

Keywords: Magnus Isacsson, Brian Winston, friendship, documentary canons, the left

This essay on my friend, the Montreal documentary filmmaker Magnus Isacsson (1948-2012), may seem a counter-intuitive choice as a contribution to a *festschrift* in honour of another friend, British documentary scholar Brian Winston. To my knowledge, Magnus has never been on Brian's radar: his references over the years to Canadian contributions to the world documentary canon are restricted to a couple of episodes in the history of our National Film Board, the cinematographers who innovated the new Direct Cinema style and technology in the late 1950s, Michel Brault and Terence Macartney-Filgate, and the transformed filmmaker-subject relations pioneered by the board's 'Challenge for Change' programme, specifically the 'Fogo Project' in the late 1960s. And finally a few times to Alan King's breakthrough independent feature *A Married Couple*, also from the 1960s, which honed the observational style of the day to accommodate more personal ethics and aesthetics than the American Wiseman model.

Even Brian's voluminous writing on his countryman John Grierson has always passed over the latter's formative impact on Canadian documentary as founding commissioner of the board beginning in 1939 – although Brian dutifully recruited my friend Ezra Winton and me to make sure the board was well covered in his wonderful anthology *The Documentary Film Book* (2013). Yet I have specifically labelled Brian and Magnus (and Ezra) my 'friends'. This essay, then, ponders the crucial – and often overlooked – place of friendship in documentary culture and scholarship.[1]

Brian and I have been 'conference friends' (especially at the annual 'Visible Evidence' conference, which he hosted twice and I once) for almost forty years, and our relationship is jovial and collaborative yet frank. He teased me repeatedly about how soporific he was sure I secretly found the 1954 Joris Ivens epic *Song of the Rivers*, a 105-minute black-and-white German-language Stalinist masterpiece, I was writing euphorically about. We even clashed one year long ago, publicly and stubbornly, over definitions and uses of the two key terms 'Direct Cinema' and 'Cinéma Vérité'. But these dynamics cemented our friendship rather than undermined it. I hope the following reflections on an unjustly non-canonical, local filmmaker serve to express my utmost respect, solidarity and affection for Brian. I hope as well they will serve as a friendly interrogation of the processes by which our international canons of documentary film are shaped and maintained.

ISACSSON'S THIRD PATH

I met Magnus Isacsson at a 1985 documentary film seminar named after Brian's exemplar and whipping boy, John Grierson, held in Brockville, Ontario. This idyllic but intense annual retreat of documentary makers and users was modelled on the American seminar named after another of Brian's figureheads Robert Flaherty. In Brockville, Magnus presented two of his fine Radio-Canada documentaries on Indigenous issues. But his frustration with the public TV framework and the space for making valid social documentary within the French-language state broadcaster was palpable, and would certainly have been familiar to Brian, an expert on and survivor of state broadcasting. Magnus made it official at that gathering that he was switching to a third path, diverging from Grierson's state sponsorship and Flaherty's corporate sponsorship models: independent work (though the first item on his 'independent' filmography is dated 1990, five years later).

I didn't especially bond with Magnus at Brockville: perhaps I was narcissistically hanging out with friends I already knew, enjoying a scrap with the Ontario film censors, flirtatiously monitoring the emergence of queer cinema in Canada, and too busy interfacing with grad students to invest in this amiable but very earnest wire-rimmed heterosexual man my own age (we were both 37 that year) – even if he was from my own Montreal neighbourhood. However, our acquaintanceship amped up to *bona fide* friendship over the next years and specifically at the 1987 seminar where, as invited programmer, I was part of a concerted collective effort to knock the socks off the seminar's conservative constituency of mostly earnest, wire-rimmed heterosexuals, feminists and librarians. Magnus, as co-animator, had to wrangle the queer and black rabble-rousers I had invited to present and did so generously and productively.

Magnus was increasingly busy far afield over the next years with his research and filming trips everywhere from Namibia to Great Whale, Quebec, to Port Radium, Northwest Territories. But whenever he was around we would cross paths at screenings and eventually nourished a relationship as weekly jogging buddies. Being neighbours encouraged this relationship – his Esplanade flat was a five-minute bike ride away and was directly on the way to the Parc du Mont-Royal, the usual site of our jogs. He commiserated with my knees and I with his big toe, increasingly in revolt, as we moved through our forties and fifties and started to creak. Being part of a sweaty butch jogging duo did a lot for my non-jock self-esteem. He even moved in with me for a year in 1999-2000, and that was also the year we shared a room in Mumbai during their documentary film festival, where he won the Golden Conch for *The Choir Boys* (1999). Back home one of the movies we saw together that same year was French 'bad girl' feminist Catherine Breillat's subversive feminist melodrama *Romance* (1999), a film that had an 'interesting' Montreal theatrical career (an angry man invaded the projection booth and ripped the print from the projectors). The final scene where the heroine incinerates her neglectful husband in a gas stove explosion left Magnus pale and silent rather than angry and violent.

This reminds me that my filmmaker friend had specialised in class and economic marginalisation and planetary survival in his work, and that for all his feminist credentials and impeccable sense of gender balance in his on-screen world, gender and sexual politics were relatively low priority. This notwithstanding the wonderful manifesto on gender and ageing that would eventually underlie his final pair of films on the naughty elderly activists *The Raging Grannies* (2010, 2014). And then there was our canoeing outing in the Laurentians where I was shocked to see this Swedish immigrant come out of the closet as a Nordic noiseless stroke absolutist, totally intolerant of my relaxed splashy – homosexual? – addling style. No wonder the narrative and analytic structures of his films were so precise!

TALKING ABOUT NON-FICTION STORYTELLING

I lay out our friendship at the start of this brief memoir-essay, in part because it entailed endless conversations about documentary practice: I guess I was one of Magnus's many sounding boards. Our conversations above all touched on non-fiction storytelling and we often came back to the strong narratives from American left filmmaker Barbara Kopple that were an inspiration for him. He also lured me on to the founding committee of what would become the *Rencontres internationales du documentaire de Montréal* festival, and I enjoyed networking and collaborating with his gang. Things often led to me throwing at him endless lists of other documentary film titles that he absolutely *had* to see as he was fine-tuning pre-production or a research shoot on this project or that one.

I insist on this personal narrative also because as I move through my seventies but continue to reflect on political documentary – even after having laid to rest my 600-page magnum opus on the topic the year before I retired – I increasingly ponder friendship and other interpersonal feelings and relationships like solidarity and empathy as the core of documentary scholarship, practice and culture. And how is it possible that I am only now getting around to writing about the engaging work of my friend, to affirming the principle of the intersection of work and friendship that I am always publicly endorsing?

My personal reflection on Magnus's practice, career and output as an independent documentarist over the last quarter-century of his life builds on this sense of his work as the outgrowth of a web of relationships, both on-camera and off-camera. Magnus himself corroborated this angle in a late interview:

> Marc Glassman: Your cinema has moved from a cinema of social issues with characters to one of characters.
>
> M. I.: I'm sure it has to do with ageing, emotional development as you get older, the impact of emotions, relationships, realising that the real substance of the films was in emotional expression and relationships.

I am also interested in Magnus's work's strong engagement and intervention with the local – not only people but also feelings, material challenges and critical social imbalances – yet also always at the same time with the global, planetary echoes and resonances of local struggles. Magnus's 'independent' career and livelihood were charged with masterful balancing – between old and new relationships, the local and the global, relations of the heart and bread-and-butter commissions. He was able to get away with the latter in part because he had somehow acquired his own camera and sound equipment, which allowed him regularly to drop everything and rush to the front line of a project that happened to be emerging on some local picket line. Except when the equipment was generously loaned out to any of his many mentees who needed it for zero-budget personal projects at the time. Magnus's activism included pedagogical transmission and hardware sharing!

At the same time, Magnus never left behind the skills in investigative journalism that endeared him to Radio-Canada, notwithstanding the minimal research time the state broadcasting system permitted and the ever-present threat there of compromise, censorship and self-censorship. No doubt this broadcast training accounted for the restrained appearance of Magnus's own authorial voice in even his most personal works, especially for the first leg of his 'independent' career. By 'voice' I mean a range of artistic options. His earlier indie productions were based on voice-over narrations that now feel distanced and formal (*Koivo*, 1990, and *Uranium*, 1991) – which were then disparaged by us recovered Griersonites as 'voice of God' – and he returned to this device as late as 2005 in *Sonny Jo and the Casino*.

But Magnus began experimenting increasingly with the use of the literal recording of his own voice as insider narrator or character, and with the adoption of a clear, articulated personal point of view. *Un syndicat avec ça?* (A trade union with that?, 1999) offers the first full-fledged voice-over narration by Magnus himself, perhaps reflecting the personal bond he developed with the doomed young McDonald's strikers. The anomalous autobiographical short *Letter to Béthièle* (2010) now stands out in the intensity of the personal, in this case paternal, feeling in its voice-over. Another film that stands out in this respect is *View from the Summit* (2002) but for the opposite reasons: its interactive narrative of activists on the street facing police and violence is so gripping that no narration whatsoever is deployed. Let me acknowledge also that Magnus himself almost never appeared visually on the screen in more than twenty films.

Magnus Isacsson on location at Great Whale, Quebec, with Indigenous collaborators Chief Matthew Mukash and René Sioui Labelle in Power, *in the early 1990s*

THE ETHICAL YET PARTISAN 'VOICE'

Aside from these questions of the incorporation of authorial voice in a narrowly literal technical sense, another broader kind of voice developed out of his abandonment of the ship of state, namely his 'authorial voice'. After all this is an essay on my friend Magnus by a reawakened romantic and old-fashioned *auteurist*! This 'voice' is distinct from what Nichols in the post-*auteurist* 1980s would have called the 'governing' 'voice of the textual system' of the film (1983). What I mean here by voice is the documentary maker's embrace of an ethical yet partisan and subjective commitment to the subjects he would meet and bond with along the way, and his cinematic articulation of the relationships he would deepen with them and with the world around them. Rather than the feigned or deluded 'objectivity' of the journalistic voice, this kind of subjective authorial voice was a feature of most of Magnus's work over the last two decades of his career.

The ideal for committed documentary that I espoused in the early 1980s entailed:

> ... an important additional assumption: if films are to be instrumental in the process of change, they must be made not only *about* people directly implicated in change, but *with* and *for* those people as well ... [filmmakers] rooting their work within actively ongoing political struggles; by making films, I repeat, not only *about* people engaged in these struggles, but also *with* and *by* them as well, ... [a] 'subject-centered' or 'contextual' ideal expressed in my string of emphasized prepositions... (1984: xiv).

Re-screening all of Magnus's intensely subject-centred and contextual work, as I have done over the last year, I have been profoundly struck by the palpable evidence of the 'with' and 'by' relationships constituting his authorial voice throughout the films, both visible onscreen. These relationships ranged from:

i) the exemplary and often heroic community activists such as Philippe, David, Yves and the artist couple Annie and Pierre whom Magnus privileged in such films as *Pressure Point: Inside the Montreal Blockade* (1999), *Waiting for Martin* (2004), *The Battle of Rabaska* (2008) and *Art in Action* (2009) respectively;

ii) reliable and recurring insider expert witnesses like Linda McQuaig, Diane Reid and Julie Roy in *The Emperor's New Clothes* (1995), *Power* (1996) and *La Grande Tumulte* (1996) respectively;

iii) gutsy but everyday heroes/social agents whose sometimes stumbling transformations provide the narrative arc of a film, like the collective protagonists of *The Choir Boys* (1999), *Maxime, McDuff & McDo* (2002) and *Ma vie réelle* (2012);

iv) those collaborators legible in the credits, as substantiated by my personal knowledge of Magnus's networks in the twenty-five-or-so years I knew him well. Here I include everyone from cinematographers (especially the faithful perennial cinematographer Martin Duckworth, fifteen years his senior, sometimes official 'co-author' of Magnus's films), producers (especially Yvan Patry, Glen Saltzman, Paul LaPointe, Marcel Simard, Malcolm Guy and Jeannine Gagné), mentees (especially Anna Paskal, Annie Jean and Simon Bujold – sometimes enlisted so deeply as to end up with their signatures as co-authors in the final credits), and translators and other crew members, to the support circles of critics, programmers and jogging partners – not to mention spouse-and-producer-editor-researcher-translator-executor, Jocelyne Clarke.

Let me interrupt the flow here with a word about Magnus's strong relations, in particular, with producers over the years, no doubt another practice he inherited from his years at Radio-Canada. I want to stress how essential they were to Magnus maintaining his quarter-century career as an independent documentary director. This achievement is much rarer than is commonly understood within the international networks of documentary scholarship or within the documentary strongholds of documentary culture within Canada and Quebec. In several cases, Magnus's producers were indicated in the credits as co-authors. Very rare are the indie documentary directors who maintain a comfortable livelihood without resort to various moonlighting options (post-secondary teaching being the most common, though Magnus almost never got caught up in what is for some indie filmmakers an exhausting distraction). Admittedly, the National Film Board's switch over the last generation away from in-house directors towards collaborations with freelances, despite its contradictions, has facilitated the pattern of indie livelihoods (at least six of Magnus's films were collaborations with the board). Typical of Canadian documentary work at large, Magnus's credits not only flagged the names of his trusted producer partners but were also inevitably a patchwork of various state funding agencies, provincial and federal. Of course, the producer's function is to put this patchwork in place, allowing Magnus over the years the time and energy to avoid fundraising and to gradually assemble and shape his intermittent and spontaneous research shoots and rushes into long-term projects and narrative patterns and voice.

BUILDING LONG-TERM RELATIONSHIPS WITH SOCIAL ACTORS

Resuming our reflection on Magnus's 'contextual' films, that is those where a long-term relationship with social actors in a continuous setting is the most palpable dynamic of his 'with' and 'for' authorial voice, the most striking examples came at the end of the filmmaker's career. A pair of films produced by Jeannine Gagné are both feature-length narratives of the lives of a group of social actors with whom Magnus and cinematographer Duckworth established trust and intimate knowledge over the course of four years. Such a period is long but not especially so in independent documentary practice if you are keeping several projects on the go, as Magnus was always able to do. Four years matches the total production period for Kopple on *Harlan County USA* (1976), Magnus's model. But it constitutes roughly only one third of their ancestor Robert Flaherty's total preparation and production time on *Nanook of the North* (1910-1922), the pioneering template for the genre.

Poster for My Real Life (2012)

Magnus's two late subject-centred films with Gagné are *L'Art en action* (*Art in Action*, 2009), a 70-minute chronicle of a duo of socially-engaged artists, Annie and Pierre, a couple in real life, over several years of their provocative creative projects in social intervention; and *Ma vie réelle* (2012), a 90-minute intimate epic of four young men, Danny, Alex, Mikerson and the latter's younger brother Michael, in the depressed and diverse neighbourhood of Montréal Nord, released the year of the filmmaker's death and recipient of the best feature-length film at the *Rencontres* festival that same year (national competition).

Both are tightly-woven narratives within a vivid social milieu, punctuated with intimate close-up conversations between off-screen Magnus and his 'stars', in whom he is able to spark profound, deeply felt personal reflections, all the while maintaining an eye on political and ethical stakes, global and local. His questions and prods are terse but brilliantly tuned to the sensibility and potential confessional positioning of each subject. The cast of *Art in Action* are well-educated activist artists from central Montreal, in whom Magnus clearly saw younger versions of himself, but the latter group could not be further from his own babyboomer, white settler demographic: four male millennials from the dispossessed and stigmatised suburb, manifesting various markers of dropout status, economic marginalisation, criminalisation, substance use and racialisation. This range is clearly one further indication of Magnus's remarkable artistic and social versatility. Perhaps the character in *Ma vie* he identified with most, the film's fifth major persona, is the mentor role played by a black community social worker type, Don Karnage, who has also 'paid the price' and basically runs a rap recording studio to encourage his struggling charges. Both films are notable for their productive alignment of seething public street life with intimate interiors and musical performances, and for a brilliant negotiation of the minefields of documentary ethics that Brian Winston will certainly admire. Otherwise, they validate the timeworn feminist principle of the personal and the political, the political dimensions of everyday life.

This embrace of the politics of the everyday gradually emerged in Magnus's career as he increasingly left behind the imprint of Radio Canada's more journalistic aesthetics, still importantly palpable in such films as *Uranium* (1991) and appearing as late as *Waiting for Martin* (2004). It was also about leaving behind or at least modulating and enlivening what his close colleague Patricio Henriquez called at Magnus's memorial event the 'Manicheanism' of left politics, and 'thesis cinema'[2] in favour of a cinema about imperfect human characters, to be made 'at home', rather than on the jaunts far afield of earlier years. Like many Quebec intellectuals in the late 1970s and early 1980s, Magnus had belonged to what were then affectionately called '*groupuscules*' (tiny groups), militant New Left cells and networks committed to revolutionary change – in Magnus's case of the Fourth Trotskyist International affiliation. And the certainties of those political cultures, Manichean and otherwise, are arguably traceable in Magnus's works of those years.

Ma vie réelle offers as a narrative climax the graphic depiction of Mikerson's son's birth (to a young woman whom we have spotted a few times but never got to know). The earlier film's *dénouement* had been no less sentimental. Annie and Pierre had kept their kids out of the film as much as possible, but they are part of a chorus of privileged school children from an 'alternative' Plateau-Mont-Royal school who perform an exalting closure, singing glowingly John Lennon utopian dream song 'Imagine' to a motley and chaotic post-dinner assemblage under the public ATSA tent. Tears are plentiful among both protagonists and spectators. The previous year's *La Bataille de Rabaska* also includes an iconography and discourse of parenthood, as if implying that the stakes of that film's exemplary activist's struggles against the fossil fuel corporations are embodied in his and his wife's loving bathing of their child in their bucolic but threatened heterofamilial home. The structural and iconographic kinship among these very different late films respectively is certainly as personal as it is generic. The 2009 and 2012 films frame chronologically what is by far Magnus's most personal video from 2010, the tender *Letter to Béthièle*. Here the filmmaker, then in remission from the cancer that would claim his life two years later, addresses his 10-year-old adoptive daughter on her birthday, and provides intimate information and questions about both her adoptive ancestry in Sweden and her blood ancestry in Haiti.

THE MIX OF EMOTION WITH LUCIDITY AND SERENITY

Biographical criticism can be a trap of course. But I do not hesitate to identify a testamentary quality in these stories and the one short epistolary video, locating in their mix of emotion with lucidity and serenity all that we saw in Magnus as he faced the end. But I allow myself the liberty also of taking at the same time a slight queer distance from them in identifying in all respect and tenderness the richly cinematic assumptions and iconographies around heterofamiliality and so-called 'reproductive futurism' that are a bond – if not liability – shared among these final works (Edelman 2004). When I say 'richly cinematic' I mean, for example, the generic impetus in the story of Alex, Danny, Mikerson and Michael, all deeply scarred by parental desertion, towards the reproductive closure of Mikerson's parenthood. I mean also Magnus's disinclination to resist the masculinist universe, dominated by hip hop, into which his four subjects are emerging and healing their scars. Beyond the counterpoint of the supporting cast of smart and strong motherly and grandmotherly characters, the film offers little critique. In this respect let's factor the riveting '*chosen* familiality' of *The Choir Boys* (1999) into this final cluster, this no less moving contextual narrative of bonding through choral singing and busking among men without offspring or family or homes, cast out from mainstream society that is as heteronormative as it is neoliberal-consumerist. This is Magnus's queerest film (though, of course, the no less homosocial *Raging Grannies* French-English diptych may not be far behind…).

Biographical criticism is, indeed, complicated but, in fact, this personal essay affirms its enduring relevance in my celebration of both a friendship including its peregrinations and contradictions, and more importantly a committed filmmaker's artistic legacy of relationships on-screen and off, of a voice, a vision, a vocation and a life. I hope this personal encounter with my jogging partner Magnus will introduce a useful dialectic into a volume celebrating the life achievement of such a prodigious and influential scholar as Brian Winston. I hope, moreover, that the prolific and inspired work of Magnus Isacsson from Montreal may soon infiltrate the canons we have built up in our centres of taste-making and gatekeeping within the empires of documentary scholarship and culture.

NOTES

[1] Brian's engagement with Canadian documentary has been heightened in recent years through his collaboration with Torontonian Gail Vanstone, an expert on another successful NFB experiment, Studio D, the Women's Studio (2017)

[2] This phrase works better in French, 'cinéma de thèse' (and in Henriquez's native Spanish, 'cine de tesis'), than it does in English, meaning a didactic cinema with a clear, thesis-style argument

MEDIAGRAPHY

Breillat, Catherine (1999) *Romance*, co-production Flach Film, CB Films, Arte France Cinéma, France, 82 min.

Flaherty, Robert (1910-1922) *Nanook of the North*, Frères Revillon, USA, 78 min.

Henriquez, Patricio (2012) Memorial tribute to Magnus, Jean, Annie (ed.) *The Cinema of Magnus Isacsson,* Pléiades Productions, Canada

Isacsson, Magnus (1990) *Toivo - Child of Hope*, Alter-Ciné, Canada, 30 min.

Isacsson, Magnus (1991) *Uranium*, National Film Board of Canada, Canada, 52 min.

Isacsson, Magnus (1996) *Power: One River, Two Nations*, Cineflix, Canada, 76 min.

Isacsson, Magnus (1996) *La Grande Tumulte (The Big Upheaval)*, Productions Virage, Canada, 52 min.

Isacsson, Magnus (1999) *Pressure Point – Inside the Montreal Blockade*, Multi-Monde production, Canada, 52 min.

Isacsson, Magnus (1999) *The Choir Boys*, Productions érézi, Canada, 75 min.

Isacsson, Magnus (2002) *View from the Summit*, Productions érézi and NFB, Canada, 75 min.

Isacsson, Magnus (2002) *Maxime, McDuff & McDo*, Les Productions Virage, Canada, 52 min.

Isacsson, Magnus (2004) *Sonny Joe and the Casino*, Pléiades Productions, Canada, 20 min.

Isacsson, Magnus (2004) *Waiting for Martin*, Lo-Tekk Productions, Canada, 52 min.

Isacsson, Magnus (2008) *The Battle of Rabaska*, ONF/NFB, Canada, 75 min.

Isacsson, Magnus (2009) *Art in Action*, Amazone Films, Canada, 70 min.

Isacsson, Magnus (2010) *Les Super-Mémés*, Island Filmworks, Canada, 45 min.

Isacsson, Magnus (2010) *Letter to Béthièle*, Pléiades productions, Canada, 8 min.

Isacsson, Magnus (2012) *Ma vie réelle (My real life)*, Amazone Film, Canada, 90 min.

Isacsson, Magnus (2014, posthumous) *Granny Power!* Productions Pléiades, Canada, 78 min.

King, Allan (1969) *A Married Couple*, Allan King Associates, Canada, 97 min.

Kopple, Barbara (1976) *Harlan County USA*, Cabin Creek Films, USA, 103 min.

REFERENCES

Edelman, Lee (2004) *No Future: Queer Theory and the Death Drive*, Durham: Duke University Press

Glassmann, Marc (2011) Interviews – Magnus Isacsson: Advocate and *Auteur*, *Point of View*, Issue 84 (Winter). Available online at http://povmagazine.com/articles/view/magnus-isacsson-advocate-and-auteur, accessed on 23 July 2021

Nichols, Bill (1983) The voice of documentary, *Film Quarterly*, Vol. 36, No. 3 pp 17-30

Waugh, Thomas (1984) Introduction: Why documentary filmmakers keep trying to change the world, *or* why people changing the world keep making documentaries, Waugh, Thomas (ed.) *'Show Us Life': Toward a History and Aesthetics of the Committed Documentary*, Metuchen, New Jersey: Scarecrow pp xi-xxvii

Waugh, Thomas and Winton, Ezra (2013) Challenges for change: Canada's National Film Board, Brian Winston (ed.) *The Documentary Film Book*, London: British Film Institute pp 138-146

Winston, Brian, Vanstone, Gail and Chi, Wang (2017) *The Act of Documenting: Documentary Film in the 21st Century*, London and New York: Bloomsbury Academic

NOTE ON THE CONTRIBUTOR

Thomas Waugh is Distinguished Professor Emeritus, Programmes in Film Studies and in Interdisciplinary Studies in Sexuality, Concordia University, Montreal. He is the author, compiler or editor of 14 books, including *'Show Us Life': Toward a History and Aesthetics of the Committed Documentary* (1984) and *I Confess: Constructing the Sexual Self in the Internet Age* (co-edited with Brandon Arroyo, 2019); co-editor with Matthew Hays of the 50-book series 'Queer Film Classics' (2008-2025) and winner of the SCMS Kovacs Book Award (2017) for *The Conscience of Cinema: The Work of Joris Ivens, 1912-1989*.

Chapter 2

Naïve Realism: Repositioning Kracauer's Theory

Deane Williams

Building on the under-appreciated intellectual rigour of Siegfried Kracauer's theoretical writings, this chapter will work towards a redemption of the term 'naïve realism'. Beginning with some notes on surrealism and photography, through the reception of documentary film in the post-World War II years, to an examination of some 'naïve' documentaries at the dawn of the digital era, such as Jia Zhangke's In Public *(2001), this chapter proposes that a thorough-going understanding of the theoretical underpinning of naïveté in relation to documentary film is needed to reposition documentary film theory and criticism in relation to cinema studies more generally.*

Keywords: documentary film, Siegfried Kracauer, naïve realism, photography, surrealism

In his 1984 book *Concepts in Film Theory*, Dudley Andrew writes that André Bazin and Siegfried Kracauer:

> … represent the realist camp finding little essential difference between perception in the cinema and in the world at large. While Bazin's notions of standard perception derive from Bergson and Sartre and are substantially more complicated than Kracauer's naïve realism, both men think of cinema as extending, rather than altering, perception (Andrew 1984: 19).

Andrew's description has haunted realist film theory ever since, diminishing the complexity of Kracauer's work as well as the productive possibilities for what might be termed naïve realist film theory. In his review of Johannes von Moltke and Kristy Rawson's edited collection *Siegfried Kracauer's American Writings*, Jeff Menne points to how Andrew's usage has been left to dangle in historical ennui, 'for the sake of distinguishing what he deemed the more salutary achievement of André Bazin and his *Cahiers du Cinéma* cohort' as a strategy in constructing 'a united front' while the 'discipline's unilateralism … took the form of obeisance to French intellectual culture' (Menne 2015: 1). Menne continues:

> ... nothing has marked the maturity of cinema studies as much as its reckoning with Siegfried Kracauer's writings. The discipline's nominal adjustment, from 'cinema studies' to 'cinema and media studies', signals its expansion; its reckoning with Kracauer, though, marks its increased conceptual and methodological sophistication (ibid).

For Menne, Andrew's term 'naïve realist' as a description of Kracauer's realist film theory, was not only a means of establishing a discipline but, more importantly, has been disproven by the discipline, by 'the greater methodological rigor in cinema studies today' where a consensus holds there to be no more misleading a tag for Kracauer's work than 'naïve realism' (ibid). Menne's review is one example of the ways in which notions of naïveté have been dealt with in cinema and media studies, whereby scholars continually look for what they consider to be the sophisticated, the complex, intricate, the knowledgeable, in the audio-visual works of others and in their own scholarship. This chapter will work towards a redemption of the term 'naïve realism' from Andrew's pejorative usage of the term and the ensuing reaction which sought to establish the under-appreciated intellectual rigour of Kracauer's work.

NAÏVE REALISM IN PHOTOGRAPHY

One way to trace the early conception of naïve realism is in photography, an apposite procedure given Kracauer's own reliance on that medium as 'a marked affinity with the visible world around us' (Bratu Hansen 1997: vii). And as Ian Walker stresses, this procedure can also be undertaken utilising the notion of 'surrealist realism' as coined by Louis Aragon to describe his book *Paris Peasant* (2004: 12). For Aragon, Walker asserts, surrealism's evocation of photography, in particular 'the realms of the instantaneous, the world of the snapshot' recalling the fervour for automatic writing, unfettered by the tenets of literary convention ... represents the idea of photographic immediacy' (ibid). According to Walker:

> To refer to a photograph as a snapshot usually implies one taken by an amateur. However deliberately made, the photograph acquires an aura of innocence, even naïvety: it is authentic precisely because its maker does not know how to contrive it (ibid).

The surrealists' re-working of the then-prevalent understandings of popular photography, in terms of immediacy and authenticity, saw an intensity of interest in everyday life, in particular the street-life of cities, the rendering of which in still-photography was a significant progenitor of naïve realism.

One of the initial and primary examples here are the street photographs taken by Jean-Eugène-Auguste Atget in the first twenty years of last century. Atget's relationship to surrealism is, at once, curious and instructive. His photographs of deserted Parisian streets were great fodder for the surrealists, in the main due to the 'objective naïveté' they conveyed. The characterising of Atget's work by commentators at the time and subsequently is instructive. Ian Walker tells us that Atget's photograph simply entitled 'Versailles' was said to be a source of amusement for the surrealist Man Ray who saw it as an indication of Atget's naïveté. Bérénice Abbott later described her encounter with Atget as 'the shock of realism unadorned' (Walker 2004: 90). In addition, Walker tells us that at the time:

> … one persistent image of Atget, within and without surrealism, was that of the naïf. The surrealists would not have intended any condescension here. They wished to erase the distinction between the self-conscious artist (such as themselves) and the artisan such as Atget whom the surrealists viewed as an unwitting avant-gardist. Both surrealist writer and poet [Robert] Desnos and [Albert] Valentin compared Atget to the obvious model of the Douanier Rousseau [Henry Rousseau]. This comparison was already common in the late 1920s; outside surrealism, other writers on Atget such as Pierre MacOrlan and Waldemar George made the link. But Desnos and Valentin placed this comparison next to more sophisticated references. Desnos wrote that Atget had the innocence of soul of a Douanier Rousseau, and the attention to detail of a Parisian *flâneur*, while Valentin made reference to Rousseau alongside the 'poètes maudits', Rimbaud, Lautréamont and Nerval as rebels whether 'conscious or unconscious' against established order (ibid: 97).

For both Desnos and Valentin, according to Walker, the paradox in Atget's work was that he had been able to present 'his viewpoint of the world, determined by an apparently mechanical medium, is also the vision of his soul' (ibid). Now this naïveté, this innocence of soul, that is assigned to Atget, has resonances for this consideration for realism. Some writers such as Walter Benjamin read in the surrealist's appreciation of Atget a revolutionary potential of 'the outmoded' – something he located in surrealism. Writing of Breton:

> … he was the first to perceive the revolutionary energies that appear in the outmoded, in the first iron constructions, the first factory buildings, the earliest photographs, the objects that began to be extinct, grand pianos, the dresses of five years ago, fashionable restaurants when the vogue has begun to ebb from them (Benjamin qtd. in ibid: 95).

Benjamin claimed that the value of Atget's work lay above all in the removal of what he famously called 'aura', writing 'he was the first to disinfect the stifling atmosphere generated by conventional portrait photography in the age of decline' (ibid). Benjamin was fascinated with Atget's fragments of Paris, writing: '… he looked for what was unremarked, forgotten, cast adrift, and thus such pictures too work against the exotic, romantically sonorous names of the cities; they pump the aura out of reality like water from a sinking ship' (ibid).

Kracauer, in his famous essay on photography that opens his *Theory of Film*, cites Atget's images of Paris streets writing that they are 'impregnated with the melancholy that a good photograph can so powerfully evoke' (1997: 16-17). For Kracauer, this melancholy is an inner disposition that not only makes elegiac objects seem attractive but also 'favours self-estrangement which on its part entails identification with all kinds of objects' (ibid: 17). In this sense, Atget's naïf-like soul comes to see itself identifying with his fragmented surroundings rendering visible a state of mind in his photographs. It is possible to see here, in a slight shift from surrealism to melancholy around Atget's work, a slippage into an indeterminate cinema, a particular approach to surrealism favoured by Kracauer and pointed out by Ian Aitken and others.

For Kracauer, photography is not simply a medium for copying, for reproduction, it is a medium for transformation, for 'rendering nature as it exists independently of us' (ibid: 18). Attending this idea is the approval of 'unstaged reality', of 'the fortuitous', 'the indeterminate', 'the endless' and 'the flow of life'. Here we need to signal the influence of Edmund Husserl, in particular his *The Crisis of European Sciences and Transcendental Phenomenology* (1970), from which Kracauer drew his *lebenswelt* or life world or 'flow of life'. For Husserl, this world of experience is a world of engagement, a world understood unknowingly, intuitively, sensorally. As Aitken tells us, Husserl argued that the objectifying abstract discourses of science obscured the more transient and subjective meanings generated within experience.

FILM – THE IDEAL MEDIUM FOR ACCESSING THE PHENOMENOLOGICAL WORLD

It is this phenomenological world which constitutes the *lebenswelt*, and Husserl argued for a return to this world – 'the world in which we live intuitively, together with its real entities – not in order to surrender to its "apparent incomprehensibility" but in order to examine its structure' (1998: 127). Of course, for Kracauer, following Husserl, film is the ideal medium for accessing this world, not because it is the same as the world but because of the structural affinities between this *lebenswelt*, with its 'transient and indeterminate structure and the suggestive indeterminacy of the film image' (see Aitken 1998: 127) and film. It is this underlying basic structure of film which brings about this affinity, it is the principles and structure of the *lebenswelt* which makes filmic realism what it is.

In some ways the launching place for the theory of film that Kracauer proposes is the phrase 'the ripple of leaves stirred by the wind' written by an enthusiastic reviewer, Henri de Parville, of the Lumière Brothers films (1997: 31). This idea of movement is crucial to Kracauer's thinking, where it is possible to see a revoicing of his writings of the 1920s and 1930s with an enthusiasm for the street where the 'flow of life' is most apparent, a place where 'the kaleidoscopic sights mingle with unidentified shapes and fragmentary visual complexes and cancel each other out, thereby preventing the onlooker from following up any of the innumerable suggestions they offer' (ibid: 72). For Kracauer, these notions are evident in the earliest cinema, particularly D. W. Griffith's where 'the medium's affinity for the flow of life would be enough to explain the attraction which the street has ever since exerted on the screen' (ibid). We can recall also Atget's photography here.

In the immediate post-war years there emerges a little cinema in New York City, where child protagonists invite us to see the world as they do. Films such as *In the Street* (James Agee and Helen Levitt, 1953), *The Quiet One* (Sidney Meyers, 1949) and *Little Fugitive* (Morris Engel, Ruth Orkin and Ray Ashley, 1953) attempted to represent a childlike world of experience in the face of modernity.

In the Street emerged out of official documentary practice and into a world of naïveté. In 1942/43 Helen Levitt was hired by the Office of War Information (OWI) in New York as assistant editor to Helen van Dongen and was eventually able to work with the likes of Helen Grayson, Henwar Rodakiewicz and Alexander Hammid, whom she came to admire for what they could do within the programmatic field of official documentary. The world of the OWI was one where films were made with a crew of up to 12 people including script girl, two camera assistants, sound recordist et al. During this time, Levitt and Janice Loeb, initially, shot footage of three gypsy kids playing in the East Bronx and a parade in Yorkville and later with James Agee and Loeb shooting in Spanish Harlem. The footage that became *In the Street,* according to Cecile Starr in the interview with Williams, eventuated because Levitt 'didn't really take to the idea that a documentary should have a script and that you should go out and know what you were going to shoot and arrange to have it there when you needed it' (2016). Levitt wanted to know what would happen if she had to improvise. Utilising a Winkelsucher attachment to a 16mm camera Levitt and Loeb were able to shoot figures at 180 degrees while the two appeared to be in conversation. This experiment was a revisitation of the method used by Walker Evans, James Mellow tells us, from as early as 1935 when he employed his friend Jane Smith Nines 'as a decoy, employing a right-angle view finder to capture the real subject while giving the appearance of taking a shot of Jane straight ahead' (1999: 237) and later Helen Levitt herself when Evans and Levitt travelled the New York subway taking candid photographs with a hidden camera which eventuated in the book *Many Are Called* (2004).

In the Street was shot by Levitt, across 1943 and 1945 and finally cut together by Levitt and completed in 1952. Initially the film is an extension of Levitt's still-photography of children and their graffiti that formed her first book *A Way of Seeing* (1989), and which, Jan Christopher Horak suggests, Agee proposed as an urban companion piece to *Let Us Now Praise Famous Men* (1995: 7). Levitt simply left the confines of the Office of War Information, went out into the street and shot footage. 'Horak understands this move on Levitt's part as a turning away from the tyranny of objectivity, which itself was a necessary toll in the social, political and propagandistic utilization of images (during the 1930s and 40s) in order to discover the personal' (ibid: 70). For Horak, Levitt's aesthetic:

> ... seemingly guarantees 'objectivity' yet ironically masks a subjectivity all its own, leaving the gaze firmly in control of the photographer, without allowing the subject to return or influence it. Thus, the ephemeral quality of those moments of action ... reflect a deeper agenda, that of a photographer looking and documenting her own subjectivity (ibid: 69).

This subjectivity is contrasted with Levitt's invisibility, her will to disappear amongst the inhabitants of 'the poor quarters of great cities' being part of the paradox; to enable her invisibility, what is rendered is a statement of Levitt's own presence. As Horak tells us, the film is shot 'mostly hand-held ... constantly moving, panning, tilting, reframing, keeping in frame moving objects, searching out new material. Moreover, the camera's nervous gaze is accentuated by jump cuts, [in the editing] which break up the action' (ibid: 74). This nervousness, born of inexperience, can also be understood in relation to Cecile Starr's belief that:

> ... it also made [Levitt] more comfortable to be on the street talking to a friend rather than looking like someone who is just hanging around trying to figure out what's going on. I think with a still camera she could make her shot and move but with a moving camera she had to get some sort of continuity or some familiarity with the scene. So Janice went with her (Williams 2016).

For *In the Street*, Levitt developed a specific, subjective method of working, of rendering images of Spanish Harlem, images of improvisation utilising the means of improvised interactive filming technique. In this regard, *In the Street* is probably the most artisanal and quotidian of the films that came to form what Jonas Mekas called a 'spontaneous cinema'. Mekas wrote in his 'New York Letter' to *Sight and Sound* (1959: 119):

> ... these films reveal an open ear and an open eye for timely, contemporary reality. They are similar in other respects: in their use of actual locations and direct lighting; their disrespect for plots and written scripts; their use of improvisation. And since their most passionate obsession is to capture life in its most free and spontaneous flight, 'to grasp life from within and not from without' (Suzuki) by loosening the sensibilities, these films could be described as a spontaneous cinema.

HOW DOCUMENTARY MOVED AWAY FROM THE 'TYRANNY OF OBJECTIVITY'

Crucial to this configuration, particularly in the post-war era, was the city and the street. Just as documentary moved away from the 'tyranny of objectivity', in Horak's words, and towards the personal and subjective, the naïve, at the same time, we witness a shift in landscape, of locale, from a rural to an urban one. In this move Siegfried Kracauer's early consideration of urban life, under the influence of

Georg Simmel, in Berlin and Paris, reinvigorated by his move to New York City with some drafts of *Theory of Film* under his arm, comes into play and knits with Mekas's pronouncements about the New American Cinema. For Kracauer:

> The street in the extended sense of the word [railway stations, dance and assembly halls, bars, hotel lobbies, airports] is not only the arena of fleeting impressions and chance encounters but a place where the flow of life is bound to assert itself. Again one will have to think mainly of the city street with its ever-moving anonymous crowds. The kaleidoscopic sights mingle with unidentified shapes and fragmentary visual complexes and cancel each other out, thereby preventing the onlooker from following up any of the innumerable suggestions they offer. What appears to him are not so much sharp-contoured individuals engaged in this or that definable pursuit as loose throngs of sketchy, completely indeterminate figures. Each has a story, yet the story is not given. Instead, an incessant flow of possibilities and near intangible meanings appears (op cit: 72).

Yet, as Horak and Starr suggest, these are still carefully constructed, framed, edited images. Kracauer provides a better understanding of this paradox between improvisation and construction. For Kracauer, film provides an image of improvisation that emerges for us, the spectators, as if it came from nowhere, or more precisely spontaneously, 'out of time' 'extempore', as Graeme Gilloch puts it. Experientially, film gives us new 'sensations, perceptions, perspectives and insights'. Films like *In the Street*, Gilloch tells us, are doubly spontaneous, both as an aspect of quotidian metropolitan experience, the incessant flow of life to which we perhaps pay little heed, (as in images of children playing in the street) but to which 'the film camera is uniquely devoted as a redeemer of the inconspicuous, disregarded and unnoticed; film is our window on the metropolitan scene' (2015: 38).

These images in many ways follow those contained in Levitt's books *In the Street* and *A Way of Seeing*: adults in conversation on stoops, children playing at hopscotch or under fire hydrants, people, young and old at window panes. Like Levitt's photography, the framing is remarkable, allowing figures in full flight to traverse the frame or shift into the foreground in their games. Without containing them, children and adults live and breathe the street life, making their daily lives out of the interactions found there. Spanish Harlem is only a small part of the buzzing metropolis, and *In the Street* never understands itself as anything more than that.

Late in *In the Street* appear images that Cecile Starr suggests were some of the earliest shot of the film taken by James Agee (Williams 2016). These are straight-on, direct, 'camera provocateur' shots of children hamming it up to the camera, individuals dissociated from their surroundings, pre-empting the Direct Cinema of the late 1950s and early 1960s. The positioning of these images later in the film enables us to relate them to the earlier 'in locale' shots, expressing a deep fascination with these child subjects, a kind of filmic discovery of life deep within these figures. Kracauer wrote specifically about *In the Street*:

> On the one hand, this film is nothing but a reportage pure and simple; its shots of Harlem scenes are so loosely juxtaposed that they almost give the impression of a random sample. A child behind a window is seen licking the pane; a woman with a terrible face passes by; a young man languidly watches the spectacle in the street; Negro children, intoxicated by their Halloween masks, dance and romp about with complete self-abandon. On the other hand, this reporting job is done with unconcealed compassion for the people depicted: the camera dwells on them tenderly; they are not meant to stand for anything but themselves (op cit: 203).

It is possible to see in these words an appreciation of the access Levitt sought to the melding of the child-like location of improvised street life. Kracauer's 'flow of life' is also about a child-like attention to detail, an intuitive childishness that Kracauer, drawing on Béla Balázs, deals with in his section on 'The Theatrical Story' in *Theory of Film*. In drawing out a distinction between theatre and film Kracauer points to what he terms the 'long shot universe of the theatre' while 'children linger over details' and 'see the world in close-ups' (ibid: 222) recalling the *mise en scène* of *In the Street*. This invocation of the child as spectator is a useful one in coming to terms with the apparent naïvete and new ways of seeing in much of the US post-war cinema that Kracauer, Mekas, Agee and others celebrated.[1]

In the Street stands as a signal film within the fervour for images of street life that characterised post-World War II New York City cultural life in which there was a fascination with the images of the city but also people's relationship with their surroundings. In this we can see Levitt's images of children, often in abject conditions, 'making do' with their surroundings, but also living in the moment, a 'moment extempore', or 'out of the time of modernity', as Gilloch puts it, where clock-watching and rationalisation are unimportant. This childlike response to modernity's regulation of time and space can be seen in Levitt, Loeb and Agee's document of spontaneity.

In the last twenty years or so of film studies, in particular, in the discipline's reflection on the digital turn, it is possible to see at least two strands of scholarship emerge. First, an attention to the high-end of Hollywood blockbusters, replete with fast-paced editing, CGI and surrounds sound. Second, a concern with smaller scale, hand-held, intimate fiction and non-fiction, something Ohad Landesman describes as 'DV Realism … utilizing the technology's immediacy and intimacy predicated upon the digital look in its various connotations of authenticity and credibility' (2008: 34). This concern can be reconsidered in terms of what we might now see as an attendant diminishing of production scale akin, perhaps, to the snapshot of the surrealists, and recalling Kracauer's interest in film's ability to diminish the distance between the spectator and the historical world, transforming our relationship with reality. Jonathan Rosenbaum writes about Abbas Kiarostami and Agnès Varda's digital cinema:

> One obvious thing that digital video does is place people on both sides of the camera on something that more nearly resembles an equal footing. A 35-millimeter camera creates something like apartheid between filmmakers and their typical subjects, fictional or nonfictional – because between them stand an entire industry, an ideology, and a great deal of money and equipment. This is the subject of many of Abbas Kiarostami's major features …; he recently shifted to DV in part because he wanted to achieve something closer to equality with whom and what he shoots. Similarly, Varda wants to be one gleaner among others – part of a spectrum of individuals, ranging from homeless scavengers to artists, who roam the street looking for 'found' objects to work with (2000).

JIA ZHANGKE AND THE RETURN OF THE AGE OF THE AMATEUR CINEMA

While Rosenbaum addresses Kiarostaimi's *ABC Africa* (2001) and Varda's *The Gleaners and I*, which sit well within this digital naïve realist moment, I would like turn to the work of Jia Zhangke, the Chinese director of films such as *Platform* (2000), *The World* (2004), *Still Life* (2005) and *24 City* (2007) and, in particular, to his *In Public* from 2001, a suitably minor work in his oeuvre. In 1999, Jia published in China's *Southern Weekend* an article entitled 'The age of amateur cinema will return' as a response to the question: 'What do you think will become the driving force for the development of films in the future?' Jia goes on to distinguish between what he terms 'the so-called professional filmmakers' and amateur cinema. By the former, he means:

> … those who strictly follow professional principles and exhaustively describe the marketing ability they possess have long lost their power of thought. They pay too much attention to whether the film is good enough to reflect their professional competencies. For example, the picture should be as delicate as an oil painting, or the *mise-en-scène* is supposed to match that of Antonioni's films, even the twinkling spotlight needs to be right on the face of the actor. They repeatedly fathom the professional mindset, cautioning themselves against any amateur act that breaks the established classical rules. Conscience and sincerity, which are crucial to filmmaking, are completely diluted by these facts.

Here, Jia is writing about a naïveté of approach, a lineage of non-professional approaches to filmmaking as an antidote to the well-worn, predictable paths of professional cinema. This amateur cinema has the potential to divine the truths and diversity of local lifeways. According to Jia:

> They ignore the so-called professional methods, so they have more chance to be innovative. They refuse to follow the standardized principles, so they acquire more diverse ideas and values. They free themselves from conventional customs and restraints to an infinite space for creation; at the same time, they are earnest and responsible because they persist with the conscience and conduct of intellectuals.

It should be pointed out that Jia's words were also a response to what he understood to be 'the trend of globalization' and a diminishing of the variety of culturally specific popular culture, including cinema. He writes:

> It is precisely in this cultural environment that only independent films that remain committed to the depiction of local culture can provide some cultural diversity. I feel more and more strongly that people can only achieve emotional communication and equal position through diversity.

In Public was commissioned by the Jeonju International Film Festival and the Sidus Corporation, South Korea. It is also a significant film in Jia's oeuvre because it is his first digital video production. Shot in Datong, in the northern Sanxi province where Jia was born and where his first films, *Xiao Wu* and *Platform*, were located, *In Public* is a melancholy, aimless and haunting observational documentary piece. The uncertain future of Datong's coal mine, crucial to the culture and economy of the area, mirrors similar images of incompleteness in his other films such as the unfinished highway of *Unknown Pleasures*, the under-construction Three Gorges Dam in *Still Life* or the half-finished luxury hotel and apartments of *24 City*. *In Public* has been described by Kevin Lee (2003) as 'a location scouting video' for Jia's following feature *Unknown Pleasures* (2002), also shot on DV signalling the film's preliminary or preparatory status. Jia has commented that the DV camera allows for quick decisions, flexible use and saving money.

However, I think there is much more to be made of this film's use of digital video than the ease of operation. The film distinguishes little between people and their locations of which there are principally four: a train station, a bus station, a bus-turned restaurant and a dance hall. The film is tentative, careful and attuned, but it is also naïve and intuitive. In this regard, Jia has found a digital cinematic style that perfectly fits the place and its people that he is rendering. In its melancholy and aimlessness, its intuition and naïveté, *In Public* utilises digital technology, not just the smaller, unobtrusive cameras and small crew but also the intuitive framing and tracing of motion specific to this location enabled by the ease of use of digital technologies. Bérénice Reynaud describes the film well in this regard:

> Unflinchingly, Jia's gaze and [his cameraman] Yu's camera captures the gap between 'life's slowness and hope's violence' (Apollinaire), between ennui, backwardness and dreary atmosphere of a small town, and the impatience, hidden desires and private concerns of its inhabitants that create as many enigmatic narrative vignettes (2002).

As well as these qualities, *In Public*'s tracing of motion represents the ceaseless change brought to bear on a provincial town necessitating the kind of cinematic approach that Zhang Zhen describes as his 'documentary method' in the earlier *Xiao Wu* as 'an aesthetic grounded in social space and experience – contingent, immanent, improvisational and open-ended' (2007: 19). The characters who inhabit this space and Jia's frame 'elude definition, in a film that thrives on indeterminacy and intuitive observation; nothing is definable, everything is mysterious and fascinating' (Lee 2003). This locating of a 'documentary method' by Zhang is useful here because it points to the taking up of DV technology by Jia in the feature *Unknown Pleasures* (2002) which followed *In Public* and has been used in all his films that followed, *The World* (2004), *Still Life* (2006), *24 City* (2008) and the documentary *Useless* (2008). Within Jia's oeuvre there is this tendency towards DV as it makes his filmic worlds real. This realism, however, provides for 'the slightest of narratives', to invoke Bazin, where Jia frames characters only for the stories they may arouse before the next character is summoned before the scene and the DV camera. In this DV world, beyond provocation, beyond the fly on the wall, Jia aestheticises experience, finding in the dun colour of Datong's environs a sense of a life tinged with the ravages of Chinese modernity.

In his essay, 'In and out of this world', Ohad Landesman ruminates on the contribution of digital video to the formal mixed-breed of documentary and fiction, including Jia's *Unknown Pleasures*. He writes:

> … on the one hand it seeks to engage the spectator in an active process of classification and framing, in which the dominant assumptions and codes behind the documentary project are exposed for re-evaluation, borrowing Barthes' famous terminology, documentary becomes not just a text but a 'writerly text' whose reader is no longer merely a consumer, but also the text's own producer. On the other hand, the viewer is invited to accept the obscurity of the distinction as an essential documenting strategy, that points to a possible failure of the traditional documentary project, and reassures the theoretical assumption many recent documentaries seem to hold; namely, that the genre cannot reveal an a-priori truth, and should therefore assert a more relative veracity by exercising strategies of fiction and exploiting the grey area between story and fact (2008: 43).

While this chapter has emphasised more than this apparent distinction and its obscurity, it seems that in films such as Jia's *In Public*, it is possible to see and feel the melding of place and people, of documentary as it gives rise to fiction, and in doing so amounts to a salient rendering of a particular, palpable, located modernity.

CONCLUSION: HOW NAÏVE REALISM OFFERS HOPE FOR THE FUTURE OF FILM

As we move further into the 21st century, it is possible to see the shining vibrancy of the turn of the century digital works such as *In Public, The Gleaners and I* and others, reflected in a some of the precious gems of naïve realism. In Australia, some of the best of Indigenous media such as the work of the Karrabing Film Collective including *Wutharr, Saltwater Dreams* (2016) or *Windjarrameru, The Stealing C*nt$* (2015) or *When the Dogs Talked* (2014) fashion youth-centred cinematic worlds born of deep Indigenous cultural lore and modernist appropriation. Maya Newell's *In My Blood It Runs* (2019) adopts the worldview of lively 10-year-old Arrente/Garrwa boy Dujuan, to fashion a vision of naïve intelligence. Both of these works, those of the Karrabing Film Collective and Newell's film, extend into the future a sense of hope and innocence born of this naïve realism.

In these moments, these historical snapshots, from the surrealist realism attributed to Jean-Eugène-Auguste Atget's photographs of Parisian streets, to Helen Levitt, Janice Loeb and James Agee's document of spontaneity, *In the Street,* and on to digital era works such as Jia Zhangke's *In Public*, it is possible to see an emerging lineage of films that can be understood as naïve realist works, following Kracauer, turning Andrew's conception into a key to not only a productive accounting for a wide-eyed rendering of innocence and discovery but also to a theoretical model for film scholarship diverging from the programmatic search for sophistication and experience.

NOTE

[1] For a consideration of the naïve qualities in Robert Flaherty's films, in particular his *The Land* (1942) and *Louisiana Story* (1948), see my Robert Flaherty (2002) *Senses of Cinema*. Available online at https://www.sensesofcinema.com/2002/great-directors/flaherty/

REFERENCES

Aitken, Ian (1998) Distraction and redemption: Kracauer, surrealism and photography, *Screen*, Vol. 39, No. 2 pp 124-140

Andrew, Dudley (1984) *Concepts in Film Theory*, Oxford: Oxford University Press

Bratu Hansen, Miriam (1997) Introduction, Kracauer, Siegfried, *Theory of Film: The Redemption of Physical Reality*, Princeton: Princeton University Press pp vii-xlv

Gilloch, Graeme (2010) Ad lib: Improvisation, imagination and enchantment in Siegfried Kracauer, *Sociétés: Revue des Sciences Humaines et Sociales*, Vol. 110 pp 29-46

Horak, Jan Christopher (1995) Seeing with one's own eyes: Helen Levitt's films, *The Yale Journal of Criticism*, Vol. 8, No. 2 pp 69-85

Jia, Zhangke (1999) The age of amateur cinema will return, *Southern Weekend* [*Nanfang Zhoumo*]. Available online at https://www.dgeneratefilms.com/post/jia-zhangke-the-age-of-amateur-cinema-will-return

Kracauer, Siegfried (1997) *Theory of Film: The Redemption of Physical Reality*, Princeton: Princeton University Press

Landesman, Ohad (2008) In and out of this world: Digital video and the aesthetics of realism in the new hybrid documentary, *Studies in Documentary Film*, Vol. 2, No. 1 pp 33-45

Lee, Kevin (2003) Jia Zhangke, *Senses of Cinema*. Available online at https://www.sensesofcinema.com/2003/great-directors/jia/

Mekas, Jonas (1959) New York Letter: Towards a spontaneous cinema, *Sight and Sound*, Vol. 28, Nos 3 and 4, Summer and Autumn pp 11-12

Menne, Jeff (2015) The critical realist in naïve New York. A review of Siegfried Kracauer's American Writings, edited by Johannes von Moltke and Kristy Rawson, *Postmodern Culture*, Vol. 25, No. 2

Reynaud, Bérénice (1996) New visions/new Chinas: Video-art, documentation and the Chinese modernity in question, Renov, Michael and Suderberg, Erika (eds) *Resolutions: Contemporary Video Practices*, Minneapolis and London: Minnesota University Press pp 229-257

Reynaud, Bérénice (2002) Cutting edge and missed encounters: Digital short films by three filmmakers, *Senses of Cinema*. Available online at http://www.sensesofcinema.com/2002/tsai-ming-liang/tsai_digital/

Rosenbaum, Jonathan (2000) Precious leftovers: *The Gleaners and I*, *Chicago Reader*, 11 May. Available online at https://jonathanrosenbaum.net/2019/05/precious-leftovers/

Walker, Ian (2004) *City Gorged by Dreams: Surrealism and Documentary Photography in Inter-War Paris*, Manchester: Manchester University Press

Williams, Deane (2016) Interview with Cecile Starr, *Framework: The Journal of Cinema and Media*, Vol. 57, No. 1 pp 58-84

NOTE ON THE CONTRIBUTOR

Deane Williams is Associate Professor of Film and Screen Studies at Monash University, Melbourne. From 2007-2017 he was editor of the journal *Studies in Documentary Film* and his books include *Australian Post-War Documentary Film: An Arc of Mirrors* (2008), *The Grierson Effect* (with Zöe Druick, 2014), the three-volume *Australian Film Theory and Criticism* (co-edited with Noel King and Constantine Verevis, 2013-2017), *The Cinema of Sean Penn: In and Out of Place* (2016) and (with Julia Vassilieva) editor of *Beyond the Essay Film: Subjectivity, Textuality and Technology* (2020).

Chapter 3

Covid-19 Conspiracy Documentary: Claiming the Real in a Context of Uncertainty

Kate Nash

The role of documentary media in conspiracy cultures represents an increasingly important field of study. This has become very clear during the Covid-19 pandemic with a number of conspiracy documentaries proving to be an important and under-explored element of the media misinformation landscape. This chapter takes four Covid-19 conspiracy documentaries as the basis for understanding how documentary might create pandemic counter-narratives. Challenging the view that conspiracy documentary can be easily dismissed as documentary's Other, it considers how they 'claim the real' by both co-opting and contesting expertise and official knowledge. The chapter argues that, in addition to mimicking the audio-visual styles and conventions of documentary, the films provide opportunities for performances of epistemic authority that position the viewer as a political agent.

Keywords: conspiracy, documentary, Covid-19, epistemology, politics

The Covid-19 pandemic has ushered in profound uncertainty and change globally. A crisis of this magnitude engages each of us in processes of questioning: What is going on? What is to be done? Is anyone to blame? The pandemic environment is rapidly changing, uncertain and emotionally charged. Documentary practices offer ways of making sense of this upheaval, from personal acts of documenting and sharing experience to televisual treatments offering explanation and investigation. This chapter will explore just one, arguably marginal, form of documentary practice. Indeed, the four films explored have a complex relationship to the idea of documentary.

Mixing fact, falsehood and exaggeration they *could* be dismissed as misinformation or 'fake news', part of an 'infodemic' that has appeared to be every bit as transmissible and dangerous as Covid-19 itself. And yet, rather than rushing to debunk the claims made in these films (a task that many others have already undertaken[1]) my aim in this chapter is to consider how they claim the real, presenting plausible counter-narratives about Covid-19 as a medical, social and political crisis. Weaving together various forms of evidence in support of their argument and performatively claiming epistemic authority, the documentaries are significant, I suggest, in prompting us to think more broadly about the significance of documentary for political engagement.

The documentaries considered offer what amount to conspiracy theories about Covid-19 in that they point, ultimately, to the secret 'machinations of powerful people' (Sunstein and Vermeule 2009) and because they present forms of 'stigmatized knowledge', truth claims that lack mainstream legitimation (Barkun 2013). Indeed, in many cases, the claims made in these documentaries have been strenuously challenged by knowledge-producing institutions. The emergence of conspiratorial thinking during a pandemic should come as little surprise given the association between conspiracy and social upheaval (van Prooijen and Douglas 2017). None of this is new, but what remains poorly understood is how conspiratorial ideas may be made plausible through forms of 'documentary' treatment. Winston and Winston (2021: 184) make an important point about those who subscribe to conspiracy theories and 'other species of alternative facts': the sense that they are somehow fundamentally different to 'the rest of us' is illusory. In the context of radical uncertainty, we are potentially all vulnerable to being convinced that things are not as they seem.

Documentaries play important, but to date under-researched, roles in conspiracy cultures. Amongst other things, documentaries help us to understand how these cultures claim the real. In his influential study of the Griersonian documentary tradition and its legacies, Winston (2008) considers how (at least in some contexts) documentary has become a means by which to claim the real. Of particular significance is the relationship (perceived and carefully negotiated) between the idea of documentary and science, journalism and the realm of politics. While the present moment is one in which these 'discourses of sobriety' have been called into question, I will show in this chapter that they remain important touchstones in understanding how documentary can work within conspiracy cultures. The films considered claim the real from a position of epistemic and political marginality, drawing on but also contesting expertise and authority. They appeal to documentary conventions, but also perform forms of journalistic, scientific and political expertise. While their claims may at times be untrue (although they rest on various truths), I hope to show that the films are not easily dismissed as documentary's 'Other'. Rather, they claim the real according to familiar logics, providing plausible narratives about events that defy easy explanation.

CONTEMPORARY CONSPIRACY CULTURES: KNOWLEDGE AND POLITICS

Conspiracy theory has generally been understood as an attempt to explain events in the world through reference to the secretive efforts of powerful, nefarious conspirators. As an attitude, conspiracy theory is built on the notions that 'things are not as they seem' and 'everything is connected' (Knight 2000: 204). While 'classic' conspiracy theories may focus on the actions of nefarious exotic 'Others', many contemporary conspiracy theories embrace a diffuse scepticism about the workings of contemporary society. As Knight (ibid: 3) suggests, contemporary conspiracy theory is less likely to focus on disruptions to the normal state of affairs, but rather give voice to 'a not entirely unfounded suspicion that the normal order of things itself amounts to a conspiracy'. In a similar vein, Melley (2000: 59) argues that conspiracy 'rarely signifies a small, secret plot anymore. Instead, it frequently refers to the workings of a large *organisation, technology* or *system,* a powerful and obscure entity so dispersed that it is the very antithesis of traditional conspiracy' (italics in the original). There is a rich literature that seeks to understand conspiracy cultures on their own terms, drawing attention to their diversity and challenging the assumption that they represent a form of epistemic and/or political pathology (Harambam 2020). Such studies aim to understand the appeal of conspiracy culture by approaching it as a reasonable response to the complexities, risks and inequalities of life in contemporary society. They provide a starting point for thinking about how conspiracy documentary negotiates expertise and positions the viewer as a political agent.

Knowledge and expertise are fundamental to contemporary conspiracy theories, including those that emerged in relation to Covid-19. Conspiracists' knowledge claims are generally dismissed as a pathological 'crippled epistemology' (Sunstein and Vermeule 2009), a 'poor person's cognitive mapping' (Jameson 1988), a throwback to a religious past and the 'pathological Other of modern science' (Harambam 2020: 14).

However, as various scholars have argued, conspiracy theories claim epistemic authority on familiar terms. As Jodi Dean (2000) suggests, conspiracy theory 'like other Enlightenment theories with claims to truth and reason', appeals to 'facticity, causality, coherence and rationality'. Indeed, given ample evidence of abuses of power by political and corporate elites, a degree of suspicion – crucial thinking – is arguably the only rational response. While trust in mainstream institutions may once have provided a foundation for knowledge, 'trusting authorities and believing "official" stories formulated by the state, politicians or the media are easily dismissed as a sign of naïvety' (Aupers 2012: 24). Many conspiracy theories, including those around Covid-19, are grounded in a critique of the social construction of 'facts', the role of commercial interests in shaping medical research and political attempts to foster compliance with public health measures. Engaging their audience as 'prosumers' (Aupers 2012: 27), conspiracy theories offer spaces for the creation of 'informational assemblages' (Dean 2000) that deploy various sources of evidence, questioning and suggesting, while (at least in some cases) acknowledging the impossibility of total knowledge.

Conspiracy theories are, like documentary, also fundamentally political. In recent years, they have come to play a more prominent, primarily de-legitimising role with respect to mainstream politics and democracy more generally (Muirhead and Rosenblum 2019). In their attack on specialist knowledge and in their ability to foster a disorienting information environment they pose a significant threat to the political process. However, it is also possible to consider how conspiracy theories and the political 'movements' they foster can provide avenues for political participation, particularly in contexts of uncertainty. Melley (2000) suggests that conspiracy theories are a response to a sense of 'agency panic' – a sense of anxiety relating to feelings of diminished agency and autonomy. In place of the traditional view of conspiracy theory as a 'paranoid' political style, Melley (and others) point to its potential value as a means by which individuals seek to reimagine their relationship to the social and political world. Certainly, for at least some conspiracy theorists, conspiracy culture provides a route into political engagement or in some cases a justification for disengagement (Harambam and Aupers 2017). It becomes relevant, therefore, to consider the ways in which conspiracy documentary might address the viewer as a political agent (or not) and the extent to which they offer a path into political engagement.

DOCUMENTARY AND CONSPIRACY CULTURE

Documentary plays important, but to date under-researched, roles in conspiracy cultures.

Sørenssen (2014) notes the emergence of a significant conspiracy video 'industry' during the 1970s that has grown as the ability to produce and distribute documentary has become easier and more affordable. Like forms of politically oriented documentary practice, there is evidence that conspiracy films play a key role in uniting and mobilising individuals around conspiracist counter-narratives. Digital technologies often play a key role, with the documentary accompanied by supporting 'evidence' that provides viewers with an opportunity for further 'investigation' of the issues raised. Harambam (2020: 53) describes conspiracy documentary as an important way in which people might encounter conspiracy ideas. Slickly produced and often presented through forms of collective viewing, they can help to unite individuals as members of a conspiracy community. In their analysis of the 9-11 conspiracy documentary *Loose Change*, Butter and Retterath (2010) similarly note the value of conspiracist documentary as a means by which 'invisible processes' are rendered visible, challenging official accounts and 'alerting' the world to what is 'really going on'. They note, too, the importance of conspiracy documentary as a means to build and sustain communities through calls to action.

These functions – revealing reality, promoting counter-narratives and analysing official discourses – align this work with the fundamental tendencies of documentary practice (Renov 1993). Achieving these functions centres on the ways in which these films seek to claim the real. While it may be tempting to approach these films as documentary's Other, as films that pervert documentary practice, it is important to recognise their kinship with conventional documentary practice. Just as it can at times be difficult (and unhelpful) to approach conspiracist ideas as reflective of epistemic failure, it is important to note the ways in which pseudo-documentary claims the real in ways that are not easily distinguished from conventional documentary. Birchall (2006), for example, locates Michael Moore's *Fahrenheit 9-11* (2004) on the 'continuum of conspiracy theory', highlighting the ways in which the film works to make connections between US President Bush and the Saudi royal family and in its scepticism over official discourse (which is rhetorically cast as patriotic). To recognise the relationship between conspiracy theory and other 'discourses of sobriety' is also to acknowledge the difficulty of distinguishing between conspiracy documentary and other forms of documentary practice.

Conspiracy documentaries tend to be formally and aesthetically conservative, very often taking an expository approach (Sørenssen 2014). A central voice-over generally frames forms of 'found' footage from news reports to political statements, readily available historic images and stock images. This audio-visual evidence has, as does all documentary evidence, a 'double existence' as 'part of the discursive chain' but also as standing outside of it (Nichols 2016: 99). As the films considered here demonstrate well, conspiracy documentaries are often informationally rich and highly analytic, building their argument in large part by re-presenting familiar material from a different point of view, in particular re-framing forms of official information. Key here are the ways in which this information is framed discursively to co-opt or contest meaning. However, also significant and as yet unexplored, are the ways in which conspiracy documentaries are performances of epistemic authority that, in the context of a struggle to define issues as significant as Covid-19, have the potential to foster political involvement.

COVID-19 CONSPIRACY DOCUMENTARIES: REVEALING 'THEIR' AGENDA (MORE OR LESS)

In the remainder of this chapter, I will focus on four documentaries that claim the real in the context of Covid-19. They do not offer a single conspiracy narrative but they often challenge mainstream narratives with suggestions, questions and suspicions that arguably fail to cohere into a narrative at all. However, as might be expected, they feature many of the same people and events and make use of similar imagery. The most high-profile of the films, *Plandemic*, has been shown to have connected anti-vaccination, QAnon and various conspiracy communities[2] suggesting the potential of the films to appeal to a wide audience. While the details differ, all the films make the claim that Covid-19 is being exploited to bring about social, political and/or economic transformation. They all seek to delegitimise official responses to the virus, drawing attention to key individuals and organisations, and promoting forms of 'resistance' from vaccine refusal to protest. The documentaries trade heavily on anti-vaccination arguments and reflect a distrust of the medical and scientific establishment. They politicise the pandemic exemplifying a 'medical populist' style (Lasco and Curato 2019) in which 'the people' must urgently reclaim power from a technocratic elite. Fostering division, appealing to fear and prejudice as well as shared values and making knowledge claims, a medical populist style seeks to offer a simple, reassuring narrative tied to political solutions.

Plandemic: InDOCTORnation is a US pseudo-documentary in two parts, a 20-minute piece based on an extended interview with Dr Judy Mikovits presented as a 'world leading' research scientist turned 'whistleblower' and a second, 75-minute pseudo-investigative documentary that builds on Mikovits's allegations, with a second 'whistleblower' (this time David Martin, described as a 'National Intelligence Analyst') who reveals 'a three-decade-long money trail' that is the 'industrial complex of coronavirus'. The investigation is wide-ranging, linking evidence of the US government's involvement in coronavirus work to a critique of mainstream media manipulation, historic examples of medical maleficence and the influence of 'corporate overlords'. The documentary focuses particularly on individuals, including Bill Gates, Anthony Fauci (chief medical advisor to the president) and Dr Tedros Adhanom Ghebreyesus (head of the WHO) whose 'corruption' offers the ultimate explanation for the pandemic, although their 'agenda' is not developed. In a similar vein, *Trail of Truth* reprises established anti-vaccination arguments – safety concerns, blind faith in the medical establishment, corporate and mainstream media corruption – extending them to suggest that Covid-19 is being exploited to 'push an agenda'. The interview-driven pseudo-documentary features prominent anti-vaccination activists Jaclyn Dunne and Professor Dolores Cahill (who features in a number of the films) along with several 'whistleblower' interviewees: an NHS surgeon suspended over comments questioning Covid-19 treatments, a health worker sacked for a social media post claiming that hospitals were not over-run and a social care worker who 'reveals' the widespread use of 'do not resuscitate' orders in care homes. The conspiracy takes the form of questions and doubts about 'what the hell is going on', giving voice to questions that, the documentary suggests, a lot of people are asking.

Wake Up Call is distinctive in its observational approach (intercut with various 'expert' interviews) with its gestures towards the traditional political campaign documentary. The film follows a self-proclaimed inter-disciplinary group called the World Freedom Alliance with close ties to the Danish JFK21 People's Party, a nascent political party led by a Danish investment banker that aligns itself politically with the French Yellow Vest movement and the Occupy movement. Indeed, the narrative arc of the film is provided by the launch of the party and a protest against Covid-19 restrictions. The documentary opens at the protest with the crowd chanting: 'This is what democracy looks like' to the sound of clanging pots and pans. This very visceral presentation of the will of the people provides the backdrop to the World Freedom Alliance's epistemic/technocratic performance. The documentary frames Covid-19 as ushering in a 'coup d'état in every country in the world' with central bankers, big pharma, tech elites and telecommunications companies colluding to destroy the middle class. However, this claim is somewhat secondary in the documentary which gives priority to medical and public health claims as well as to the broader discourse that pits humans as sovereign and free against technology and humans 'as a resource'.

The New Normal offers the most elaborate conspiracy narrative, exploring the possibility that Covid-19 is part of a plan by world governments, global corporations and tech elites to accelerate radical social, economic and political change and bring about a fourth industrial revolution. Presenting, somewhat ironically, a corporate plan to undermine capitalism, the documentary focuses on technology (AI in particular) suggesting the emergence of a global 'useless class' (the work of Israeli intellectual Yuval Noah Harari provides a foundation for this critique) and new possibilities for total surveillance and global totalitarian government. The documentary is produced entirely with pre-existing footage, with an authoritative but reassuring female voice-over that would not be out of place on the BBC. The effect is a professional look and feel that performs a pseudo-journalistic objectivity by using questioning to suggest investigation. For instance, 'If the pandemic *was* planned why would now be the perfect time to activate it? Is their intention to boost infection rates to justify more lockdowns?' As with *Wake Up Call*, the conspiracy is one in which global elites are presented as using Covid-19 as a way to destroy the middle class and create a compliant population who will accept the new social and political controls required to realise the fourth industrial revolution.

The films claim epistemic authority in a number of ways. Firstly, they all seek to convince the viewer through the richness of the evidence offered. Drawing on academic studies, personal experience, archival material and news content, the films address the viewer as a rational sceptic who needs to be actively convinced. This strategic deployment of multiple sources of evidence, that appeal to different members of the conspiracy community, has also been observed in the creation of conspiracy 'shows' (Harambam and Aupers 2019). Further, there is an analytic impulse across all of the films that taps into expectations about documentary as challenging authority, taking a critical approach to its subject matter. Of course, in practice this impulse is often more style than substance but, nevertheless, the documentaries mimic this orientation.

What I want to consider in the remainder of this chapter are the ways in which the documentaries navigate their relationship to established authority. On the one hand, all the films seek to challenge and re-frame 'official' information and governance. And yet, they also appeal to it in strategic ways.

PERFORMING THE REAL: CREATING, CONTESTING AND CO-OPTING EXPERTISE

As conspiracy narratives, the Covid-19 documentaries challenge the authority of knowledge-producing institutions and processes, particularly in relation to medicine and science. However, the films are not 'anti-science' *per se*. As observed in other conspiracy cultures, a distinction is drawn between the scientific establishment, which is criticised for its corruption by vested (commercial and political) interests, and scientific concepts and values that are very often co-opted by conspiracy theorists (Harambam and Aupers 2015). *Plandemic*, exemplifies this tension. On the one hand it discredits the scientific establishment by revealing historic and contemporary maleficence. Dramatic images of DDT being sprayed on children and references to the Tuskegee Syphilis Study cast doubt on the trustworthiness of government, patent applications and other documents that seem to show evidence of 'secret' research into coronavirus similarly suggests corruption. And yet at the same time, as Prasad (2021) argues, the film constructs an ideal of science and scientific expertise, presenting Dr Judy Mikovits as a scientist/hero who was not only ahead of her time in terms of scientific understanding but also willing to take on the scientific establishment for the good of others (and at personal cost). Her credibility is established both through her scientific understanding (evidenced in her appeal to scientific language and concepts) and in her commitment to the values of scientific enquiry: 'I will never stop telling the truth.'

All of the documentaries contrast an ideal of scientific neutrality and beneficence with the corruption of the medical establishment. Whistleblower doctors feature prominently, their credentials foregrounded (although the loss of those credentials is often presented as evidence of censorship), offering explanation and advice that calls public health measures (mask wearing, lockdowns and vaccination) into question. Public health materials are re-presented as manipulative and unethical (*Trail of Truth*) and government communication is framed as 'disease mongering' (*The New Normal*). The documentaries present the corruption of the medical establishment as so total that most medical professionals are unaware of the extent to which they, too, are being misled. Both *Plandemic* and *The New Normal* point to corporate involvement in the professionalisation of medicine (including the role of the Rockefeller Foundation in medical education) while *Plandemic* and *Wake Up Call* make a direct appeal to medical practitioners to 'wake up'.

And yet, while the medical establishment is called into question, the documentaries all appeal to scientific language, concepts and norms. Significantly scientific publications are used selectively to evidence the documentaries' claims. In *Wake Up Call*, for example, an editorial from the *British Medical Journal* accusing the UK government of 'suppressing science' is given particular prominence. 'It's not conspiracy,' the speaker emphatically claims, 'it's in the *British Medical Journal*' (the citation details are very prominently displayed).[4] This logic permeates the films which appeal selectively to scientific institutions, experts and 'facts' in supporting the conspiracists' claims. On the one hand the scientific establishment is presented as so completely co-opted by powerful interests that censorship is total, on the other any disagreement with the mainstream narrative coming from elite sources is presented as powerful evidence.

Conspiracy cultures typically encourage adherents to 'do their own research', with documentary forming an important part of the information ecology. The Covid-19 documentaries position the viewer as an epistemic agent, charged with making sense of the pandemic on her own terms. The viewer is implored to 'be critical, do your own research and don't let the media manipulate you' (*The New Normal*). *Plandemic*, Part 2, begins, for example, by pointing the viewer to the other resources that have been made available to satisfy her of the truth of the documentary's claims. In *Trail of Truth*, anti-lockdown activist Jaclyn Dunne performs this ideal of 'lay expertise'. The film opens with Dunne asking questions about Covid-19: 'They,' she warns, 'are not on our side … this is about money and control.' She then goes on to explain how she came to her critical perspective through personal experience – her daughter's negative reaction to a vaccine and the sudden death of her parents. This becomes a catalyst for her own 'medical' research. 'I'm just a mum, but I can read; I can find out what's best,' she tells the viewer. Her blind faith gives way to a questioning attitude and a growing expertise.

This expertise is performed early in the documentary as Dunne unravels a scroll consisting of numerous pages of links. She explains that this is not the research itself, but 'lists of links for the research' that she has done. As the list of links unravels and falls on the floor it serves as evidence of the research underpinning Dunne's claims, serving as a kind of performative bibliography. She makes knowing reference to the idea of 'going down the rabbit hole' and notes that she is often criticised for having a 'Google degree', and yet her performance serves to dismiss such concerns. Throughout the film, her claims are backed up by images of medical publications and data. Dunne's performance challenges the monopoly of the 'establishment' when it comes to medical authority, highlighting the significance of first-hand experience and maternal understanding. Now, her experience serves to frame the viewer as an authority who in the current environment needs to 'start questioning what the hell is going on'.

Journalistic expertise is also both claimed and challenged in the documentaries. As with scientific expertise, the documentaries seek to de-legitimise the mainstream media, 'following the money' to demonstrate that powerful interests control the public conversation. In some cases (*Plandemic* and *The New Normal*), the films offer a performance of journalistic investigation. *Plandemic* offers something like a documentary 'quest' to delve 'behind the headlines' (Corner 1995: 84). Drawing together the different threads of the narrative, the process of investigation becomes one of joining the dots to reveal the conspiracist agenda. Audiences may be cued to take up new content as evidence of maleficence (e.g. daily death tolls as fear mongering) or as revelation (clips of journalists interrogating elites are very often used to suggest incompetence). News reports also prove the reality of things that may be beyond the viewer's personal experience, such as implanted digital identification devices or provide historic proof of wrongdoing. Within each of the films the viewer is encouraged both to recognise the mainstream media as manipulative and to accept it as offering credible, verified information.

Appeals to what appears to be 'citizen journalism' provides highly emotive 'first-hand' evidence of state violence in both *Trail of Truth* and *The New Normal*. Amateur footage of police crackdowns at anti-lockdown protests and the removal of elderly relatives from their families carries the authority of direct observation, immediate and authentic. This amateur journalistic work, as a form of alternative media, also implicitly critiques the mainstream media for not representing the experience of the people.

Finally, the documentaries both critique and perform technocratic responses to the pandemic. As previously noted, the World Freedom Alliance is a self-declared inter-disciplinary panel of experts who feature in several of the documentaries (*Wake Up Call, Trail of Truth* and *The New Normal*). The group critiques mainstream solutions to the pandemic, but it does so by performing a very familiar form of technocratic expertise. As the group's website[5] proclaims: 'We will offer transparent evidence-based solutions and encourage robust debate with media, scientists and governments, to ensure our fundamental freedoms of the people of the world are restored and maintained.' From photo-ops (see Figure 1.) to conference presentations and round-tables, the group performs a very familiar form of professional governance. In their appeal to expertise, they offer a technocratic solution. While medical populism is generally understood as the antithesis of technocratic responses to medical crises, the World Freedom Alliance blends these two political styles. The WFA is populist in that it is opposed to the (corrupt) institutions of contemporary society and their response to the pandemic, but at the same time they appeal to technocracy as an ideal for dealing with medical crises.

Figure 1: Trail of Truth – The World Freedom Alliance 'experts' panel

CONCLUSIONS

It is easy to dismiss conspiracy documentary as the work of fringe lunatics and to assume that what is needed is factual correction. The Covid-19 documentaries point to the complexities of claiming the real in the context of uncertainty and in an environment where the various discourses of sobriety with which documentary has claimed kinship have lost at least some of their epistemic authority. Hence, the conspiracist's essential dilemma: how to appeal to established authority to claim the real, while also de-legitimising it? Documentary provides a valuable window into conspiracy culture that allows us to understand better how it is that they might serve to convince. Of course, this is not their only function and further attention to the contexts of distribution and political mobilisation will also be important. While each of the Covid-19 documentaries addresses its audience as a political actor and seeks to foster forms of political participation (from the very personal to the collective) we know little about their success in doing so. We do have some evidence, however, that these documentaries have played a role in spreading counter-narratives about Covid-19 and for this reason they are worthy of scholarly attention.

NOTES

[1] Comedian John Oliver debunked *Plandemic* (see https://www.youtube.com/watch?v=0b_eHBZLM6U) and Reuters has 'fact-checked' *The New Normal* (https://www.reuters.com/article/uk-factcheck-reset-idUSKBN29O228

[2] https://onezero.medium.com/facebook-groups-and-youtube-enabled-viral-spread-of-plandemic-misinformation-f1a279335e8c. See also https://www.nytimes.com/2020/05/20/technology/plandemic-movie-youtube-facebook-coronavirus.html

[3] The Tuskegee Study of Untreated Syphilis in the Negro Male (informally referred to as the Tuskegee Experiment or Tuskegee Syphilis Study) was ethically abusive research conducted between 1932 and 1972 by the United States Public Health Service (PHS) and the Centers for Disease Control and Prevention (CDC) on a group of around 400 African Americans with syphilis

[4] The *BMJ* editorial is available online at https://www.bmj.com/content/371/bmj.m4425

[5] https://worldfreedomalliance.org

REFERENCES

Aupers, Seth (2012) Trust no-one: Modernisation, paranoia and conspiracy culture, *European Journal of Communication*, Vol. 27, No. 1 pp 22-34

Barkun, Michael (2013) *A Culture of Conspiracy: Apocalyptic Visions in Contemporary America*, Berkeley: University of California Press

Birchall, Claire (2006) *Knowledge Goes Pop: From Conspiracy Theory to Gossip*, Oxford and New York: BERG

Butter, Michael and Knight, Peter (2015) Bridging the great divide: Conspiracy theory research for the 21st century, *Diogenes*, Vol. 62, Nos 2 and 3 pp 17-29

Butter, Michael and Retterath, Lisa (2010) From alerting the world to stabilizing its own community: The shifting cultural work of the *Loose Change* films, *Canadian Review of American Studies*, Vol. 40, No. 1 pp 25-44

Corner, John (1995) *Television Form and Public Address*, London and New York: Edward Arnold

Dean, Jodi (2000) Theorizing conspiracy theory, *Theory and Event*, Vol. 4, No. 3. Available online at muse.jhu.edu/article/32599

Harambam, Jaron (2020) *Contemporary Conspiracy Culture: Truth and Knowledge in an Era of Epistemic Instability*, London and New York: Routledge

Harambam, Jaron and Aupers, Stef (2015) Contesting epistemic authority: Conspiracy theories on the boundaries of science, *Public Understanding of Science*, Vol. 24, No. 4 pp 466-480

Harambam, Jaron and Aupers, Stef (2017) 'I am not a conspiracy theorist': Relational identification in the Dutch conspiracy milieu, *Cultural Sociology*, Vol. 11, No. 1 pp 113-129

Harambam, Jaron and Aupers, Stef (2019) From the unbelievable to the undeniable: Epistemological pluralism, or how conspiracy theorists legitimate their extraordinary truth claims, *European Journal of Cultural Studies*. Available online at https://doi.org/10.1177/1367549419886045

Jameson, Frederic (1988) Cognitive mapping, Nelson, Cary and Grossberg, Lawrence (eds) *Marxism and the Interpretation of Culture*, Chicago IL: University of Illinois Press pp 347-359

Knight, Peter (2000) *Conspiracy Culture: From Kennedy to the* X-Files, Abingdon and New York: Routledge

Lasco, Gideon and Curato, Nicole (2019) Medical populism, *Social Science and Medicine*, Vol. 221 pp 1-8. Available online at https://doi.org/10.1016/j.socscimed.2018.12.006

Melley, Timothy (2000) *Empire of Conspiracy: The Culture of Paranoia in Postwar America*, Ithaca, NY: Cornell University Press

Muirhead, Russell and Rosembaum, Nancy (2019) *A Lot of People are Saying: The New Conspiracism and the Assault on Democracy*, Princeton and Oxford: Princeton University Press

Nichols, Bill (2016) *Speaking Truths with Film: Evidence, Ethics, Politics in Documentary*, California: University of California Press

Prasad, Amit (2021) Anti-science, misinformation and conspiracies: Covid-19, post-truth and Science and Technology Studies (STS), *Science Technology and Society*. Available online at https://journals.sagepub.com/doi/full/10.1177/09717218211003413

van Prooijen, Jan-Willem and Douglas, Karen M. (2017) Conspiracy theories as part of history: The role of crisis situations, *Memory Studies*, Vol. 10, No. 3 pp 323-333

Renov, Michael (1993) Towards a poetics of documentary, Renov, Michael (ed.) *Theorizing Documentary*, New York and London: Routledge pp 12-36

Sørenssen, Bjørn (2014) Digital diffusion of delusions: A world wide web of conspiracy documentaries, Nash, Kate, Hight, Craig and Summerhayes, Catherine (eds) *New Documentary Ecologies: Emerging Platforms, Practices and Discourses*, New York and Hampshire: Palgrave Macmillan pp 201-218

Sunstein, Cass R. and Vermeule, Adrian (2009) Symposium on conspiracy theories. Conspiracy theories: Causes and cures, *The Journal of Political Philosophy*, Vol. 17, No. 2 pp 202-227

Winston, Brian (2008) *Claiming the Real: The Documentary Film Revisited*, London: BFI, second edition

Winston, Brian and Winston, Matthew (2021) *The Roots of Fake News: Objecting to Objective Journalism*, New York and Abingdon: Routledge

THE COVID-19 DOCUMENTARIES

Wake Up Call: https://brandnewtube.com/watch/wake-up-call-covid-19-documentary-world-freedom-alliance-copenhagen-banned-from-youtube_W8lovFZazi8y2JP.html

Plandemic: https://www.peepstv.org

The New Normal: https://www.youtube.com/watch?v=E0cbIzJy-R0

Trail of Truth: https://vimeo.com/493774491

NOTE ON THE CONTRIBUTOR

Kate Nash is an Associate Professor in Media and Communication at the University of Leeds and Co-Editor (with Craig Hight) of the journal *Studies in Documentary Film*. Her research centres on documentary media and its social impacts, with a focus on digital media and audiences. Her recent book, *Interactive Documentary: Theory and Debate*, traces continuities and transformations in documentary practice in the digital realm, using key debates in the field as an opportunity for theoretical intervention.

Chapter 4

The Act of Watching Documentary

Annette Hill

In The Act of Documenting *(2017), Winston, Vanstone and Chi connect production studies with reception studies in docmedia. This work signals how the act of documenting, a performative practice within the media industries, is intrinsically connected with the act of watching, a performative practice within cultures of viewing. There are challenges in conducting documentary audience research, in particular reflecting on the meaning of engagement for documentary studies. A pragmatic meaning of engagement as a metric or marker of impact limits our ability to capture the complex engagement of audiences as they reflect on the meaning and value of documentaries that matter to them. The act of watching documentary is a multi-faceted performance that signals the significance of context and subjectivity for audiences of factuality. By asking audiences themselves about their documentary engagement hopefully we can expand our understanding of the resonance of documentary in people's lives.*

Keywords: documentary audiences, media engagement, qualitative research

INTRODUCTION

When we consider the rich range of research in documentary, from ethics and film making, to aesthetics and soundscapes, it's surprising to find that audience research occupies a small part of the academic landscape. Studies on documentary audiences by, for example, Austin (2007), Ellis (2011) and Bondebjerg (2014) have explored cognitive engagement, emotion and cinema reception; and there are studies on strategic impact documentary, public engagement and social activism by Nash and Corner (2016) and Nash, Hight and Summerhayes (2014). These rich studies occupy a relatively small space in documentary research. In this chapter, I address how further empirical and theoretical research on the act of watching documentary would open up a wider semantics of engagement than we currently use when thinking about how documentary forms meaningful relations with its audiences and publics.

One scholar who has inspired my own work on documentary is Brian Winston. He was always curious about audiences and how they engaged and disengaged with documentary – not imagined audiences, but real people and their everyday lives at particular moments in time. My early research on audiences of hospital docusoaps in the 1990s was connected to Winston's writings on truth claims in documentary (Hill 2000); later I followed up on this work by going deeper into news, documentary and reality TV, considering how audiences explore questions of referential integrity (see Hill 2005, 2007). I used Winston's work by asking similar questions about truth claims, authenticity and performance, but from the reverse perspective of audiences. More recently, in *The Act of Documenting* (2017), Winston, Vanstone and Chi have connected production studies with reception studies in their research on a broad area of docmedia. This work signals how the act of documenting, a performative practice within the media industries, is intrinsically connected with the act of watching, a performative practice within cultures of viewing.

There are challenges in conducting documentary audience research, in particular reflecting on the meaning of engagement for documentary studies. A pragmatic meaning of engagement as a metric, or marker of impact, limits our ability to capture the complex engagement of audiences as they reflect on the meaning and value of documentaries that matter to them. The act of watching documentary is a multi-faceted performance that signals the significance of context and subjectivity for audiences of factuality. Our starting point is to ask audiences about their documentary engagement and hopefully what we find expands our understanding of the resonance of documentary in people's lives.

CONTEXTS AND DOCUMENTARY ENGAGEMENT

If we want to examine documentary audience engagement, it's important to start with the premise that engagement is more than a measurement of interest, or a statistic for public impact and policy intervention. Certainly, if we consider a pragmatic meaning of the word engagement then it is often used as shorthand for audience attention or public and policy impact. In this meaning of the word, audience information systems, from ratings data to social media analytics and ticket sales, attempt to measure and secure engagement for audiences and consumers of documentary. Policy engagement by filmmakers and advocacy groups (such as citizen's campaign groups and lobby groups) usually means a form of public engagement that aims to make an impact on an intended audience, for example to make an intervention into norms, values and policies for the environment and animal rights (see Corner and Nash 2016). Another meaning of engagement is that of consumption, an aspect of engagement that relates to commercial logics, most often in the form of advertising. Whilst not the focus of this chapter, there are ways in which documentary connects with consumption, for example ethical consumption and eco-tourism which also promote certain brands, or lifestyle gurus within popular documentary.

The pragmatic meaning of engagement in the media industry and policy arena runs parallel to cultural engagement: by audiences, fans, users and so forth, whose choices about what they engage or disengage with influence the ways in which the media industries, and media policies and strategies around content, are managed (see Hill and Steemers 2017). Cultural engagement, usually a term applied within audience and cultural studies, draws on a tradition that looks at processes and practices, that is to say the dynamic and often contradictory ways people encounter and experience cultural artefacts (see Hermes 2005). Thus, when the term engagement is used in relation to media audiences it means a dimension of human experience, in particular the subjective realities that shape our relationships with, for example, documentary.

A more political meaning of media engagement can be traced to the work of Dahlgren (2009) who roots the word in democratic and cultural theory. There are rational and subjective dimensions of media engagement, linking processes of engagement to civic subjectivity and reflections on normative visions of democracy. Dahlgren's recognition of the role of passion and subjective experience within political engagement is key to understanding what drives political and social activism. In the case of documentary audience engagement, the ways in which producers invite citizens to engage with documentary is a significant part of understanding affect and passion as a motivation to engage. This meaning of engagement, with a perspective from democratic and cultural theory, captures the power of the concept as constituting in itself forms of agency (see Dahlgren and Hill 2020).

In the case of documentary audience engagement this would mean understanding it as protean, that is to say not a fixed metric but a subjective process where there are shifting connections and meanings that are highly sensitive to context. It is the last part, context, that forms the basis of the reflections in this chapter. In *The Act of Documenting*, the politics and reception of documentary film in the Global South and North is addressed. The generic, industrial and regional contexts for engagement, regarding information and public knowledge, help to shape reception practices. Winston, Vanstone and Chi (2017: 173) note how documentary reception involves an assessment of authenticity within a film or television series, for example, involving genre recognition regarding a documentary's claims for representing reality. They also note a degree of trust by audiences in the claims made by a filmmaker, participants, and marketing and dissemination around a documentary. Thus, documentary reception is a process between producer, text and audience: '... their interactivity with the film conditions it, they influence the documentary as much as it does them' (ibid: 173).

In a section of the book dedicated to documentary reception, the authors consider the slippery terms of engagement and impact, noting how there is some confusion in the use of these terms by filmmakers and broadcasters, commissioning bodies and by other stakeholders (e.g. policy groups and non-governmental organisations). They critically analyse Joshua Oppenheimer's film *The Act of Killing* (2012) that draws on enactments, directed by perpetrators of violence during the time of the Indonesian genocide of 1965, as part of a performance documentary about the imaginary, impunity and amnesty. This film is related to a second documentary *The Look of Silence* (2014), also directed by Oppenheimer, that addresses a family and generational trauma as they search for victim recognition.

A key point for Winston, Vanstone and Chi is that engagement relates to consciousness raising and opinion formation, such as increased understanding and public opinion, whereas impact is connected to discernable outcomes, such as changes in policy. Whilst documentary films do not need to demonstrate impact and provide evidence of visible outcomes of the power of a documentary within a particular societal arena or policy and advocacy group, it is often something that commissioning bodies and funders require. Winston, Vanstone and Chi argue that 'impact is rare and the determination of engagement fraught' (ibid: 222). Audience engagement (as consciousness raising) and public impact (as social effectiveness) are connected: '… impact and engagement are intertwined, the former cannot happen without the latter' (ibid: 198). However, methods and theories for how to study documentary audiences are still relatively absent from the field. Thus, there is some pressure on the meaning of the terms engagement and impact and how to research and measure this for documentary.

AUDIENCE ENGAGEMENT WITH *THE ACT OF KILLING*

In this section, I would like to add to this discussion on engagement and impact from the perspective of audience studies by reflecting on two pieces of research published on *The Act of Killing* and *The Look of Silence*. These journal articles, one on performance, memory and audiences (Hill et al. 2019), and the other on the documentary imaginary (Hill 2021), both explore affect and subjectivity as key to understanding documentary engagement. In light of Winston, Vanstone and Chi's discussion on engagement and impact, this audience research suggests that there is a space in between engagement and impact, that of resonance, that can be useful in gaining empirical and analytical purchase on audiences. We can define engagement as the affective and cognitive work of documentary audiences, resonance as the quality of a documentary in its meaning and value for audiences in their lives, and impact as the observable outcome of documentary engagement. By introducing the connections across engagement as resonance, and impact as a consequence of engagement, we can begin to see one of the ways through the fraught discussions on engagement and impact.

A brief note on the methods for the audience study. The project started with discussions on the production of the documentaries, leading to two in-depth interviews with Oppenheimer in 2013-2014. From these interviews, a team, led by myself and involving three other researchers, piloted audience interviews, using a semi-structured, flexible guide. We recruited transnational audiences, including 21 viewers in Denmark and Sweden, 12 viewers from the United Kingdom, 10 from Colombia and nine from Japan, with an equal gender mix of 26 males and 26 females, aged from 20 to 60-years-old, during a long data collection phase from 2014-2016. The researchers for the project were living in Denmark, Sweden, the United Kingdom, Japan and Colombia, so there was a flexible and pragmatic approach to the sampling; we followed the films in their cinema and DVD distribution within these countries and interviewed audiences, not directly after they had seen the films, but over a period of time. Our audiences had found *The Act of Killing* at the cinema, on DVD and streaming from online platforms, some seeing the full-length version, others the shorter version, and some both versions. Our audiences had also paid attention to reviews and word-of-mouth, thus coming to the film with some information and expectations about the style of the film and its subject matter (for more details see Hill et al. 2019, Hill 2021).

The moments before engagement can often be crucial to the act of watching documentary and help to shape the moment of engagement itself. The context of engagement, such as the cinema where audiences watch *The Act of Killing*, or the online platform where they find the film, will already affect audiences, helping to shape an affective climate for the act of watching documentary. The moment of engagement itself is an immersive experience. Elsewhere I have analysed modes of engagement for documentary (see Hill 2007, 2008, 2013), arguing for physical, cognitive, affective and emotional modes of engagement. Certainly, this documentary invites audiences to immerse themselves in a shocking experience, one that asks them to engage in all sorts of ways through the body, mind and heart. We find audiences expressing their engagement through their bodies, articulating their engagement in moral discussion of the ethics of documentary or performances of people in the films, and reflecting on their engagement as audiences themselves. Thus, we can trace engagement across several sites of analysis, from the moment prior to engagement – and then with the content of the film, the genre of documentary and the wider societal context for audiences.

Documentary engagement and impact are contingent on the subjective positions of audiences and the place of engagement. Watching the film in Indonesia, where it was screened by student and civil society groups, for example, has its own challenges in terms of collective engagement and societal or policy impact. Heryanto's (2014) reflections on *The Act of Killing*, and the audience's expectations for the film's impact within Indonesia highlight these challenges. He hoped the film might provide 'a new weapon for those seeking justice for the victims of 1965, both past and present' (ibid: 163). But, despite his own contributions to journal articles and press reports, his expectations were not met, and demands for justice continue in an on-going struggle for recognition and action.

Watching the film from other regions, with different memories and experiences of war, violence and trauma is also significant and makes engagement and impact fraught with other kinds of difficulties and problems. For example, we found that Colombian audiences thought *The Act of Killing* a shocking film – typically describing it as a 'what the fuck doc'. The film invited them to engage with the act of documenting genocide through the aesthetics and direction, and the act of watching within the context of their lives in a country struggling for peace and in a society scarred by war. Diana Taylor's research on performance and memory (2003) was helpful in understanding the way audiences engaged with the embodied and performed acts of the perpetrators and victims in the films; this performance of violence and impunity generated a broader repertoire of knowledge among audiences. 'The act of watching these documentaries is so challenging that it provokes audiences to become engaged not only with the aesthetics and subject matter, and the subjectivity of the filmmaker but also the subjective positions of viewers themselves' (Hill et al. 2019: 674).

If we briefly address the Japanese audiences of *The Act of Killing*, we can see the context to engagement is significant – from before the act of watching through to the immersive experience of engagement and its resonance with audiences. The distributor of the film in Japan certainly saw the potential for provocation in the style and subject matter of the film: 'I myself was knocked out of my wits after viewing it. Initially I assumed that the audience will be limited because the content was political' (interview, 5 December 2014). However, to their surprise, the film, showing in art house and independent cinemas in various cities, did well in terms of ticket sales (approximately 50,000 at the time of the interview) and managed to reach beyond the original target audience of older cinema-goers to attract younger audiences: 'There were many young people beyond my expectation. It must be because the film is so powerful.'

One audience member (a 39-year-old male) managed to attend the late-night screening at an independent cinema in the region of Kyushu. He started watching the film, thinking it was about the genocide in Rwanda, a country he was interested in, only to find it was about something else. He found the double subjectivity of the documentary moving: he engaged with emotional and moral conflicts through the person of Anwar as a perpetrator of mass killing. And he reflected on connections with perpetrators of violence in Japan: 'We can see many of these gangs in Kawasaki. … Once you create vigilantes the violence becomes their main power.' Here, we can see how this audience member's watching the documentary late at night in the cinema creates an affective climate that amplifies the visceral shock of the film: he was expecting a more expository style of documentary about genocide but, instead, encountered a more performative style: 'I had never seen such a style of documentary film before. … There was no such film which made me so exhausted after viewing. … It upset my mind. It comes to my heart.'

A radio presenter and film critic (a 47-year-old living in Kawasaki), who interviewed the film distributor about *The Act of Killing* for her programme, noted how word-of-mouth, critics' reviews and press reports all helped give the film the reputation for being shocking, thus shaping the affective climate in advance by preparing audiences for a visceral experience. She promoted the film with a warning to her listeners that they could expect to be shocked by the style of the film and its subject matter. Moreover, *The Act of Killing*, in her view, was a resource for conversations on Japanese and American complicity in the Indonesian genocide (Blum 2003; Dewi 2014). She considered the film 'a rare documentary' while the act of watching was a performative process of immersion in the 'painful experiences' as imagined and felt in and through the film. She was deeply troubled by the 'relationship between murderers and victims' as represented in the film which provoked, for her, thoughts about the atrocities committed during and after World War II by Japanese troops in Korea and China: 'I really feel that Japan came to be wicked.' The context prior to engagement shapes the immersive mode of engagement with the film, which resonates for her with regard to memory and forgetting in Japanese post-war culture (Tsutsui 2009). Here, then, engagement is not only shown through ticket sales, or the cinema experience, but also as cultural resonance: what the film means to her and her lived realities. Although her individual engagement does not lead directly to a policy impact, the radio programme she hosts about the film is a good example of the consequences of her engagement, as she becomes a participant in the media debates about *The Act of Killing* and she creates a mediated space for public conversations about the film.

In another example, a 19-year-old female student saw *The Act of Killing* at her local independent cinema in Kawasaki. Before watching the film, she had followed a celebrity figure, Madame Dewi, and her blog, referring to comments on the film and criticism of the Japanese government's support for the Indonesian government at the time: 'This fact has not been widely known in Japan. I really felt that Japan needs to accept properly this history.' After seeing the film, she wrote a course report on the Indonesian genocide, and afterwards went on a trip to Beijing, visiting the Museum of the War of Chinese People's Resistance against Japanese Aggression, where she 'saw how the Chinese looked at the Shino-Japanese war'. Engagement is more than purchasing a cinema ticket, or attention to the film and its marketing online: the moral issues within the film resonate and fuel curiosity for more knowledge.

Two female friends, a 33-year-old school administrator and a 39-year-old part-time worker in a family business, engaged with the film and reflected on its resonance for their inter-generational memories of war. They spoke of how the film showed morality as 'fragile and rotten' in society. They connected their experience of watching the film with their lack of knowledge about the perpetrators of violence during World War II or victims of the atomic bomb attack on Hiroshima on 6 August 1945:

We also did the same thing in Japan. It makes me think that we don't hear at all from grandfathers about the war, saying 'I killed people' to their sons or grandchildren (33-year old-school administrator).

The real victims who had really bad experiences rarely talk about it. They don't want to remember or even talk about it. They just want to forget about it, but cannot forget … now they started talking about it before they die… I lived with my grandmother, but she hardly talked about it. But, once she happened to tell us a of a person who was burnt all over their body and their skin came off, trying to find water… My grandmother said that the real victims avoided registering for compensation because they were discriminated as atomic bomb victims outside of Hiroshima. Then, these people were hiding that they were exposed to radiation and later on symptoms appeared. … I think we should make a film based on such ugly stories rather than romanticising the post-war period (39-year-old part-time worker in a family business).

Taylor's research on enactments shows how 'embodied and performed acts generate, record and transmit knowledge' (2003: 21). Whilst Taylor is referring to participants and performers within live events, placing emphasis on acts of transfer that draw on the power of live performance, we can extend this idea to audiences as performers. The act of watching documentary generates knowledge, in this case disputed knowledge about Japanese cultural memory and practices of forgetting.

In some final reflections on the meaning of engagement, resonance and impact for documentary, it is worth considering resonance in more detail in relation to audiences. Two relatively recent studies on normative and empirical meanings of resonance point to the value of the term for understanding documentary experiences in societal and cultural contexts. Rosa's (2019: 58) sociological inquiry into resonance notes how the idea means 'an intrinsic connection or correspondence of mutual relation', an idea counter to theories of alienation, for example. Bogart's (2021: 3) artistic inquiry into resonance notes how the idea means 'what ripples and radiates: one energetic being influences the vibrations of another'. Bogart identifies particular qualities in artistic work, such as curiosity or presence, that can offer audiences pathways to resonance, to be affected, to feel connected to an art work although not necessarily to be in agreement with it.

In the audience comments above, coming from outside Indonesia and another place of engagement, we could possibly expect the film to be watched in a distanced way, for example, with people experiencing a disconnect between memories of genocide in Indonesia and those of war in Japan. *The Act of Killing* is a disturbing documentary, one that audience members find so shocking it can make them feel physically sick. For Bogart (2021), artworks that provoke feelings of pain or sickness are less likely to generate resonance. But this film ripples and radiates through audiences, provoking engagement and offering pathways to resonance. Japanese audience members are stimulated to call for documentaries about morality since these 'ugly stories' offer a darker picture of how humans relate with, or turn against, each other, as part of political and social realities.

CONCLUSION

In sum, when Winston, Vanstone and Chi argue for the act of documenting as a significant development in the study of docmedia, the act of watching documentary can also be included in this analysis of documentary. As commissioners and funders for documentary place emphasis on measurable engagement and demonstrable impact, the vexed issue of what engagement means and methodological questions of how to substantiate claims of impact will continue to challenge filmmakers and researchers. Documentary audience research can contribute to these discussions. In particular, widening our understanding of engagement to include affect and the potential for audience agency will open up a more multi-faceted type of audience research into engagement, resonance and impact as connected. Audiences make those connections when they engage and reflect on the power of documentary to 'show us life' (Winston, Vanstone and Chi 2017: 217).

REFERENCES

Austin, Thomas (2007) *Watching the World: Screen Documentary and Audiences*, Manchester: Manchester University Press

Blum, William (2003) *Killing Hope: US Military and CIA Interventions Since World War II*, London: Zed Books

Bogart, Anne (2021) *The Art of Resonance*, London: Methuen Drama

Bondebjerg, Ib (2014) *Engaging with Reality: Documentary and Globalisation*, Bristol: Intellect

Coleman, Stephen (2013) *How Voters Feel*, Cambridge: Cambridge University Press

Corner, John (2017) Afterword, *Media Industries*, Vol. 4, No. 1 pp 1-6

Dahlgren, Peter and Hill, Annette (2020) Parameters of media engagement, *Media Theory*, Vol. 4, No. 1. Available online at http://journalcontent.mediatheoryjournal.org/index.php/mt/article/view/107

Dahlgren, Peter (2009) *Media and Political Engagement*, Cambridge: Cambridge University Press

Dewi, Madam (2014) Tairyo-gyakusatsu wo seitouka shita documentary eiga [A documentary film which shows how Indonesia justified genocide], Blog, 4 April. Available online at http://ameblo.jp/dewisukarno/entry-11805347817.html, accessed on 11 September 2016

Ellis, John (2011) *Documentary Witness and Self-revelation*, London: Routledge

Hermes, Joke (2005) *Re-reading Popular Culture*, London: Wiley-Blackwell

Heryanto, Ariel (2014) Great and misplaced expectations, *Critical Asian Studies*, Vol. 46, No. 1 pp 162-166

Hill, Annette (2000) Fearful and safe: Audience response to British reality programming, *Television and New Media*, Vol. 1, No. 2 pp 193-214

Hill, Annette (2007) *Restyling Factual TV: Audiences and News, Documentary and Reality Genres*, London: Routledge

Hill, Annette (2008) Documentary modes of engagement, Austen, Thomas and de Jong, Wilma (eds) *Rethinking Documentary: New Perspectives, New Practices*, Maidenhead and New York: Open University Press

Hill, Annette (2013) Ambiguous audiences, Winston, Brian (ed.) *The Documentary Film Book*, London: British Film Institute pp 83-88

Hill, Annette and Steemers, Jeanette (2017) Introduction to media engagement, *Media Industries*, Vol. 4, No. 1 pp 1-5

Hill, Annette, Askanius, Tina, Kondo, Koko and Urueta, José Luis (2019) Provocative engagement: Documentary audiences and performance in *The Act of Killing* and *The Look of Silence*, *International Journal of Cultural Studies*, Vol. 22, No. 5 pp 662-677

Hill, Annette (2021) Documentary imaginary: Production and audience research of *The Act of Killing* and *The Look of Silence*, *European Journal of Cultural Studies*, Vol. 24, No. 4 pp 801-815

Nash, Kate, Hight, Craig and Summerhayes, Catherine (2014) *New Documentary Ecologies: Emerging Platforms, Practices and* Discourses, London: Palgrave Macmillan

Nash, Kate and Corner, John (2016) Strategic impact documentary: Contexts of production and social intervention, *European Journal of Communication*, Vol. 31, No. 3 pp 227-242

Rosa, Hartmut (2019) *Resonance: A Sociology of our Relationship to the World* (translated by Wagner, J.), Cambridge: Polity

Taylor, Diana (2003) *The Archive and the Repertoire: Performing Cultural Memory in the Americas*, Durham, NC: Duke University Press

Tsutsui, Kiyoteru (2009) The trajectory of perpetrators' trauma: Mnemonic politics around the Asia Pacific War in Japan, *Social Forces*, Vol. 87, No. 3 pp 1,389-1,416

Winston, Brian, Vanstone, Gail and Chi, Wang (2017) *The Act of Documenting: Documentary Film in the 21st Century*, London: Bloomsbury

NOTE ON THE CONTRIBUTOR

Annette Hill is a Professor of Media and Communication at Lund University, Sweden, and Visiting Professor at King's College London. Her research focuses on audiences and popular culture, with interests in media engagement, everyday life, genres, production studies and cultures of viewing. She is the author of nine books and many articles and book chapters in journals and edited collections, which address varieties of engagement with reality television, news and documentary, television drama, entertainment formats, live events and sports entertainment, film violence and media ethics. Her latest book is *The Handbook of Mobile Socialities* (with Hartmann and Andersson, Routledge, 2021).

SECTION 2

Free Expression, Offence and Critical Human Rights

Chapter 5

Humans as Cultural Beings in Theory and Practice

Clifford Christians

The philosophy-of-the-human as cultural beings emphasises the intrinsic importance of our symbolic and interpretive capacities. Humans are the one living species constituted by language; therefore, humans are fundamentally cultural beings. Communication is the catalytic agent in cultural formation, and its most explicit expressions are symbolic creations such as the dramatic arts, public discourse, oral-aural language, electronic entertainment, live streaming and digital networks. Our linguistic nature means that interpretation is the key to understanding human consciousness. Interpretation takes seriously lives that are grounded in cultural complexities and, therefore, critical inquiry is interpretation's key modality. As media writer and producer, in ethics and critique, teaching and administration, Brian Winston exemplifies this humanities perspective.

Keywords: critical inquiry, cultural being, interpretation, philosophy of language, symbol

THE PHILOSOPHY-OF-THE-HUMAN

The philosophy-of-the-human concerns itself with the deepest questions human beings have faced since history began. In the philosophy-of-the-human's most credible forms, the interdependence of people, animals and plant life is supposed, rather than the human species considered dominant over other animate forms. The philosophical perspective developed here privileges human mediations while committed to the unified web of organic existence.

The philosophy-of-the-human investigates the status of mortal beings in the universe and the purpose and meaning of human life. In contrast, the empirical sciences are said to be concerned with the physical, chemical and biological properties of things. The philosophical approach of this chapter denies this dualism. Humans are seen as an indivisible whole, an organic unity with multi-sided sociocultural and physical capacities. The various dimensions of humanness express themselves in and through one another. Language and society are not two separate realms, with relationships that require specification; they are interactive in human livelihood. The ethnographic is embodied in human experience rather than becoming statistically abstract empiricism. Defining humans as cultural beings does not commit the fallacy of naturalistic theorising, where rationality determines both the genesis and the conclusion.

The philosophy-of-the-human presupposes that it makes sense to argue for a human reality and that philosophical scholarship is able to contribute to its comprehension. David Hume's *Treatise of Human Nature* (1739-1740) and Immanuel Kant's *Anthropology* (1798) took these presumptions to be uncontested. In the twentieth century, Ernst Cassirer summarised his four-volume *The Philosophy of Symbolic Forms* (1923-1929) as an *Essay on Man* and Michael Landman presents a standard label for this tradition with his title *Philosophical Anthropology* (1974) (cf Ricoeur 1967; Schacht 1990). Søren Kierkegaard's *Concluding Unscientific Postscript: Philosophical Fragments* (1941 [1846]) conceives the truth of humanity phenomenologically, as subjectivity rather than as capacities that determine actual human contingencies. For Karl Marx, in *Sixth Thesis of Feuerbach* (1845), humanity does not consist of metaphysical or in-born traits, but humans are an ensemble of social relations that are historically contingent. Jean-Paul Sartre's *Existentialism and Humanism* (1973 [1946]) insists that we 'exist first and define ourselves afterwards' acquiring an essence through choices and projects, with nothing to be explained by something outside ourselves. In Friedrich Nietzsche's best-known *Human All Too Human: A Book for Free Spirits* (1908 [1878]), the human analytical awareness that he called 'psychological observations' enables humans to control the narrative of their own existence. Reinhold Niebuhr's theological two-volume *The Nature and Destiny of Man* (1943) presumes human reality also, as do *The Philosophy of Human Nature* (2008), by Howard Kainz, and Michael Ruse's *The Philosophy of Human Evolution* (2012) in contemporary terms. The philosophy of the human as an intellectual idea has developed a significant account of what human being entails. Without exception these works verify the philosophy-of-the-human's conceptual foundation that human reality is theoretically consequential.

EXISTENCE VERSUS ESSENCE

As philosophers have searched for the characteristics that are both common and exclusive to human beings, one answer has focused on the epistemic category 'essence'. Essences are considered determinative of the phenomenon called humankind. To understand human nature is to grasp the necessary constituents of this bounded entity. The idea of human nature as essence is metaphysical in character, with the natural aspects of human beingness typically self-interest, humanity-interest and life-interest. The Marxist tradition is highly critical of an unalterable inner being, for example; confined to human nature, inquiry regarding essence is reductionistic. The dualisms that result from the essential approach to human nature have been dissentious and generally unproductive.

Existentialism contradicts the essentialist tradition. From Martin Heidegger's revolutionary *Being and Time* (1927), the philosophy-of-the-human's prevailing emphasis has been existential Being. Heidegger's redefinition 'does not conceive of human beings in relation to a reality that transcends and constitutes them as those they are' (Schacht 1990: 161). In this new paradigm, human beingness is not an immutable essence but an animated existent expressing the meaning of things. In the existential terms of this essay, essences cannot be determinative of humankind; being-in-the-world is the primary given.

The existentialist framework views relational reality as a complex of congruent dimensions. Thus, the philosophy-of-the-human does not illuminate a static substance; rather, the reality it proposes is a multi-faceted complex of coherent dimensions. In explicating the properties of the human condition, the processes and engagements of human life are its determinants. The major concern of philosophical exploration of human existence is inter-personal relationships, that is, the ontology of communalism. Among these relationships, inter-subjectivity is the primary theme. The existential philosophical approach emphasises the cultural and historical nature of human beings, and the intrinsic importance of the symbolic and interpretive capacities, as seen in communicative action. The perspective of humans in ontological terms avoids intellectual dualisms such as formal rationality versus subjectivism.

When the philosophy-of-the-human is considered across geography and history, three properties of human existence are understood: the universal human species in cultural terms, the interpretive mode of philosophical hermeneutics, and the authentic identity of critical theory as the linguistic framework for cross-cultural theorising.

CULTURAL SPECIES

The philosophy-of-the-human identifies the necessary and sufficient conditions of human existence; in so doing four perspectives have dominated – biological organism, rational agent, social beings and cultural species. This intellectual history is summarised here in comparative terms, with a rationale given for the preferred definition of humans as cultural beings.

Humans-as-biological-organisms is one of the foremost definitions in the philosophical literature. Humans are considered living entities within the biosphere. This understanding emphasises the continuity of human life with other animate forms, those ranging from embryonic organisms to the sophisticated systems of human agency. The biological organism scholarship includes human evolution, human evolutionary biology, population genetics, paleontology and the study of biological relatives.

In the philosophy-of-the-human tradition that considers humans to be rational beings, reasoning centres on autonomous actors. Classical Greek philosophy was committed to a basal rationalism; that is, the identity of being and reason as our essential humanness. For René Descartes (1596-1650), the essence of selfhood is thinking substance (*res cogitans*); the human species is rationality interiorised, *cogito ergo sum*. As the eighteenth century congealed around Cartesian rationality, Kant lectured in his early career on mathematics, logic and Newtonian physics at the University of Königsberg. His first major book, *Universal Natural History and Theory of the Heavens* (1755), described the universe's structure in terms of Newton's cosmology (Kant 1781, 1785). John Stuart Mill's *Utilitarianism* (1979 [1861]) is rooted in the inductive reasoning of his *System of Logic* (1843) so that an exclusive formal principle constitutes rational judgments. Based on August Comte's *A General View of Positivism* (1910 [1848]), social research is neutral for Mill, ordered with statistical precision on the sophisticated procedures of inferential logic.

In the post-Enlightenment West for natural science and empirical social science, genuine knowledge is testable and, therein, objectively true. It is cognitively precise, but in linear fashion with a non-contingent starting point. Truth was explained in scientific terms and rational calculation was accepted as modernity's ideology. Rationality was understood through analytic calculation that divided natural reality into quantitative items that are to be managed technically.

The definition of humans as social beings is philosophically derived from Aristotle, in the 4th century BC. As he argues in his *Politics* (1992 [350 BC]), human beings are social and political by nature, 'an animal intended to live in a *polis*' (ibid: 123a). Philosophers who define humans as social beings accentuate the constitutive role of social structures in human experience and action, which they find more compelling than explanations centred on the biological or rational. In this definition, as members of particular societies, human beings are 'producers as well as the products of the conditions of their existence', whose consciousness is informed by social formations and whose lives are bound up with the domain of social relations (Schacht 1990: 165). In Aristotle's tradition, the concept of essentialist human nature is presumed. Even as the tradition expands conceptually – imagination, wisdom, discernment – the notion of essence remains the intellectual core.[1]

Philosophers committed to the idea of 'social beings in the world' discuss among themselves the overriding issue whether situated existence necessitates realisation. Given the complex circumstances involved in particular situations, and contending that identity is not determined by such circumstances, what relational stances, then, does this definition entail? In Heidegger's state of fallenness, for example, wherein is resistance? Can there be distancing from social contexts without transcendence outside the situatedness? What is the alternative to illusions of false security when beingness is under assault? In what capacity is consciousness critical when insisting on cognitive neutrality?

From the perspective of humans as cultural beings, the idea of rational being is reductionistic, accounting for the epistemic but not for a holistic humanity of emotions, will and *techne*. In the symbolic approach to communication, concepts are not separated from their representations. The social and personal dimensions of language are in unity.

Humans-as-biological-organisms continues to be productive, with neuroscience advancing its complexity. But the foundational concepts for the human condition remain elementary in character. Beyond the quest for survival is the need for meaningful human interaction; we comprehend ourselves by interpreting the symbolism that our lifeworld represents.

SYMBOLIC EXPRESSIONS

In the philosophy-of-the-human tradition that inspires this chapter, humans know themselves through their symbolic expressions. Communication is the creative process of building and affirming the human order though symbols, with cultures the human habitat that results. Language does not merely reflect reality from the outside; events must be recomposed into narratives in order for humans to comprehend reality at all. In Richard Schacht's summary definition: 'Humans are language-using and culture-incorporating creatures whose form of experience, conduct and interaction take shape in linguistically and culturally structured environments, and are conditioned by the meanings they bear' (Schacht 1990: 173).

Communication is the public agency through which human identity is realised. Language is not a vehicle of individuated cognition and subjective preference as the epistemology of rational choice assumes, but belongs to the community's reflection and action. As the alphabet organises the complex world of sound into its audiological units, humans as cultural beings use lingual formations to initiate and maintain a liveable environment.

In Ernst Cassirer's *Philosophy of Symbolic Forms* (1953-1957, 1966 [1923-1929]), the symbolic realm is unique to the human species. Humans alone of living entities possess the creative mind, the capacity to construct the domain of human understanding typically called 'culture'. Humanity has no essential static nature in itself, only history. History is a precondition of all thought including critical reflection. That which appears to humans in their modality of understanding is gained from history's pre-given context. Reason is not ensconced in innermost being, isolated from communication, as John Locke (1632-1704) argued; nor is reason a separate faculty. As humans create lifeworlds through language, these creations are permeated by epistemic properties such as rationale, judgment, examination and discovery.

Human beings are a cultural species, enabling them to represent different cultural identities, all of which transcend the natural behaviour of other species.

To contemplate this reality philosophically is to examine such questions as: What makes cultural forms of life possible? What distinguishes culture from natural organic forms? And what is a valid reason for acting? Moreover, the phenomenon of human intersubjectivity is philosophically interesting. Human expressions develop into further expressions and intentions are registered intermittently; together they produce other expressions that include intentionality, with all levels and dimensions conditioned by symbolic conventions.

Linguistic capacity is a structural property of cultural beingness; perception, emotion, planning and thought are all plausibly transformed into linguistic creations. Transformed connections between perception and belief are also conceivable, as are the manifold relationships between thought and action. For Michael Tomasello's *A Natural History of Human Thinking* (2014), the lingual capacity enables joint intentionality, peculiar to humans as collaborators. Non-linguistic animals cooperate in the sense that participants in a functional task carry out their part in a social process. Collaboration goes beyond cooperation by linking the collaborators together in a form of networked minds with cognition distributed across the participants. Tomasello argues that collaborative activity creates a more permanent shared world, that is to say, a culture.

INTERPRETIVE BEINGS

The symbolic, linguistic character of the human species means that interpretation is indispensable for understanding anthropological capacities, the vicissitudes of life and moral requisites. When humans are defined as cultural beings, human affairs are fundamentally interpretive, rather than a matter of scientific explanation presuming neutrality. Since humanity is embedded in an existing cultural world, its sense of being is necessarily historical. The world orientation of humans-in-relation is a primordial given, and no one ever stands outside an evolving interpretation of his or her humanness. It is illusory to claim a pure understanding of human reality that is non-interpretive. Because all experience is linguistic, humans understand themselves as subjects, and the world in which they live, only through the symbolic meanings that represent the world. Therefore, philosophical analysis of and everyday observation of human affairs are both matters of interpretation rather than of rational calculation.

In the philosophy-of -the-human in the West, classical Greece established the process of interpretation as ascetically radical to human life and consequently considered it an intellectual problem. Thus, Aristotle wrote a major treatise on interpretation (*hermeneia*), that is, the erudite *Peri hermeneias,* 'On Interpretation', in the *Organon.* In so delineating the conditions of understanding, Aristotle centred on the human ability to interpret languages, to make linguistic expressions meaningful. The art of *hermenia* is the key to moral judgments in the *Nicomachean Ethics*. Plato had already established in the *Phaedrus* (370 BC) that messages of expression are distinct from acts of interpretation. Presuming the validity of his distinction, in the *Ion* (380 BC), Plato focuses on the role of the interpretive process within the broader category, understanding. The idea of interpretation, with varying emphases, appears in the classical literature of Lucretius, Plutarch, Euripedes, Xenophon and Epicurus.

RICOEUR'S THEORY OF INTERPRETATION

The philosopher of language, Paul Ricoeur, reconstructs the philosophy of the human around the interpretive modality. Interpretation is dialogue with human existence past and present; therefore, epistemic certainty is impossible (Ricoeur 1967). No facts exist that speak for themselves. Actualities of human existence must be symbolised as interactive voices to be understood. Interpretation is a multi-dimensional activity; the materials available for interpretation are themselves interpreted: memories, beliefs, heterodoxies and perceptions, for example (cf. Gadamer 1975, 1989).

In Ricoeur's *Conflict of Interpretations* (1974) and *Interpretation Theory* (1976), the ontological character of his philosophy of language is developed explicitly. The awareness of humans as beings-in-the-world is based on the lingual reality of belongingness for *homo sapiens*. Human existence is a composite of present-day socioculturalism and of civilisations past that continue to exist in art, music, literature and philosophy. Self-being is always interpreted within a community of interacting beings. 'The subject that interprets himself while interpreting signs is no longer the *cogito*; rather, he is a being who discovers by the exegesis of his own life, that he is placed in Being before he places and possesses himself.' Our manner of existence 'remains from start to finish a being-interpreted' (Ricoeur 1974: 11).

Humans understand themselves as situated in time and space by interpreting the symbolic meanings that constitute the world of species existence. Subjectivity is a person's existential awareness in the ongoing interpretive process. It is invalid to assume that there is direct knowledge of our selfhood or that the self is autonomous, since conscious awareness is a construal of our cultural situatedness.

The idea of metaphor is the centrepiece of Ricoeur's theory of interpretation. The semantic power of metaphor engenders a surplus of meaning in the linguistic imagination. In *The Rule of Metaphor* (1981), he defends a new understanding of metaphor's lingual purpose. Ricoeur argues that classic rhetoric presupposed two levels of signification for metaphor – the primary literal level and the other symbolic level which is secondary. As obvious from Ricoeur's theory of interpretation, dividing metaphor into these two domains as separate, unequal steps is erroneous. The interpretive process is fluid, with interpreters interacting between levels both erratically and simultaneously within the semiotic context. As denotation and inference indicate, words are polysemic. All languages provide metaphorical resources that can be used creatively to produce new meanings. Surplus of meaning expands and extends the original without abandoning it; there is a root idea of meaningfulness across cultures, though elaborations are multiple.

Ricoeur does not limit our understanding of discourse to its correspondence with facts or to the author's intent or to one literal meaning; he sees all forms of communication in terms of the 'principle of plentitude', that is, 'a text means all that it can mean' (Ricoeur 1981: 176). Meaning is constrained by the dialectic of context, by the history of the narrative and by the boundaries of actual experience, but the pivotal feature of interpretation is the extravagance of significations. For Ricoeur, our spatiotemporal location and transcending the local are an integrated composite. Surplus of meaning is not 'simply different meanings appended to different beliefs' (Lynch 2011: 6). Ricoeur's surplus of meaning gives multiple realisability in narrative a credible form.

Interpretation is not abstractionism; the human species cannot withdraw from its linguisticality to determine what something actually means. Interpretation is always at the level of the lingual world native to us. For Ricoeur, language is the vehicle that makes the intelligible accessible for use, with all lingual exercises interpretive. As Heidegger puts it: 'All language … interprets. It is an interpretation at one and the same time of a reality and of the one who speaks about this reality' (1971a: 89). Interpretation opens up the immanent properties of public life in its dynamic dimensions. The livelihood of humans as cultural beings is characterised by multiple interpretations and grounded in cultural diversity.

CRITICAL INQUIRY

The philosophy-of-the-human as cultural being entails critical forms of knowledge production in both cognition and practice. The symbolic theory of communicative forms, and the interpretive modality that this approach requires, is the lingual arena in which critical inquiry has epistemological priority.

Critical theories share the ideas and methodologies of interpretive theories. Interpretive and critical approaches do not merely explain but establish commitments between interpreters and the interpreted. Interpretation and critical inquiry are not reportage, but both are claims of linguistic philosophy. Critical scholarship differs in that its interpretive acts are symbolic constructs to critique the ways that societies encumber and subjugate. Critical perspectives aim to change human conditions by emphasising the social structures of society as a whole.

Critical inquiry enriches interpretativeness by specialising in dialectical analysis. The art of knowing truth, by uncovering the contradictions in adversarial reasoning and in underlying commonplace ideologies, exposes the oppositional struggles for power. When people become aware of the dialectic of opposing forces, they are able to liberate themselves and change the existing order. Critical inquiry is reflective assessment that exposes power ensembles, contending as it does that a society's social degradations arise more decisively from hidden structures and cultural assumptions than from individual psychological factors.[2]

HABERMAS AND CRITICAL INQUIRY

The philosophical problem that emerges in critical inquiry is identifying those aspects of its theories and methods that are adequate for underwriting social criticism. Jürgen Habermas is the principal second generation critical theorist to accomplish this task. Habermas's *Knowledge and Human Interests* (1968) established that critical knowledge is based on principles that differentiate it from natural science and from the liberal arts by its reflection and emancipation. Habermas's philosophical endeavour from *Knowledge and Human Interests* in 1968 to *Moral Consciousness and Communicative Action* in 1990 has been to develop an interactive, fallibilist and ethnographic account of rationality, pushing critical inquiry in a naturalist direction. From the 1960s onwards, language, symbolism and meaning have been developed as the theoretical foundation of the humanities through the influence of Ludwig Wittgenstein, Ferdinand de Saussure, Hans-Georg Gadamer and other thinkers in linguistic philosophy, symbolic interactionism and hermeneutics. Habermas's project reflects this philosophy-of-language trajectory.[3]

Already with Max Horkheimer (1895-1973) in the early days of the Frankfurt School, positivist social science was rejected for its reductionistic study of issues in isolation and its separation of facts from values through quantitative techniques. Habermas endorses the Frankfurt epistemology. For him, likewise, rationality is not the possession of knowledge. The issue is communicative rationality, that is, 'how speaking and acting subjects use knowledge' (Habermas 1984: 11). In this view, speech acts ought to reconstruct an equalitarian domain in which participants are 'attributed the capacity to produce valid utterances and are considered capable of distinguishing valid from invalid expressions' (Habermas 1990: 31). Acquiring the abilities needed for communicative rationality enables critical inquiry.

Thus, Habermas redefines critical inquiry as reconstructive science. Habermas's reconstructionism explicates the conditions for incorrect or correct utterances; reconstruction also explains why some utterances distort, some speech acts are unsuccessful and argumentation frequently inadequate. Habermas uses formal pragmatics philosophically to identify the justifications used in various forms of argumentation; these reflections yield semantic rules that organise discursive communication which, in turn, can reform discursive institutions (Habermas 1996: 230n). Reconstructive theory and practice 'explain deviant cases and through this indirect authority acquire a critical function' (Habermas 1990: 32). As noted regarding ideological speech, Habermas calls narrative that is not dependent on the conditions of communicative rationality distorted communication. In such communication, interactants are not able to participate fairly regardless of the outcome.

IDEOLOGY OF INSTRUMENTALISM

Ideology is the central concept in the scholarship of critical inquiry, that is, ideology as ideas that configure societies' notion of reality. In critical inquiry, ideology as a system of representations that governs how social orders are constructed is the principal obstacle to human liberation. Although Habermas quarrelled with marginal issues in Adorno and Horkheimer's *Dialectic of Enlightenment* (2003 [1944]), he reiterated their historical treatment that modernity's reason and freedom have turned into their opposites; rather than liberating, the Western Enlightenment's worldview – that the mind deliberates impartially — has become a dominating and controlling ideology.[4]

The prevailing ideology in the industrial West is instrumentalism – the idea that technology is neutral and expands in terms of its own technical character without conditioning our humanness. Technologies are considered artifacts of science apart from values. Technological products are thought to be independent, being used to support both positive and negative lifestyles and cultures. 'Technology, as pure instrumentality, is indifferent to the variety of ends it can be employed to achieve' (Feenberg 1991: 5). Websites provide both the lives of heroes and the rancorous hate speech of fundamentalist sects. As ideology, the idea of instrumental neutrality is taken for granted.

In instrumentalism, or its cognate technicism, as digital technologies represent reality they do so with a technological rhythm. Human values are replaced by efficiency, that is, by the machine's defining feature. This is a mechanical model where the capabilities of media technologies set a society's agenda and establish the cultural issues. With its diffusion-of-tools mentality, instrumentalism begins and ends with the technological reality itself and offers strategies for accomplishing technical goals through it. In the ideology of instrumentalism, scientific prowess and financial resources are channelled into high technology, into improving the power and speed of technological instruments. Humans participate in cyberspace as the facilitators of networks. Critical inquiry, in exposing the ideology of neutral instruments, examines symbolic systems in their historical and institutional contexts – instead of a preoccupation with subsets of hardware and software.[5]

MONOPOLY OF KNOWLEDGE

The Canadian communications theorist, Harold Innis, has expanded critical inquiry with his concept 'monopoly of knowledge'. Critical inquiry has included a psychological orientation since Erich Fromm's *Escape from Freedom* (1941) and Innis's *The Bias of Communication* (1951) benefits from that intellectual trajectory. But his major influence on critical perspectives is sociological, clarifying in *Empire and Communication* (1952) the compositional and historical dimensions of media ecology. For Innis, media technologies do not exist innocuously alongside one another. As his historical studies elaborated, new technologies of communication tend to monopolise human knowledge and reduce existing media forms to a supplementary role.

From the introduction of cuneiform writing to contemporary communication satellites, fibre optics and the algorithmic digital, scholars in the Innis tradition examine all important shifts in symbolic forms, associating them with differentiations in culture and in social organisation. The conceptual demand is to identify the distinctive properties of particular media technologies such as books, magazines, radio, cinema, television, live stream, Facebook, WhatsApp, Twitter, YouNow and WeChat. As Innis concludes, oral culture continued after print became the dominant medium, but the oral-aural mode was no longer the standard of truth or the centrepiece of medicine, engineering, law and politics. In the era of ideological instrumentalism, digital knowledge is primary and other print and broadcast forms become secondary. Cyberspace monopolises our livelihood and institutions now.

A credible critical approach in the internet age must account for this monopoly-of-knowledge phenomenon. Learning from the Innis tradition, the imperative for critical inquiry in the ideological era of instrumentalism is multimedia abundance instead of the Web 2.0's monopoly of knowledge.

PERSPECTIVISM

Perspective-taking is implicit in the reflexivity of critical inquiry. Since the critical approach focuses on social relationships, such relationships can be specified in terms of perspective-takers by those who are included in the interpretations. Habermas calls the social inquiries 'technocratic' that use methodologies for problem-solving in terms of third-person knowledge of impersonal consequences. For critical inquiry, reflective participants are contextualised in the social relationships they constitute, enabling them to discern across various perspectives in their acts of social criticism. When there is multimedia abundance, it is possible to replace the social scientist as detached observer with a diversity of critical perspectives.

Critical perspectives disclose; they open up the inside meaning to critique the heart of the matter. Critical perspectives see beneath the surface of everyday affairs, taking account of the interactional context, motives and presuppositions. Thus, authentic disclosure is opposed to the ideology of instrumentalism. These inside perspectives that reveal the inner meaning of the lingual world in which humans exist are presented in the natural languages of human interaction. Natural language rather than the artificial languages of mathematical statistics or linear induction is the mode of perspectivism.

Critical perspectives in narrative form are a society's critical discourse and mediated technologies are the principal public forum of critical discourse.[6] Given humans as cultural beings and technologies as processes of cultural formation, communication technology is not a tool *per se*, but a cultural process of making meaning. From the perspective of technology as a cultural enterprise, media technologies symbolise human events without which the human species cannot exist. Thus, communicative events such as educational pedagogy, medical networks and entertainment programming are not driven by context-free abstractions, but resonate with the breadth of human agency in its interactions with animate and inanimate reality. The existence of culture presupposes the reflexive ability of the human mind to interpret culture and its contexts. The interpretive turn recovers history and biography, so that complex perspective-taking and multi-layered events and cultures are represented adequately, with critical discourse the result.

SYMBOLIC SYSTEMS

As contended above, the philosophy-of-humans as the cultural species considers the lingual arts as the defining characteristic of human existence, language referring in expansive terms to the full range of symbolic forms. Stated differently, communication is the catalytic agent in cultural formation and its most explicit expressions are symbolic formations: the dramatic arts, news narrative, oral-aural language, electronic entertainment, live streaming and digital networks. Since language is the material of human exchange, symbols create what humans view as reality. The primary constituents of human livelihood are religion, myth, art, science and history; symbols are the facilitator of all such creations. Symbols are not identical to the actualities they symbolise, but they do participate in the authentication of that which they represent. In literature and cinema or YouTube Live, as examples of symbolic formations, their inner dialectics – point of departure, setting, tone, digital coding and resolution of conflict – reflect their culture's value system.

Symbolic systems of critical discourse in the public forum will follow the interpretive arts to sufficiency. Mediations that inform the public adequately aim for interpretive adequacy. Interpretation with a critical perspective is not preoccupied with specific struggles, but addresses the dominant and resilient crises of having social science, education, neighbourhoods, religious centres and voluntary associations co-opted by the ideology of technicism. What Clifford Geertz (1973) calls 'thick description' replaces the thinness of statistically precise objectivism. Accounts that meet the principle of sufficiency put specifics in their context of meaning. Sufficiency entails credible interpretations of the attitudes, language and cultural forms of the social group being reported. News as critical discourse means distinguishing the major components of the lifeworld being investigated from digressions and parentheses. Interpretive adequacy in the public arena challenges the injustices of hegemonic alliances and supports movements opposing these disenfranchisements, recognising the activists as reflective participants in cultural formation.

Critical inquiry appeals to the knowledge that reflective agents already possess to a greater or lesser extent. Critical social scientists participate in the creation of the contexts in which their perspective-taking is publicly verified. The emphasis in interpretation is on discovery rather than administering routinised procedures. According to Habermas's communicative rationality, the goal of critical inquiry is not to manipulate or control sociocultural processes, but to initiate and foster critical discourse so that there is adequate participatory reflection by all those affected (Habermas 1971: 40-41).

CONCLUSION

For the philosophy-of-the-human, the issue is not the certainty of knowledge but theory as inquiry into the meaning of metanarratives. Theorising discloses the fundamental conditions of existential reality. The suggestiveness of theoretical claims derives from the interpretive domain that is symbolised in human culture. Theories are not scholastic paradigms of mathematical precision, but theorising is the imaginative power that gives an inside perspective on reality.[7] Critical theory, as in Habermas, is based on the philosophy of cultural beings as its existential ground. Thus, its orientating basis affirms the need for a strong claim of rightness in critical discourse, without which it would be invalid to engage in social criticism.

As the intellectual history of the philosophy-of-the-human documents, the question of theory is finally ontological, that is, theory concerns the nature of organic being, specifically the character of human beingness. Following Heidegger and Ellul, as argued in Innis's theory of communication, and presumed in Habermas's communicative rationality, technologies and beingness are interwoven. Therefore, mechanistic and bureaucratic standards for judging communication phenomena are decidedly secondary to cultural humanity as a normative ideal. Reality is not to be understood as a raw aggregate of the inanimate, but a converged order of material and organic that makes critical theory intelligible.[8] Knowledge is incoherent if infinite regression is presumed. Interpretation is impossible without a given. Theories are perspectival schemes for elaborating basic values.

As interpretive formulae, theories are validated by the extent to which they open up possibilities of action. Theories are not epistemically independent, but forms of discovery that are tested by the criterion of interpretive adequacy. The ethnographic is grafted into human existence rather than isolating itself as regression vectors, syllogisms and statistical correlations. The philosophy of humans as cultural beings defines agency within the ideology of instrumentalism. This philosophy-of-the-human perspective avoids the logical mistake of interpreting cultural diversity as moral relativism. It recognises that asserting prescriptive claims from the experiential commits the fallacy of confused categories.

Brian Winston, as media writer and documentary film producer, in ethics and critique, teaching and administration, exemplifies the humanities perspective of this essay. As a world class critical theorist, his hermeneutical depth on mediated symbolic systems demonstrates how interpretive scholarship ought to be done in a global era of cross-cultural complexity.

NOTES

[1] Marx's existentialism is an alternative to Aristotelian essence, contending that the social organism is greater than the sum of its parts. According to this organicist model originating with Hegel, what is real to the social organism's members can only be real in relation to the whole. Society is not a conglomerate of atomistic individuals as in Locke's contractual notion of society

[2] The history and content of critical theory is well known and, therefore, acknowledged in this footnote rather than elaborated in the text. The Frankfurt School of Critical Theory is the most influential tradition, founded in 1923 at the Institute of Social Research of the University of Frankfurt. Max Horkheimer was director from 1930 to 1958 stressing interdisciplinary scholarship, with Theodor Adorno (philosopher and sociologist) and Erich Fromm (psychologist) early collaborators, and literary critics, Walter Benjamin and Leo Lowenthal, later associates. The institute disbanded in 1969 but its transformations continued in new and extensive form with Jürgen Habermas. Habermas's communicative rationality, politics of textuality and dialectical discourse are particularly relevant to the philosophy of humans as cultural beings

[3] Social philosopher Max Weber is also influential for Habermas. Weber's critical perspective resulted from his recognising social science as causal and interpretive and uniting both dimensions in such publications as his *Protestant Ethic and the Spirit of Capitalism* (1904-1905), multiple chapters in *The Methodology of the Social Sciences* (1949) and his essay 'Science as a vocation' in his *From Max Weber: Essays in Sociology* (1916)

[4] René Descartes's *Discourse on Method* (2021 [1637]) establishes and elaborates on this objectivism, with pure mathematics the least touched by circumstances (see also Descartes 1964). For the Enlightenment mind, Descartes defines out of existence the brilliant thinking of earlier cultures and non-Western peoples

[5] In the scholarship of French philosopher, Jacques Ellul, modern means of communication are not neutral instruments. Media systems are absorbed into an efficiency-dominated culture. In his *Propaganda, Humiliation of the Word* (1965) and *The Technological Bluff* (1990), Ellul defines the electronic media in terms of *la technique*. This concept is for him an internal bureaucratising that saturates culture and institutions. Humans are absorbed into a data world of one-dimensional shibboleths and memes. News and entertainment media provide a rationale for human existence, with communication technologies the public perimeter of the technological order

[6] The Frankfurt School considers the mass media an oppressive technological system. Habermasian critical inquiry uses a broader definition of the mass media as a 'consciousness-shaping institution'

[7] In Thomas Kuhn's classic *The Structure of Scientific Revolutions* (1996), theories as paradigm constructions are a complex of politics, creativity, intuition and beliefs. For Kuhn, as with this chapter, theories are constructed paradigms rather than the normal science of verifying hypotheses

[8] Zgymunt Bauman's (2005) liquid modernity as an intellectual framework is also consistent with the philosophy of cultural beings. In Bauman's *Liquid Life*, cultural systems and social structures have become fluid. In Grant Kien's *Global Technography: Ethnography in the Age of Mobility* (2009), there has been a paradigmatic transformation to instability in the social media era. He follows Heidegger's *On the Way to Language* (1971a) and his *Poetry, Language, Thought* (1971b) in arguing that humans require the structure of time and a sense of distance to avoid solipsism. However, with the compression of history into the momentary and the demise of spatial limits, our basis

of knowing shifts to an anywhere, anytime experience with humans seeing themselves as existing everywhere always and nowhere never

REFERENCES

Aristotle (1992 [350 BC]) *The Politics*, trans. Sinclair, T. A., London: Penguin Books

Aristotle (1998 [340 BC]) *The Nicomachean Ethics*, trans. Ross, W. D., New York: Oxford University Press

Bauman, Zgymunt (2005) *Liquid Life*, Cambridge, UK: Polity Press

Cassirer, Ernst (1944) *An Essay on Man: An Introduction to a Philosophy of Human Culture*, New Haven, CT: Yale University Press

Cassirer, Ernst (1953-1957, 1966 [1923-1929]) *The Philosophy of Symbolic Forms*, trans. Manheim, R. and Krois, J. 4 Vols, New Haven, CT: Yale University Press

Comte, Auguste (1910 [1848]) *A General View of Positivism*, trans. Bridges, J. H., London: George Routledge & Sons

Descartes, René (1964) *Rules for the Direction of the Mind: Philosophical Essays*, trans. Lafleur, L. J., Indianapolis: Bobbs-Merrill pp 147-236. Original work began in 1628 but not published in his lifetime

Descartes, René (2021 [1637]) *Discourse on Method*, trans. Veitch, J., Ottawa: East India Publishing Company

Ellul, Jacques (1954) *The Technological Society*, trans. Wilkinson, J., New York: Random Vintage

Ellul, Jacques (1965) *Propaganda: The Formation of Men's Attitudes*, trans. Kellen, K. and Lerner, J., New York: Alfred A. Knopf

Ellul, Jacques (1985) *The Humiliation of the Word*, trans. Hanks, J. M., Grand Rapids, MI: Eerdmans

Ellul, Jacques (1990) *The Technological Bluff*, trans. Bromiley, G. W., Grand Rapids, MI: Eerdmans

Feenberg, Andrew (1991) *A Critical Theory of Technology*, New York: Oxford University Press

Fromm, Erich (1941) *Escape from Freedom*, New York: Henry Holt & Co

Gadamer, Hans-Georg (1975) The problem of historical consciousness, *Graduate Faculty Philosophy Journal*, New School for Social Research, Vol. 5, No. 1 pp 8-52

Gadamer, Hans-Georg (1989) *Truth and Method*, trans. Weinsheimer. J. and Marshall, D. G., London: Continuum, revised edition

Geertz, Clifford (1973) *The Interpretation of Cultures*, New York: Basic Books

Habermas, Jürgen (1968) *Knowledge and Human Interests*, Boston: Beacon Press

Habermas, Jürgen (1987 [1984]) *The Theory of Communicative Action*, Vols 1 and 2, Boston: Beacon Press

Habermas, Jürgen (1990) *Moral Consciousness and Communicative Action*, Cambridge, MA: MIT Press

Habermas, Jürgen (1996) *Between Facts and Norms*, Cambridge, MA: MIT Press

Heidegger, Martin (1962 [1927]) *Being and Time*, trans. Macquarrie, J. and Robinson, E., New York: Harper & Row

Heidegger, Martin (1971a) *On the Way to Language*, trans. Hertz, P. and Stambaugh, J., New York: Harper & Row

Heidegger, Martin (1971b) *Poetry, Language, Thought*, trans. Hofstader, A., New York: Harper &

Row

Heidegger, Martin (1977) *The Question Concerning Technology and Other Essays*, trans. Lovitt, W., New York: Harper & Row

Horkheimer, Max and Adorno, Theodor W. (2003 [1944]) *Dialectic of Enlightenment*, trans. Jephcott, E., Stanford, CA: Stanford University Press

Innis, Harold (1951) *The Bias of Communication*, Toronto: University of Toronto Press

Innis, Harold (1952) *Empire and Communication*, Toronto: University of Toronto Press

Kainz, Howard P. (2008) *The Philosophy of Human Nature*, Chicago: Open Court Publishing

Kant, Immanuel (2016 [1781]) *Critique of Pure Reason*, trans. Meiklejohn, J., Auckland, NZ: Pantianos Classics

Kant, Immanuel (2009 [1785]) *Groundwork of the Metaphysic of Morals*, trans. Paton, H. J., New York: Harper Perennial

Kien, Grant (2009) *Global Technography: Ethnography in an Age of Mobility*, New York: Peter Lang

Kierkegaard, Søren (1941 [1846]) *Concluding Unscientific Postscript: Philosophical Fragments*, Princeton, NJ: Princeton University Press

Kuhn, Thomas S. (1996) *The Structure of Scientific Revolutions*, Chicago: University of Chicago Press, third edition

Landman, Michael (1974) *Philosophical Anthropology*, trans. Parent, D. J., Philadelphia: Westminster Press

Lynch, Jake (2011) *Truth As One and Many*, New York: Oxford Clarendon

Mill, John Stuart (1888 [1843]) *A System of Logic, Ratiocinative and Inductive*, New York: Harper & Brothers, eighth edition

Mill, John Stuart (1979 [1861]) *Utilitarianism*, Indianapolis: Hackett

Niebuhr, Reinhold (1964 [1941]) *The Nature and Destiny of Man. Vol. 1: Human Nature, Vol. 2: Human Destiny*, New York: Scribner's

Nietzsche, Friedrich (1908 [1878]) *Human All Too Human: A Book for Free Spirits*, trans. Harvey, A., Chicago: Charles H. Kerr & Company

Ricoeur, Paul (1967) The antinomy of human reality and the problem of philosophical anthropology, Lawrence, N. and O'Connor, D. (eds) *Readings in Existential Phenomenology*, Englewood Cliffs, N. J.: Prentice-Hall pp 390-402

Ricoeur, Paul (1974) *The Conflict of Interpretations: Essays in Hermeneutics*, Ihde, D. (ed.) Evanston, Ill: Northwestern University Press

Ricoeur, Paul (1976) *Interpretation Theory: Discourse and the Surplus of Meaning*, Fort Worth: Texas Christian University Press

Ricoeur, Paul (1981) *The Rule of Metaphor: The Creation of Meaning in Language*, London: Routledge

Ruse, Michael (2012) *The Philosophy of Human Evolution*, Cambridge, UK: Cambridge University Press

Sartre, Jean-Paul (1973 [1946]) *Existentialism and Humanism*, trans. Mairet, P., London: Methuen

Schacht, Richard (1974) On existentialism, *existenz*-philosophy, and philosophical anthropology, *American Philosophical Quarterly*, Vol. 11, No. 4 pp 291-305

Schacht, Richard (1990) Philosophical anthropology: What, why and how, *Philosophy and Phenomenological Research*, Vol. 50 (Supplement) pp 155-176

Tomasello, Michael (2014) *A Natural History of Human Thinking*, Cambridge, MA: Harvard University Press

Weber, Max (1992 [1904-1905]) *The Protestant Ethic and the Spirit of Capitalism*, trans. Parsons, T., London: Routledge

Weber, Max (1946 [1919]) *From Max Weber: Essays in Sociology*, Gerth, H. H. and Wright Mills, C. (eds) Oxford, UK: Oxford University Press

Weber, Max (1949) *The Methodology of the Social Sciences*, Shils, E. A. and Finch, H. A. (eds) New York: The Free Press

NOTE ON THE CONTRIBUTOR

Clifford G. Christians (PhD, LittD, DHL) is Research Professor of Communications, Professor of Journalism and Professor of Media Studies Emeritus at the University of Illinois USA, where he was Director of the Institute of Communications Research and Head of the PhD in Communications for 16 years. His recent publications as author or co-author include *Key Concepts in Critical Cultural Studies, Ethics for Public Communication, Normative Theories of the Media, Media Ethics: Cases and Moral Reasoning* (11th edition) and *Media Ethics and Global Justice in the Digital Age*.

Chapter 6

Doing Harm: How the UK Government Threatens to Impose Online Censorship

Julian Petley

In this chapter, I examine Brian Winston's defence of freedom of expression as a key Enlightenment principle and his criticisms of broadcasting regulation in the UK for departing from it. I also focus on the notion of harm, deriving from John Stuart Mill, that Winston employs to indicate where the limits of freedom of expression should lie. Winston complains that notions of offence and insult have increasingly expanded definitions of harm and so narrowed the bounds of freedom of expression. I use this critique as the starting point for an analysis of the regime of online regulation currently being proposed by the UK government in the form of the Online Safety Bill. This, I argue, threatens to create an unwieldy, unaccountable and unnecessary state apparatus of online censorship, operates with far too broad and vague a notion of harm, and will see material expelled from the online world which is entirely legal in the offline world. I conclude by examining recent proposals from the Law Commission for bringing the regulation of certain categories of online and offline communications into line, and for clarifying what is actually meant by harm in certain specific pieces of legislation. I argue that the commission's carefully delimited approach to the issue of harm in the communications sphere is greatly preferable to the regulatory Behemoth proposed by the Online Safety Bill, which would very seriously endanger the communicative freedoms espoused by Brian Winston.

Keywords: harm, offence, freedom of expression, Online Safety Bill, Ofcom

ON FAILING TO OBTAIN FREEDOM OF EXPRESSION

Brian Winston has always been a redoubtable defender of freedom of expression, both as a television practitioner and as an academic, and a severe critic of those who deny or backslide on this key Enlightenment principle.

Quoting Tom Paine's observation that 'what we obtain too cheap, we esteem too lightly', he lamented in *Messages: Free Expression, Media and the West from Gutenberg to Google* that:

> For the West, there is little or no sense that we have 'obtained' free expression and the rest of the Enlightenment's cluster of fundamental rights cheaply, or indeed at any price at all. They are simply 'there' and, 50 years after the defeat of totalitarianism in the West and some years since its fall in Eastern Europe, the struggles that secured those releases are sufficiently forgotten for these rights to be subjected to fundamental criticism and dismissal. It becomes respectable for repressive opinion once more to question their very validity as concepts; or, at best, to demand that 'responsibilities', beyond those required in general by civil society, 'pay' in some way for such rights (2005: 396).

In Winston's view, the media today enjoy less freedom than did the press in the nineteenth century, 'partial and inadequate' though this was in practice: 'Beyond its extension from person to press, the universality of free expression was not established. It remains not established today' (ibid.: 397). Such an argument would appear to fly in the face of those who still argue, like latter-day Mary Whitehouses, that the modern media are far too 'permissive', as Winston himself admits:

> In a world awash with pornography, telephoto lenses and audio bugging devices, where indeed anything seems to go, there would seem to be no basis for concern for media liberty; yet behind this flood the basics of free expression, as a concept receiving widespread support, are being eroded (ibid: 399).

Thus, while there has undoubtedly been a superficial liberalisation of the rules governing entertainment on the numerous screens which increasingly dominate our lives, at the same time the laws relating to official secrecy, terrorism, academic practice and the right to protest, for example, are being relentlessly tightened in a manner that severely limits freedom of expression in matters which are vital to the health of a democratic society (Article 19 2020). Yet, particularly in the UK, these fail to excite critical comment in much of the mainstream media. Indeed, in the case of sections of the Conservative press, such measures are all too frequently advocated and welcomed.

'AN APPROPRIATE LEVEL OF FREEDOM OF EXPRESSION'

Nor is it the case, as is all too often supposed, that, because of the nature of the technology involved, newer media are less easy to regulate than their predecessors. To illustrate this point, Winston takes the case of television as regulated by the Communications Act 2003. This created the Office of Communications (Ofcom) and laid down that one of its duties was 'the application, in the case of all television and radio services, of standards that provide adequate protection to members of the public from the inclusion of offensive and harmful material in such services' and that it carried out this function 'in the manner that best guarantees an *appropriate level of freedom of expression*' (emphasis added). Winston's objection to Ofcom is that the regulation of the media for which it is responsible is:

> ... determined by statutory bureaucratic structures beyond the courts. Such a situation would not be acceptable if applied to the press or stage, but a slough of reasons is usually given to justify why, in a liberal society, supposedly committed to free expression, differences of treatment between media can be justified (2005: 397).

Chief amongst these are the allegedly harmful 'effects' of the electronic media:

> The influence of non-print mass-communication systems is deemed so vast that they cannot be allowed to function without special extra control. Yet, it is not an absolute given that, for example, the newer media are more 'influential', for all that they are certainly more pervasive (ibid: 397-398).

In Winston's view, however, 'free expression should not be abridged by assumptions about the supposed "power" and pervasiveness of different media. Technology should have nothing to do with it as a principle'. Instead, 'the media – new, old and to come – like all individual citizens, should stand equal before the law' (ibid: 399).

TOLERATION'S LIMITS

In *The Rushdie* Fatwa *and After: A Lesson to the Circumspect*, Winston returns to the notion of harm as a common justification for censorship. He begins by stating that 'toleration is the foundation of a right of free expression; without the one there cannot be the other' (2014: 8), before going on to note that 'toleration's limit is most clearly reached when any sort of demonstrable damage can be proved, whatever its cause' (ibid: 10). Here, Winston is drawing on J. S. Mill's famous dictum that 'the only purpose for which power can be rightfully exercised over any member of a civilised community, against his will, is to prevent harm to others' (1985 [1859]: 68). Mill also describes harmful actions as those which are 'calculated to produce evil to someone else' (ibid) or which are 'hurtful to others' (ibid: 70). Winston argues that 'harm' here equates to 'perceptible hurt' and that as 'remedies exist at law for the perceptible hurts arising from violence', so they should for speech if:

… damage flows from it and is externally verifiable, 'perceptible'. There is a difference between the impact of a word and that of a closed fist, but words do impact none the less and their damage can be perceptible. Therefore they can be censored (Winston 2014: 11).

As an example of a law designed to deal with such damage, Winston cites the Defamation Act 2013. This lays down that a statement is defamatory if it has caused, or is likely to cause, serious harm to the claimant's reputation – a factual proposition which can be established only by referring to the actual impact of the words used. For example, a company claiming that it had been defamed would have to show that the material in question had caused it, or was likely to cause it, serious financial loss. One might also point to the Suicide Act 1961, which makes it an offence to encourage or assist suicide.

'A RIGHT NOT TO BE OFFENDED OR INSULTED'

However, for Winston the problem is that, in practice, matters have been moving away from considering speech to be damaging only if its deleterious impact is externally verifiable and that:

> … now the 'hurts' arising from speech are not necessarily at all perceptible and indeed do not have to be present. That they could occur is enough. … Expression's potential for causing damage without specific actual damage being demonstrated is enough (ibid: 11).

Winston was particularly concerned about the Rushdie affair because, for him, it demonstrated that the principle of 'do no harm' had expanded 'to encompass a right not to be offended or insulted' (ibid: 17). It is important to understand here that he was not denying that words may, indeed, insult and offend, but, rather, arguing that these are 'effects which cannot be determined by the measure of externally verifiable damage. … Feelings, in the nature of the case, must be self-attested; they cannot be unambiguously externally verified as can the effects of "violence"' (ibid). In Winston's view, expanding the notion of harm into what he calls this 'evidence-free, ill-defined terrain' is to give the censor:

> … entrance to the country of offence unless the damage is perceptible (that is, externally evidenced) or perceptible damage is probable. (The law knows how to deal with probabilities). Simply to state that words can be (and do) evil in no way addresses how to deal with them in a free society (ibid: 87).

THE ONLINE HARMS WHITE PAPER

However, the principles enunciated by Winston threaten to be effectively trampled underfoot by the manner in which the present government proposes to censor the internet, which also provides ample confirmation of Winston's contention at the start of this chapter that 'there is little or no sense that we have "obtained" free expression' and that 'the influence of non-print mass-communication systems is deemed so vast that they cannot be allowed to function without special extra control'.

Successive British governments have threatened to impose internet censorship ever since the World Wide Web began to enter everyday use in 1993-1994, and although various piecemeal forms of censorship have been introduced since then, nothing as totalising and all-embracing as the system outlined in the Online Harms White Paper in April 2019 has been attempted in the UK – or, indeed, in any other democratic country. As the White Paper itself put it:

- There is currently a patchwork of regulation and voluntary initiatives aimed at addressing these problems, but these have not gone far or fast enough to keep UK users safe online.

- The UK will be the first to tackle online harms in a coherent, single regulatory framework that reflects our commitment to a free, open and secure internet (Department for Digital, Culture, Media and Sport/Home Office 2019: 30).

Just how the degree of censorship outlined below can also be squared with a commitment to freedom and openness is not explained. But it is clear from the White Paper that the government intends to legislate for a statutory 'duty of care' on social media platforms and a wide range of other internet companies that 'allow users to share or discover user-generated content, or interact with each other online' (ibid: 8). This duty would require them to 'take more responsibility for the safety of their users and tackle harm caused by content or activity on their services' (ibid: 7). Crucially, it would apply not only to illegal content but also to lawful material regarded as harmful under the new legislation. The duty would be overseen by a regulator (later designated as Ofcom) armed with the power to fine companies for non-compliance. Again, anything further away from Winston's contentions that all media should stand equal before the law, and that only illegal material should be subject to censorship, is extremely hard to imagine.

The White Paper provides a list of specific harms that would be in scope of the new legislation. However, it also notes that the list is neither exhaustive nor fixed, 'as a static list could prevent swift regulatory action to address new forms of online harm, new technologies, content and new online activities' (ibid: 30). Thus, the regulator will be able to add new harms at will. The harms with which the measure is concerned are of three kinds: 'harms with a clear definition', 'harms with a less clear definition' and 'underage exposure to legal content' (ibid: 31). The first category is concerned with content that is already illegal under existing laws, and consists of:

- Child sexual exploitation and abuse.
- Terrorist content and activity.
- Organised immigration crime.
- Modern slavery.
- Extreme pornography.
- Revenge pornography.
- Harassment and cyberstalking.
- Hate crime.
- Encouraging or assisting suicide.
- Incitement of violence.
- Sale of illegal goods/services, such as drugs and weapons (on the open internet).
- Content illegally uploaded from prisons.
- Sexting of indecent images by under-18s (creating, possessing, copying or distributing indecent or sexual images of children and young people under the age of 18).

'Harms with a less clear definition' are:

- Cyberbullying and trolling.
- Extremist content and activity.
- Coercive behaviour.
- Intimidation.
- Disinformation.
- Violent content.
- Advocacy of self-harm.
- Promotion of Female Genital Mutilation (FGM).

Finally, 'underage exposure to legal content' is defined as:

- Children accessing pornography.
- Children accessing inappropriate material (including under-13s using social media and under-18s using dating apps; excessive screen time).

Clearly, the second category of harms brings within the scope of the Bill a whole host of material which is currently legal but is nonetheless to be banished from vast swathes of the internet as far as its UK users are concerned because it is considered harmful.

'AN AMORPHOUS CONCEPT'

The Online Harms White Paper and the subsequent Online Safety Bill raise with glaring clarity all the problems associated with allegedly harmful media content noted repeatedly by Brian Winston. Indeed, one of the most authoritative critics of this measure, the lawyer Graham Smith (2019), echoed Winston in a blog posted just after the publication of the White Paper:

> Harm is an amorphous concept. It changes shape according to the opinion of whoever is empowered to apply it. Even when limited to harm suffered by an individual, harm is an ambiguous term. It will certainly include objectively ascertainable physical injury. ... But it may include also include subjective harms, dependent on someone's opinion that they have suffered what they regard as harm. When applied to speech, this is highly problematic. ... Harm as such has no identifiable boundaries, at least none that would pass a legislative test.

Just how broadly the government wished at this point to define harm can be illustrated by the inclusion in the White Paper of 'threats to our way of life'. This is defined in a highly Panglossian manner with which many would strongly disagree ('our society is built on confidence in public institutions, trust in electoral processes, a robust, lively and plural media, and hard-won democratic freedoms that allow different voices, views and opinions to freely and peacefully contribute to public discourse'). The main harm to this idealised vision is seen as stemming from inaccurate information and disinformation, the latter defined here as 'information which is created or disseminated with the deliberate intent to mislead; this could be to cause harm, or for personal, political or financial gain' and material which 'can threaten public safety, undermine national security, fracture community cohesion and reduce trust' (2019: 22). In which case, the legally proper solution would be to frame legislation making it a specific offence to spread inaccurate information and disinformation in any form of media whatsoever – a measure which, of course, would never be introduced as it would cause apoplexy amongst the government's many supporters in the national press. Thus, the government finds it more convenient to stigmatise the internet while banging the patriotic drum and, as Smith (2019) puts it, to engage in the kind of prose that 'may benefit the soapbox or an election manifesto but has no place in or near legislation'.

Similar points about the need for specific legislation to tackle specific harms were made by, amongst many others, Index on Censorship and the Open Rights Group. The former argued that:

> The wide range of different harms which the government is seeking to tackle in this policy process require different, tailored responses. Measures proposed must be underpinned by strong evidence, both of the likely scale of the harm and the measures' likely effectiveness. ... Any legislative or regulatory measures should be supported by clear and unambiguous evidence of their need and effectiveness (2019).

Likewise, the Open Rights Group stated:

> Any policy intervention must be underpinned with a clear, objective evidence base which demonstrates that actions are necessary and proportionate. Regulation impacting on citizens' free speech needs to be based on evidence of harm traceable to specific pieces or types of content, activity or behaviour, rather than expectations or social judgements that these may be related to possible harms. ... Any policy intervention must be defined and limited by precise terminology. Imprecise language risks dangerous overreach. If the harms-based model of regulation is used, tighter identification/definition of types of harms and their natures is vitally needed (2019: 4-5).

THE DRAFT ONLINE SAFETY BILL

In its Full Response in December 2020 to the consultation process initiated by the White Paper, the government narrowed its definition of harmful online content and activity to material which 'gives rise to a foreseeable risk of significant adverse physical or psychological impact on individuals' (Department for Digital, Culture, Media and Sport/Home Office 2020: 24). It also made it clear that 'the duty of care will apply to content or activity which could cause significant physical or psychological harm to an individual' (ibid: 50). The proposed measure was now more focused on personal safety as properly understood rather than vague and unbounded notions of harm – which is presumably why it was renamed the Online Safety Bill. However, as Smith (2020) points out:

> The definition of harm remains problematic: not least because inclusion of 'psychological impact' may suggest that the notion of harm is still tied to variable, subjective reactions of different readers. Subjectivity opens the door to application of a standard of the most easily upset user.

The Draft Online Safety Bill was published in May 2021. According to its Impact Assessment, it seeks to address the following broad categories of harmful online content:

- Illegal user-generated content and activity: user-generated content and activity which is an offence under UK law – such as child sexual exploitation and abuse, terrorism, hate crime and sale of illegal drugs and weapons.

- Legal but harmful user-generated content and activity: user-generated content and activity which may not be illegal under all circumstances, but which gives rise to a foreseeable risk of psychological and physical harm to adults – such as abuse or eating disorder content.

- Underage exposure to user-generated content and activity which gives rise to a foreseeable risk of psychological and physical harm to children – such as pornography, violent content (Department for Digital, Culture, Media and Sport/Home Office 2021: 20).

It also refers back to the White Paper's list of harms of various kinds, which shows that these are still very much in play. Furthermore, the problematic phrase 'legal but harmful' occurs no less than 97 times, although the document is worryingly short on specific examples of such material, other than 'abuse, harassment and intimidation directed towards public figures' and 'cyberbullying'. Harm is defined in the Bill at section 137(1) as simply 'physical or psychological harm', which is a shortened version of the definition proposed by the government in its Full Response. However, as Smith (2021) notes:

> The draft Bill does not stipulate that 'harmful' should be understood in the same limited way. The result of that omission, combined with other definitions, could be to give the Secretary of State regulation-making powers for legal but harmful content that are, on the face of them, not limited to physical or psychological harm.

On the other hand, in the case of legal but harmful content it does provide a more developed version of the Full Response's general definition of harm by specifying that the impact of allegedly harmful material must be on a hypothetical adult or child 'of ordinary sensibilities', that is, not the most easily upset user.

'WORKING OUT WHAT HARM MEANS'

At the time of writing, the Online Harms Bill has only just begun its journey through parliament, thus making it impossible to know exactly what final form it will take. However, it can be safely asserted that its conception of harm will bear little or no relation to the one advanced by Brian Winston, that it will take no account of his (and others') argument that specific harms should be the subject of specific laws and turn on its head his contention that all media should be treated equally before the law. Indeed, all of these ideas are summarily dismissed in the report by Lorna Woods and William Perrin for the Carnegie UK Trust, *Online Harm Reduction? A Statutory Duty of Care and Regulator*, which was published concurrently with the White Paper and greatly informed government thinking on this matter. They state:

A traditional focus for the debate on internet harms has been the 'if it is illegal offline it should be illegal online' and then to focus on the removal of content that is contrary to the criminal law. While the criminal law may identify types of content that cause significant harm, and would therefore fall within the scope of the regime, the criminal law does not constitute a complete list of harms against which we would expect a service provider to take action. Nor is harm caused only by content but also by the *impact of the underlying systems* such as software, business processes and their resourcing/effectiveness. We therefore do not think that the question of whether an action constitutes a criminal offence is helpful in determining harms (2019: 40, emphasis added).

Dismissing the idea that in the interests of legal and democratic legitimacy the level of harm should be specified in detail in statute, Woods and Perrin argue, instead, that 'the detail of the harms should be derived from high level statements of relevant harms by the regulator and set down in code' (ibid: 41). They also airily note that 'in our experience of regulation, competent regulators have had little difficulty in the past in working out what harm means' and add:

If in 2003 there was general acceptance relating to content of programmes for television and radio, protecting the public from offensive and harmful material, why have those definitions changed, or what makes them undeliverable now? Why did we understand what we meant by 'harm' in 2003 but appear to ask what it is today? (quoted in ibid).

The answer is provided by Graham Smith (2019), who points out that:

… in 2003 the legislators did not have to understand what the vague term 'harm' meant because they gave Ofcom the power to decide. It is no surprise if Ofcom has had little difficulty, since it is in reality not 'working out what harms means' but deciding on its own meanings. It is, in effect, performing a delegated legislative function.

As noted earlier, the Act refers to 'offensive and harmful' material. However, it makes no attempt to define it. Instead, in section 319(1)(h), Ofcom is charged with ensuring that 'generally accepted standards are applied to the contents of television and radio services so as to provide adequate protection for members of the public from the inclusion in such services of offensive and harmful material'. And section 319(4)(a) insists that in setting and securing these standards, Ofcom must have regard to 'the degree of harm or offence likely to be caused by the inclusion of any particular sort of material in programmes generally, or in programmes of a particular description'.

'GENERALLY ACCEPTED STANDARDS' AND 'BROAD PUBLIC OPINION'

How Ofcom operationalises these (and other) legal requirements laid down in the Act can be understood by referring to its *Broadcasting Code* (2020), section two of which is entitled 'Harm and Offence'. Paragraph 2.3 states that:

> In applying generally accepted standards broadcasters must ensure that material which may cause offence is justified by the context. …. Such material may include, but is not limited to, offensive language, violence, sex, sexual violence, humiliation, distress, violation of human dignity, discriminatory treatment or language (for example on the grounds of age, disability, gender reassignment, pregnancy and maternity, race, religion or belief, sex and sexual orientation, and marriage and civil partnership). Appropriate information should also be broadcast where it would assist in avoiding or minimising offence.

This part of the code also includes sections on violence, dangerous behaviour and suicide; exorcism, the occult and the paranormal; and hypnotic and other techniques, simulated news and photosensitive epilepsy.

From this, it is clear that the manner in which Ofcom has 'decided on its own meanings' of harm has considerable potential impact on a very wide range of programme content – perhaps far wider than most people realise. Of course, Ofcom, unlike its predecessors – the ITA, IBA and ITC – does not have the power to pre-censor programmes, but it most certainly has the power of post-broadcast sanction, and the vast majority of UK programme-makers know exactly what is and is not acceptable, and thus abide by Ofcom's standards. The point at which editorial judgement shades over into self-censorship is very hard to locate.

A similar point about a broad regulatory remit being granted by legislation which specifically mentions harm is the Video Recordings Act 1984. As amended in 1994, this requires the British Board of Film Classification (BBFC), when classifying videos, to have:

> … special regard … to any harm that may be caused to potential viewers or, through their behaviour, to society by the manner in which the work deals with – (a) criminal behaviour; (b) illegal drugs; (c) violent behaviour or incidents; (d) horrific behaviour or incidents; or (e) human sexual activity.

Admittedly the notion of harm here is rather more specific than in the Communications Act but, as in the case of Ofcom, it is significant that the BBFC feels that the legislation entitles it to cast the regulatory net widely. Its current *Guidelines* define harm thus:

> In relation to harm, we will consider whether the material, either on its own, or in combination with other content of a similar nature, may cause any harm at the category concerned. This includes not just any harm that

may result from the behaviour of potential viewers, but also any moral or societal harm that may be caused by, for example, desensitising a potential viewer to the effects of violence, degrading a potential viewer's sense of empathy, encouraging a dehumanised view of others, encouraging anti-social attitudes, reinforcing unhealthy fantasies, or eroding a sense of moral responsibility. Especially with regard to children, harm may also include impairing social and moral development, distorting a viewer's sense of right and wrong, and limiting their capacity for compassion (2019: 7).

It could be argued, and doubtless Brian Winston would do so, that under the aegis of preventing harm, these regulatory authorities are going beyond the bounds of what is acceptable or desirable in a democratic society. Admittedly these are not latter-day versions of Oscar Wilde's Miss Prism, for whom the mark of fiction was that the good ended happily and the bad unhappily, but they are still encroaching on broadly moral and ethical issues which some may feel should be none of their business. It might also be objected that Ofcom's 'generally accepted standards' and the BBFC's 'broad public opinion' (ibid: 7) are extremely difficult to identify and satisfy in a society as heterogeneous and diverse as our own.

NEW MEDIA, OLD PROBLEMS, NEW LAWS

However, this is by no means an argument against media regulation *per se*, nor to deny that the internet has, if not created new problems in the realm of media content, then certainly greatly exacerbated already-existing ones (and not simply in the media field, either). Child-abuse materials (which, it should be remembered, are the actual records of an extremely serious crime), bullying, harassment, threats, incitement to commit acts of terrorism, dissemination of deliberate disinformation, all can most certainly be considered as harmful in Winston's sense, and thus should be the subject of specific legislation (as, indeed, some already are). For example, if someone is bullied and then, as a direct result of that bullying, commits suicide or has a nervous breakdown, that is clearly harm by any definition. Take, for example, the harms caused by the online bullying of Caroline Criado-Perez after she had campaigned for a woman to appear on a banknote, harms which were recognised as such (albeit belatedly) by both the police and the Crown Prosecution Service and which caused two people to be charged and found guilty under section 127(1)(a) of the Communications Act, of which more below. (For further details of this case see BBC (2014) and Topping (2014)).

This is the kind of approach outlined by Law Commission's 2021 report *Modernising Communications Offences*, which represents an attempt to deal with the subject of harm and offence in a more measured and nuanced way than that proposed by the White Paper and the Online Safety Bill, with their elaborate regulatory structure, sweeping scope and apparent disregard of the many dangers posed to freedom of expression by the measures which they blithely propose.

The report addresses itself, in particular, to the need to reform current laws which have been used against abusive behaviour online of one kind or another. In the commission's view, 'the existing patchwork of criminal law is unclear and has an unduly broad scope' (2021: 4). Indeed, they are 'concerned that the current offences are so broad that they could, in certain circumstances, interfere disproportionately with the right to freedom of expression protected under Article 10 of the ECHR' (ibid). They also make it clear that their aim is 'to modernise the framework of criminal offences that target communications and ensure only sufficiently harmful communications are criminalised' and, in doing so, 'to ensure our recommendations do not extend inappropriately the reach of the existing communications offences or overlap significantly with other crimes' (ibid).

The commission is particularly exercised by two offences. The first concerns Section 1 of the Malicious Communications Act 1988, which makes it a criminal offence to send someone, by any means, a message which is indecent, grossly offensive, a threat, or false, and if the purpose of sending the message was to cause 'distress or anxiety' to the recipient. The second is the above-mentioned section 127(1)(a) of the Communications Act 2003, which criminalises the sending, via a 'public electronic communications network', of a message which is 'grossly offensive or of an indecent, obscene or menacing character'. The commission argues that:

> Reliance on vague terms like 'grossly offensive' and 'indecent' raises concerns that the offences criminalise some forms of free expression that ought to be protected. Simply put, these adjectives do not always correspond to harm. For example, consensual sexting between adults could be 'indecent', but is not obviously worthy of criminalisation (ibid: 6).

On the other hand, however, the commission also feels that offences do not always effectively target the harms arising from online abuse, because too often the threshold of criminality is set too low.

FROM CATEGORIES OF CONTENT TO THE CONSEQUENCES OF COMMUNICATION

The commission seeks to address these problems by shifting away from assessing categories of content, such as 'indecent' or 'grossly offensive', to assessing the consequences of communication in cases where these can be defined as harmful. But whilst bearing in mind that online abuse is one of the major challenges for the current law, the commission is keen to stress that it has 'tried not to constrain the offences to particular forms of communication', so that they 'do not arbitrarily criminalise communications differently based on the mode of communication' (ibid: 8).

Turning to specifics, the commission sets out the details of a new offence based on likely psychological harm to replace the offences in the Acts noted above. This, it contends, 'will more effectively protect freedom of expression and avoid over-criminalisation while better targeting the myriad types of harmful communications' (ibid: 9). Briefly, this offence would be committed by someone who sends a communication that is deliberately intended to cause harm to a likely audience, with harm being defined here as psychological harm amounting at least to serious distress. When deciding whether such a communication was likely to cause harm to its likely audience, a court would have to have regard to the context in which the communication was sent, including the characteristics of the likely recipient or recipients (ibid: 7).

The commission also proposes a new offence involving threatening communications. Here the defendant would be liable if they sent – by any means – a communication that conveys a threat of serious harm, and if, in conveying the threat, they intended its object to fear that it would be carried out, or was reckless as to whether they would fear that this would happen. For the purposes of this offence, serious harm would include serious injury (amounting to grievous bodily harm as understood under the Offences Against the Person Act 1861), rape and serious financial harm (ibid: 13).

CONCLUSION

Brian Winston may regard the Law Commission's definitions of what constitute harmful forms of communication as still pushing too far beyond the perceptible and verifiable. But one feels that at least he would welcome its attempt to define what it means by harm in relation to certain specific offences and that he would endorse its media-neutral approach which stresses that what is illegal offline is also illegal online – something which is all too often forgotten or ignored in endless jeremiads against the evils of the online world. These are a particular speciality of sections of Britain's national press which, of course, have their own reasons for advocating the censorship of those areas of the internet which they do not own and control. Yet this has led such doughty enemies of the 'nanny state' and 'red tape' to argue for and endorse a measure such as the Online Safety Bill (from which, of course, they have successfully lobbied to exempt themselves) – an act of arrant hypocrisy remarkable by even their debased standards.

REFERENCES

Article 19 (2019) *Freedom of Expression in the UK: Policy Briefing*. Available online at https://www.article19.org/wp-content/uploads/2020/03/Fex_UK_briefing.pdf, accessed on 2 September 2021

BBC News (2014) Two guilty over abusive tweets to Caroline Criado-Perez, 7 January. Available online at https://www.bbc.co.uk/news/uk-25641941, accessed on 2 September 2021

British Board of Film Classification (2019) *Classification Guidelines*. Available online at file:///C:/Users/owner/Downloads/bbfc-classification-guidelines%20(1).pdf, accessed on 2 September 2021.

Department for Digital, Culture, Media and Sport/Home Office (2019) *Online Harms White Paper*. Available online at https://assets.publishing.service.gov.uk/government/uploads/system/uploads/attachment_data/file/944310/Online_Harms_White_Paper_Full_Government_Response_to_the_consultation_CP_354_CCS001_CCS1220695430-001__V2.pdf, accessed on 2 September 2021

Department for Digital, Culture, Media and Sport/Home Office (2020) *Online Harms White Paper: Full Government Response to the Consultation*. Available online at https://www.gov.uk/government/consultations/online-harms-white-paper/outcome/online-harms-white-paper-full-government-response, accessed on 2 September 2021

Department for Digital, Culture, Media and Sport/Home Office (2021) *The Online Safety Bill: Impact Assessment*. Available online at https://assets.publishing.service.gov.uk/government/uploads/system/uploads/attachment_data/file/985283/Draft_Online_Safety_Bill_-_Impact_Assessment_Web_Accessible.pdf, accessed on 2 September 2021

Index on Censorship (2019) Online harms proposals pose serious risks to freedom of expression, 8 April. Available online at

https://www.indexoncensorship.org/2019/04/online-harms-proposals-pose-serious-risks-to-freedom-of-expression-online/, accessed on 2 September 2012

Law Commission (2021) *Modernising Communications Offences: Summary of the Final Report*. Available online at https://s3-eu-west-2.amazonaws.com/lawcom-prod-storage-11jsxou24uy7q/uploads/2021/07/Summary-of-Modernising-Communications-Offences-2021.pdf, accessed on 2 September 2021

Mill, John Stuart (1985 [1859]) *On Liberty*, London: Penguin Books

Ofcom (2020) *Broadcasting Code*. Available online at https://www.ofcom.org.uk/tv-radio-and-on-demand/broadcast-codes/broadcast-code, accessed on 2 September 2021

Open Rights Group (2019) *ORG Policy Responses to Online Harms White Paper*, May. Available online at https://modx.openrightsgroup.org/assets/files/reports/report_pdfs/ORG_Policy_Lines_Online_Harms_WP.pdf, accessed on 2 September 2021

Smith, Graham (2019) Users behaving badly – the Online Harms White Paper, *Cyberleagle*, 18 April. Available online at https://www.cyberleagle.com/2019/04/users-behaving-badly-online-harms-white.html, accessed on 2 September 2021

Smith, Graham (2020) The Online Harms edifice takes shape, *Cyberleagle*, 17 December. Available online at https://www.cyberleagle.com/2020/12/the-online-harms-edifice-takes-shape.html, accessed on 2 September 2021

Smith, Graham (2021) Harm version 3.0: The draft Online Safety Bill, *Cyberleagle*, 16 May. Available online at https://www.cyberleagle.com/2021/05/harm-version-30-draft-online-safety-bill.html, accessed on 2 September 2021

Topping, Alexandra (2014) Jane Austin Twitter row: Two plead guilty to abusive tweets, 7 January. Available online at https://www.theguardian.com/society/2014/jan/07/jane-austen-banknote-abusive-tweets-criado-perez, accessed 2 September 2021

Winston, Brian (2005) *Messages: Free Expression, Media and the West from Gutenberg to Google*, London and New York: Routledge

Winston, Brian (2014) *The Rushdie Fatwa and After*, Basingstoke: Palgrave Macmillan

Woods, Lorna and Perrin, William (2019) *Online Harm Reduction – a Statutory Duty of Care and Regulator*, Carnegie UK Trust. Available online at https://d1ssu070pg2v9i.cloudfront.net/pex/pex_carnegie2021/2019/04/06084627/Online-harm-reduction-a-statutory-duty-of-care-and-regulator.pdf

NOTE ON THE CONTRIBUTOR

Julian Petley is Emeritus and Honorary Professor of Journalism at Brunel University London. The second edition of his *Culture Wars: The Media and the British Left* (with James Curran and Ivor Gaber) was published by Routledge in 2019. He is a member of the editorial board of the *British Journalism Review* and the principal editor of the *Journal of British Cinema and Television*. A former journalist, he contributes to online publications such as *Inforrm*, *Byline Times* and *openDemocracy*.

Chapter 7

The Price of Ridiculing the Prophet: The *Charlie Hebdo* Affair

Raphael Cohen-Almagor

This chapter analyses the terror attack on the Charlie Hebdo *offices, in Paris, on 7 January 2015, through several prisms: freedom of expression, the principle of profound offence, the fallacy of universal liberalism, globalisation and the era in which we live of violence and terror. It is argued that after the violent episodes following the publications of* The Satanic Verses, *the Danish cartoons and the* Hebdo *cartoons we need to understand that freedom of speech has a price. Responsible people should weigh the consequences of their conduct – action and speech. We should learn from these affairs, take offence seriously, acknowledge the fallacy of universalism and the reality of globalisation where speech in the liberal part of the world may provoke negative and violent reaction worldwide. We should assert our principles while being cognisant of the price tag which may be high and bloody.*

Keywords: *Charlie Hebdo*, freedom of expression, offence, social responsibility, terror

John is standing in the city square and sings loudly. He holds a baseball bat and carries a big sign that says: 'I dare you to criticise my singing.' John is 2 metres tall and his physique suggests that he spends many of his free hours in a gym. It seems he enjoys many free hours. The expression on his face leaves little doubt as to the likely consequences of such a dare. You have the freedom and choice to ridicule him, even more so because you do find his singing most disturbing. Still, would you dare him?

Liberal democracies do not address the issue of offence adequately. Proponents of free speech speak on 'the right to offend' and 'the right to ridicule' (Winston 2012; Dworkin 2006). Brian Winston (2012: xiv) premises his book, *A Right to Offend*, on the assumption that freedom of expression 'can only be said to exist if it encompasses a right to offend. The right to offend is the right of expression's touchstone, just as the right of expression is the touchstone to human rights in general'.

A right is an entitlement. It is a strong claim to do a certain thing. Dworkin (2006) argues that in a democracy no one, however powerful or impotent, can have a right not to be insulted or offended. We cannot argue that religious matters are exceptional and deserve a special status. Religion, any religion, must observe the principles of democracy which include, according to Dworkin, the right to free expression and the right to ridicule. No religion can be permitted to legislate for everyone about what can or cannot be said. Dworkin argues categorically that no one's religious convictions can be thought to trump the freedom that makes democracy possible.

While I agree that there is a right to freedom of expression, I do not think people have a 'right' to ridicule. People should be able to discuss and debate sensitive matters, and the long list of such matters includes race, religion, nationalism, culture, misogyny, bigotry, sex, pornography, human trafficking, prostitution crime, capital punishment, suicide, colonialism, exploitation, slavery, euthanasia and traumatic life experiences such as abortion, bullying, rape, abuse, illnesses, homelessness, death, violence, war, drugs and alcohol. This is not an exhaustive list. When such issues are discussed, the conversation should be done in a civil and sensitive manner. Still, some people may be offended by the very fact that certain sensitive or taboo issues are discussed; but the speaker's intention should always be to treat people with dignity and respect, not to offend or ridicule them and/or matters that are important to them. We should perceive our fellow humans as worthy of respect, recognising the inner spark, the dignity of the person. We are endowed with dignity and have the right to be treated with dignity and respect.

The language of rights makes a powerful claim that I wish to reserve to truly important matters, such as the right to life, right to freedom of expression, right to health or the right to education. When one uses the term 'right' to something, one considers that something should be upheld and promoted. Therefore, I would not assign ridicule the same degree of importance that is assigned to life, freedom of expression, health and education. Ridicule is one category of freedom of expression and, to my mind, not a very important category, certainly not an essential part of the right to free expression. My conception of a good life does not include ridicule in the top one hundred things that constitute goodness. While I would not object to a healthy dose of cynicism and think that a witty criticism of politicians can potentially be fun, I would not use the language of rights in this context. Whereas Dworkin and Winston argue that people should enjoy the right to offend and ridicule as a matter of principle, notwithstanding consequences, my viewpoint is consequentialist in nature and involves a balancing act: weighing on the scales the benefits of ridicule *vis-à-vis* the risks involved.

In this chapter, I analyse the terror attack on the *Charlie Hebdo* offices through several prisms: freedom of expression; the principle of profound offence; the fallacy of universal liberalism; globalisation and the era in which we live of violence and terror. I suggest that a balance needs to be struck between political satire and social responsibility. Political satire is defined as 'the use of humour, irony, exaggeration or ridicule to expose and criticize people's stupidity or vices, particularly in the context of contemporary politics and other topical issues' (Lexico 2020). While acknowledging the importance of political satire as a tool aimed at provoking and challenging opinions by making people think about certain contested issues or people in a controversial, different way, it is argued that after the violent episodes that followed the publication of *The Satanic Verses*, the Danish cartoons and the *Hebdo* cartoons, we know full well that freedom of speech has a price. Responsible people should weigh the consequences of their conduct – action and speech. We should learn from these affairs, take offence seriously, acknowledge the fallacy of universalism and the reality of globalisation where speech in a liberal part of the world may provoke negative and violent reaction worldwide. We should assert our principles while being cognisant of the price tag which may be high and bloody. And the price will not necessarily be paid only by the speaker. The speaker also endangers others. Responsible speakers should ask themselves whether their struggle to express outrageous ideas freely justifies putting other people's lives as risk. Our freedoms should always be tempered by social responsibility.

THE TERROR ATTACK

On 7 January 2015, two terrorists armed with automatic rifles stormed the office of the satirical magazine *Charlie Hebdo*. The weekly first appeared in 1970 after the monthly *Hara-Kiri* magazine was banned for mocking the death of former French President Charles de Gaulle. Its main aim was to direct satirical attacks on the government, its motto being b*ête et méchant* – or 'mean and nasty' (Devichand 2016). The magazine printed cartoons that ridiculed the Prophet Muhammad (also spelled Mohammed) in 2006 and 2011. By the time the terrorists had left, eleven cartoonists and satirists whose names were called out were shot dead. Among them were the then-magazine editor Stéphane Charbonnier and the famous cartoonist Cabu. Eleven other people were injured. 'We have avenged the Prophet!' the killers shouted (Rayner et al. 2015; *Sky News* 2015). Later the terrorists also killed a policeman. The Muslim community was at the eye of the storm as public debate denounced 'perverted Islam' that negated the message of the *Quran*. The French President, François Hollande, indulged in 'us' versus 'them' rhetoric: French national identity against the terrorist other; the French Republic that stood for freedom *vis-à-vis* jihadist murderers who sought to challenge the spirit, unity and the values that enshrined the nation (Bogain 2019).

OFFENCE

The *Charlie Hebdo* affair is concerned with the issue of offence. Offence is distinguished from harm. It refers to the impact of a conduct that a doer inflicts on his or her target/s, causing them discomfort, aversion, disgust, humiliation and other similar mental states. The offender causes the targets some degree of suffering. Offence is subjective and requires psychological evaluation.[1] Generally speaking, courts do not take offence seriously. Offence is not considered as grounds for limiting speech because what offends one may enchant another. Judges are not thrilled to let another profession decide constitutional matters, thus usually dismiss offence (Goldberger 1991). But when does offence matter?

Offence should be taken seriously and can set boundaries to freedom of expression provided that some preconditions are satisfied. First under consideration is *profound* offence, to be distinguished from mere annoyance or nuisance. In other words, the offence should be significant and serious, *morally on a par with physical harm*. Second, profound offences are such that people take offence of the troubling words even when they are not exposed to that offence directly. They feel deep relation to the attacked whether or not they witnessed the offensive attack themselves. The very fact that the offence is taking place moves and shakes their moral sensibilities because they feel that the offence in itself is fundamentally wrong. The offended feel moral shock, indignation and revulsion (Cohen-Almagor 2006: 77-122). The foundations of their very well-being are threatened.

People may feel profound offence as a result of many problematic forms of expression. France has a rich tradition of a cynical and even outrageous press that mocks anything and everything. *Le Charivari, Charlie Hebdo, Le Canard enchaîné* are well-known examples of great satirical magazines that have practised freedom of expression to the extreme. Their editors believe that taking offence is the decision of the one who decides to be offended. If people decide to take offence, this is *their* problem.

Other liberals may take the issue of offence more seriously. But they qualify the application of restricting speech on grounds of offence by insisting that the offensive speech should concern a person *directly*. The 'offence to sensibilities' argument in and of itself can serve as grounds for restricting freedom of expression in extreme cases when the offence is severe and the target group (individual or individuals) cannot avoid being exposed to the offence (Cohen-Almagor 2002). In order to determine how offensive the expression is, we must examine its content and manner of expression, and the speaker's intention. As for the circumstances, these must be such that the target group cannot avoid being exposed to the expression. Under the 'offence to sensibilities' argument, when the content or manner of expression is designed to cause severe psychological offence against a target group, and the objective circumstances make that group inescapably exposed to that offence, then the expression in question has to be restricted (Cohen-Almagor 1993; 2005; 2020).[2]

According to this formulation, the crude *Charlie Hebdo* cartoons cannot be seriously and significantly offensive. Muslims can easily avoid reading the offensive cartoons. They *choose* to relate to the cartoons. No one forced them to read *Charlie Hebdo*. They could have easily avoided being subjected to the offence. They decided not to. Thus, liberals will fight for the right of the *Charlie Hebdo* writers to continue to ridicule anything and any person they wish. But this is only the start of the discussion, not the end of it. There is a difference between civil and respectful speech, on the one hand, and divisive, inflammatory and rowdy speech on the other. Liberal democracies uphold and promote the right to freedom of expression. They have an obligation to do so as part of the *raison d'être* of liberal democracy. But they should not allow *carte blanche* to abuse free speech in a way that is likely to stir hatred and violence. Freedom is not a licence to anarchy.[3]

Marliere (2017) argues that, generally speaking, French people do not support unqualified freedom of expression. While they defend the principle of free speech, many of them do not believe there is a right to embrace and publish offensive ideas. In Marliere's view, this explains why the whole French nation did not support the *Charlie Hebdo* cartoons (ibid). On the political left, there was unease regarding the Islamophobic sentiments. Immediately after acts of terrorism, people took to the streets to express their repulsion at the brutal violence. While many of them would not endorse unlimited speech, the French message solidified the view that no one should be murdered because they hold ideas that someone abhors. Cynical and upsetting satire does not justify murder.

THE FALLACY OF UNIVERSAL LIBERALISM

A common liberal fallacy is the belief in universalism. Liberals believe that there are universal ethical values that withstand borders and are shared by all humans. Our membership in the human species creates the notion of universal moral obligation and a belief in shared universal values (Christians et al. 1997; Swidler 1999; Titley et al. 2017; Christians 2019). This belief, however, is more a wishful thinking than an acknowledgment of reality. I believe that there are some basic universal needs that all people wish to secure such as food, raiment and shelter; I believe that sexual drives are universal and that people need to have some sleep to be able continue functioning; I also believe that we should strive to universalise moral principles. But our ability to universalise our moral principles will be bettered by emphasising the differences between liberal and non-liberal values, not by blurring them and confusing the ideal and the real.

Sociologically speaking, we cannot ignore the fact that universal values do not underlie all societies. Ideally there are some ethical concerns that should be accepted by all societies, but in reality we know this is not the case. Some cultures do not adopt liberal democracy as a way of life (Baghramian et al. 2000; Parekh 2005, 2019; Modood 2013; Cohen-Almagor 2015, 2021). Instead, they adhere to other forms of authority that are alien to the underpinning values of liberal democracy: liberty, equality, tolerance and pluralism. Some cultures do not accept the norms of respecting others and not harming others that form the *raison d'être* of liberal democracy. Their principles do not encourage autonomy, individualism, pluralism and openness, and their behaviour is not in tune with the so-called universal concepts of human dignity and caring. Non-liberal cultures, based on authoritarian conceptions and principles, do not abide by the Judea-Christian values and norms.

Some cultures despise these norms and wish to undercut them. Muslims, for the large part, value freedom of expression that enables them to disseminate the messages of Islam and the teachings of the Prophets. But many Muslims question the scope and limits of freedom of expression and wish to draw them differently than liberals. Some Muslims are not willing to criticise Islam and are particularly sensitive to everything that concerns the Prophet Muhammad. Some Muslims retaliate with extreme violence when their religion is mocked in a way they deem disrespectful and deriding. Those who violently react to what they see as blasphemy ought to be aware that they are presenting a very negative picture of Muslims to the world.

GLOBALISATION

The fallacy of universalism relates to the third major concern: globalisation. We are living in a global village where people across the globe are aware of what is happening in other parts of the world. Thus, contrasts between different systems of belief can easily become apparent. No religious group has a *right* not to be ridiculed. French and other presses are free to express outrageous views but they need to bear in mind that not everyone lives and abides by the same liberal concepts. Some people, in France and anywhere else in the global village that is facilitated by rapid communication and transportation, may decide to react very negatively to mockery and spite. Those people are not guided by the principles of liberty and tolerance, and do not think that freedom of speech should be protected no matter what. *The Satanic Verses* (Rushdie 1988; Slaughter 1993; Green 2013), the Danish cartoons (*Telegraph* 2015; Mohammed Image Archives n/d; McGraw et al. 2012; Lægaard 2007; Cram 2009; Pinto 2010) and the *Hebdo* cartoons have shown us that freedom of speech has a price. Some 150 people died in violent demonstrations sparked by the *Jyllands-Posten*'s publication of the twelve cartoons in September 2005 (Bruck 2012) and dozens of people died since then in related events. A Pakistani religious leader, Mohammed Yousaf Qureshi, announced a *fatwa* and offered a $25,000 reward to anyone who killed one of the cartoonists (Klausen 2009). The German newspaper, *Hamburger Morgenpost*, that decided to republish the offensive cartoons, was subjected to an arson attack (ABC 2015).

Responsible people should weigh the consequences of their conduct – action and speech. We should learn from these affairs, take offence seriously, acknowledge the fallacy of universalism and the reality of globalisation where speech in a liberal part of the world may provoke negative and violent reaction worldwide. We should assert our principles while being cognisant of the price tag. After the above incidents, people who adhere to unrestrained speech should not say anymore: 'I had no idea that my freedom to speak might provoke such a violent reaction.' Now we know that the price may be high and bloody. And the price will not necessarily be paid only by the speaker. The speaker also endangers others. Before publication, prospective speakers should ask themselves whether the likely consequences are less important than their freedom to spite. The decision is theirs. They should bear in mind that the outcomes may also affect innocent bystanders and policemen rushed to restore order. Responsible speakers should ask themselves whether their struggle to express outrageous ideas freely justifies putting other people's lives as risk. It is one thing to be willing to pay a price for your own conduct. It is quite another to expect others to back a cause that they do not endorse as strongly as the speaker. They may simply be in the wrong place and time to earn the title 'victims who fought for the right to free speech'.

Some six months after the terrorist attack on the magazine, the editor of *Charlie Hebdo* declared that he *would* not publish any more cartoons of the Prophet Muhammad (Kassam 2015). In April 2015, cartoonist Luz, who drew *Charlie Hebdo*'s front cover picture of Muhammad following the massacre of the satirical weekly's editorial team, said in the same vein he would no longer draw the prophet (Spencer 2015). In between these two declarations, the American Freedom Defence Initiative (AFDI) hosted a contest that awarded $10,000 for the best cartoon depicting Muhammad. Two armed men shot the security guard and injured him. The police later shot and killed both men (Bever and Murphy 2015; Buncombe 2015).

However, in 2020 *Charlie Hebdo* published the same offensive cartoons to mark the opening of the trial of 14 people accused of aiding and abetting those involved in the 2015 massacre. *Charlie Hebdo*'s editors justified their controversial decision by saying that, in their view, it was 'unacceptable to start the trial' without showing the 'pieces of evidence' and that refraining from republishing the caricatures would have amounted to 'political or journalistic cowardice'. They added: 'Do we want to live in a country that claims to be a great democracy, free and modern, which, at the same time, does not affirm its most profound convictions?' (Onishi 2020).

By their act the editors showed that they were not cowards. Their act also showed irresponsibility if not recklessness. A violent response soon arrived. A young Muslim stabbed two random people at the entrance of the magazine's old offices (Ynet 2020; Walla 2020). Those two people, who had nothing to do with the *Hebdo* publications or their decision-making processes and considerations whether to republish or not republish, paid dearly for the editor's so-called bravery.

CONCLUSION

The *Charlie Hebdo* affair has brought to the fore major issues: freedom of expression, offence, the fallacy of universal liberalism, globalisation and sombre yet sober thoughts about the era in which we live. There is a difference between freedom of expression and freedom to ridicule. Exchange of ideas should have bounds of decorum and civility. Ridicule should be confined to certain forums in which it is understood by all parties concerned that in those specific circumstances it is possible to say things that are perceived offensive and even intolerable in other circumstances. Consent is important. While, for instance, a lecturer should not ridicule her student in class, lecturers and their students may agree to entertain in a comedy store theatre setting and say things that would carry severe penalties if they were said in an academic setting. Granted that satirical journals, such as *Charlie Hebdo*, are special forums in which people are depicted as caricatures, events are exaggerated and the confines of free expression are stretched to the limit. Granted also that people do not have to read these journals. A person who buys the journal or visits its website voluntarily subjects herself to offensive content that might hurt her sensibilities. However, sometime the 'sacred cows' that are slaughtered on the pages of satirical magazines are so sacred that the outrage expands beyond the confines of the journal. Editors and authors have common sense to project the impact of their ridiculous statements. If they know that certain provocations are likely to lead to violence against themselves and against innocent bystanders, then they responsibly need to weigh the pros and cons of the so-called 'right to ridicule' versus the well-recognised right to life and make a reasonable judgement call. I leave it to the editors to decide. I do not suggest that the law should be involved. I call for prudent, responsible thinking before rushing to provocations that are likely to yield violence. Mechanisms of deliberative democracy in promoting civilised debates and discourse are preferable to legal censorship.

If the publisher of this volume where to put one of the Muhammad cartoons on the book cover in order to receive attention and possibly increase the sales of this *festschrift* then I would perceive this act as unreasonable, callous, irresponsible and dangerous. I would then swiftly withdraw my chapter from this volume. Like the vast majority of John's audience in the example that opened this chapter who did not dare to criticise John's singing, I do not see the point of aggravating tensions and unnecessarily bringing about potential violence. The *Charlie Hebdo* editors may be courageous but I doubt their prudence. There is no need to inflame and outrage people. Instead, we need to establish an atmosphere of peace and tranquillity where people of different conceptions of the good can converse in safety. Instead of creating cleavages we need to build bridges. When discussing highly sensitive issues, what is required is caution rather than carelessness, sticking to the facts rather than exaggerating and falsifying them.

Worryingly, the slogan that many people in the West adopted to identify with the satirical magazine and express their revulsion regarding the terror attack, 'Je Suis Charlie', was embraced by the Front National and other extreme right parties and movements in France and elsewhere to harbour Islamophobia and hatred and, at the same time, to popularise and normalise their radical and extreme agendas. In Germany, the Patriotic Europeans against the Islamisation of the West movement, Pegida, rode the 'Je Suis Charlie' wave to rally thousands of supporters, calling for Germany's awakening while accentuating the difference between the German nation and Islam (*Augsburger Allgemeine* 2015). Behind the banner of 'Je Suis Charlie' a strange union emerged between some liberals, who stand for freedom of expression, and racists, who abuse freedom of expression to promote bigotry and hostility against Muslims.

One may argue that many of recent years' terrorists were Muslims. But certainly not every Muslim is a terrorist. Violence preceded Islam. Like all other religions, Islam is grand in its preaching, dictates, stories, parables and statements. Like all religions, Islam is open to contradictory interpretations. Luckily, the vast majority of Muslims are peaceful, law-abiding citizens who believe that life is a special gift to be promoted and cherished. Defaming religion on the premise of a 'right', no less, to ridicule and offend is questionable. Defaming Islam when we know the results might be terror and mayhem is simply irresponsible.

In October 2020, French history teacher Samuel Paty was beheaded after he showed some of the Prophet Mohammed cartoons to his class. The context was free speech, religion and secularism in France. In this era of violence and political extremism, a small and determined minority has no qualms in killing their target groups and innocent civilians to promote its aim. Zealots are certain that they have complete hold of the truth, that they know better and that they should use coercive means in hammering their value system into all societies. We should be aware of their determination and willingness to inflict violence and try to lower the flames, not to provoke and raise them. At the same time, we should also clearly and explicitly declare that there is a zero-sum game between liberal democracy and terrorism.

Therefore, it is incumbent on the forces of democracy and freedom to protect liberal cultures from enemies and to stand strong against those who wish to destroy liberal democracies. While there is no 'right' to offend and social responsibility and civility are required when we make satire, we should also make clear that there is no room for violence. As we acknowledge that boundaries of civility should be introduced to freedom of expression so we acknowledge that boundaries should be introduced to freedom of action. Both boundaries are necessary to assure our existence and well-being. Nothing short of the future of our children is at stake.

- This is an expanded and updated version of a short article that was published in The Great War Series (Part II), *The Critique* (7 January 2016). The author wishes to thank Ejan Mackaay and participants of the International Society for Public Law's ICON•S Annual Conference (July 2021) for their constructive comments.

NOTES

[1] Very few books were published about offence. These include Feinberg (1985); King (2014); Hatzis (2021)

[2] For a different view, see Simpson (2018)

[3] For further discussion, see Bonotti and Seglow (2021) pp 72-91

REFERENCES

ABC (2015) German regional newspaper *Hamburger Morgenpost*, the target of an arson attack, *ABC*, 11 January. Available online at https://www.abc.net.au/news/2015-01-11/hamburger-morgenpost-arson-attack/6011370?nw=0

Augsburger Allgemeine (2015) Pegida supporters run with 'Je Suis Charlie' posters, 12 January. Available online at https://www.augsburger-allgemeine.de/politik/Pegida-Pegida-Anhaenger-laufen-mit-Je-suis-Charlie-Plakaten-id32620562.html

Baghramian, Maria and Ingram, Attracta (eds) (2000) *Pluralism: The Philosophy and Politics of Diversity*, London: Routledge

Bever, Lindsey and Murphy, Brian (2015), Gunmen shot dead in Texas after opening fire outside prophet Muhammad 'cartoon' show, *Washington Post*, 4 May. Available online at https://joemiller.us/2015/05/gunmen-shot-dead-in-texas-after-opening-fire-outside-prophet-muhammad-cartoon-show/

Bogain, Ariane (2019) Terrorism and the discursive construction of national Identity in France, *National Identities*, Vol. 21, No. 3 pp 241-265

Bonotti, Matteo and Seglow, Jonathan (2021) *Free Speech*, Cambridge: Polity

Bruck, Jan (2012) Mohammed cartoons have lasting effect, *Deutsche Welle*, 13 April. Available online at https://www.dw.com/en/mohammed-cartoons-have-lasting-effect/a-15878492

Buncombe, Andrew (2015) Garland shooting: Prophet Mohamed cartoon contest organisers condemn attack as 'war on free speech' after police kill two gunmen, *Independent*, 5 May. Available online at https://www.independent.co.uk/news/world/americas/texas-shooting-organisers-prophet-mohamed-cartoon-contest-condemn-attack-war-free-speech-after-police-kill-two-gunmen-10223333.html

Christians, Clifford and Traber, Michael (eds) (1997) *Communication Ethics and Universal Values*, Thousand Oaks: Sage

Christians, Clifford (2019) *Media Ethics and Global Justice in the Digital Age*, Cambridge and New York: Cambridge University Press

Cohen-Almagor, Raphael (1993) Harm principle, offence principle, and the Skokie Affair, *Political Studies*, Vol. 41, No. 3 pp 453-470

Cohen-Almagor, Raphael (2002) The offense to sensibilities argument as grounds for limiting free expression: The Israeli experience, *International Journal of Politics and Ethics*, Vol. 2, Nos 2 and 3 pp 101-117, 189-209

Cohen-Almagor, Raphael (2005) *Speech, Media, and Ethics: The Limits of Free Expression*, Houndmills and New York: Palgrave-Macmillan

Cohen-Almagor, Raphael (2006) *The Scope of Tolerance: Studies on the Costs of Free Expression and Freedom of the Press*, London and New York: Routledge

Cohen-Almagor, Raphael (2015) *Confronting the Internet's Dark Side: Moral and Social Responsibility on the Free Highway*, New York and Washington DC.: Cambridge University Press and Woodrow Wilson Center Press

Cohen-Almagor, Raphael (2020) Taking profound offence seriously: Freedom of speech v. human dignity, *Journal of Hate Studies*, Vol. 16, No. 1 pp 1-11

Cohen-Almagor, Raphael (2021) *Just, Reasonable Multiculturalism*, Cambridge and New York: Cambridge University Press

Cram, Ian (2009) The Danish cartoons, offensive expression, and democratic legitimacy, Hare, Ivan and Weinstein, James (eds) *Extreme Speech and Democracy*, Oxford: Oxford University Press pp 289-310

Devichand, Mukul (2016) How the world was changed by the slogan 'Je Suis Charlie', *BBC*, 3 January. Available online at https://www.bbc.co.uk/news/blogs-trending-35108339

Dworkin, Ronald (2006) The right to ridicule, *New York Review of Books*, Vol. 53, No. 5 p. 44. Available online at https://www.nybooks.com/articles/2006/03/23/the-right-to-ridicule/

Feinberg, Joel (1985) *Offense to Others*, Oxford and New York: Oxford University Press

Goldberger, D. (1991) Sources of judicial reluctance to use psychic harm as a basis for suppressing racist, sexist and ethnically offensive speech, *Brooklyn Law Review*, Vol. 56 pp 1165-1212

Green, Todd (2013) *The Satanic Verses* 25 years later: Why the Rushdie Affair still matters, *Huffpost*, 26 November. Available online at https://www.huffpost.com/entry/the-satanic-verses-twenty_b_3965066

Hatzis, Nicholas (2021) *Offensive Speech, Religion, and the Limits of the Law*, Oxford: Oxford University Press

House of Commons and House of Lords Joint Committee on Human Rights (2018) *Free Speech: Guidance for Universities and Students Organising Events*, London: House of Commons and House of Lords. Available online at https://publications.parliament.uk/pa/jt201719/jtselect/jtrights/589/589-annex.pdf

Kassam, Raheem (2015) *Charlie Hebdo* editor: No more Mohammed cartoons, *Middle East Forum Blog*, 17 July. Available online at https://www.meforum.org/5387/charlie-hebdo

King, Richard (2014) *On Offence: The Politics of Indignation*, London: Scribe

Klausen, Jytte (2009) The Danish cartoons and modern iconoclasm in the cosmopolitan Muslim diaspora, *Harvard Middle Eastern and Islam Review*, Vol. 8 pp 86-118

Lægaard, Sune (2007) The cartoon controversy: Offence, identity, oppression? *Political Studies*, Vol. 55 pp 581-498

Lexico (2020) Satire. Available online at https://www.lexico.com/definition/satire Marliere, Philippe (2017) The meaning of 'Charlie': The debate on the troubled French identity, Titley, Gavan, Freedman, Des, Khiabany, Gholam and Mondon, Aurélien (eds) (2017) *After* Charlie Hebdo*: Terror, Racism and Free Speech*, London: Zed pp 46-62

McGraw, Peter and Warner, Joel (2012) The Danish cartoon crisis of 2005 and 2006: 10 things you didn't know about the original Muhammad controversy, *Huffington Post*, 25 September. Available online at https://www.huffpost.com/entry/muhammad-cartoons_b_1907545

Modood, Tariq (2013) *Multiculturalism*, Cambridge: Polity Press

Mohammed Image Archives (n/d) The *Jyllands-Posten* cartoons. Available online at http://www.zombietime.com/mohammed_image_archive/jyllands-posten_cartoons/

Onishi, Norimitsu (2020) *Charlie Hebdo* republishes cartoons that prompted deadly 2015 attack, *New York Times*, 1 September. Available online at hhttps://www.nytimes.com/2020/09/01/world/europe/charlie-hebdo-cartoons-trial-france.html?campaign_id=2&emc=edit_th_20200902&instance_id=21796&nl=todaysheadlines&regi_id=33802468&segment_id=37315&user_id=4f90d90719be4cf835ad78a361c068b1

Parekh, Bhikhu (2005) *Rethinking Multiculturalism: Cultural Diversity and Political Theory*, London: Palgrave

Parekh, Bhikhu (2019) *Ethnocentric Political Theory*, London: Palgrave

Pinto, Meital (2010) What are offences to feelings really about? A new regulative principle for the multicultural era, *Oxford Journal of Legal Studies*, Vol. 30, No. 4 pp 695-723

Quran (n/d) *The Holy Quran*. Available online at https://www.clearquran.com/042.html

Rayner, Gordon, Samuel, Henry and Evans, Martin (2015) *Charlie Hebdo* attack: France's worst terrorist attack in a generation leaves 12 dead, *Telegraph*, 7 January. Available online at http://www.telegraph.co.uk/news/worldnews/europe/france/11331902/Charlie-Hebdo-attack-Frances-worst-terrorist-attack-in-a-generation-leaves-12-dead.html

Rushdie, Salman (1988) *The Satanic Verses*, London: Viking

Simpson, Robert Mark (2018) Regulating offence, nurturing offence, *Politics, Philosophy and Economics*, Vol. 17, No. 3 pp 235-256

Sky News (2015) *Charlie Hebdo* attacks: Two suspects arrested, 18 June. Available online at https://news.sky.com/story/charlie-hebdo-attacks-two-suspects-arrested-10355465

Slaughter, M. M. (1993) The Salman Rushdie affair: Apostasy, honor, and freedom of speech, *Virginia Law Review*, Vol. 79, No. 1 pp 153-204

Spencer, Robert (2015) Top *Charlie Hebdo* cartoonist Luz says will no longer draw Muhammad, *JihadWatch*, 29 April. Available online at http://www.jihadwatch.org/2015/04/top-charlie-hebdo-cartoonist-luz-says-will-no-longer-draw-muhammad

Swidler, Leonard (1999) *For All Life: Toward a Universal Declaration of a Global Ethic*, Ashland, OR.: White Cloud Press

Telegraph (2015) Prophet Mohammed cartoons controversy: Timeline, *Telegraph*, 4 May. Available online at http://www.telegraph.co.uk/news/worldnews/europe/france/11341599/Prophet-Muhammad-cartoons-controversy-timeline.html

Titley, Gavan, Freedman, Des, Khiabany, Gholam and Mondon, Aurélien (eds) (2017) *After Charlie Hebdo: Terror, Racism and Free Speech*, London: Zed

Walla (2020) The terrorist from Paris admitted: The attack – revenge for the publication of the *Charlie Hebdo* Muhammad illustrations, 27 September. Available online at https://news.walla.co.il/item/3389095

Winston, Brian (2012) *A Right to Offend*, London: Bloomsbury

Ynet (2020) After the attack in Paris: Increased security in synagogues, 26 September. Available online at https://www.ynet.co.il/news/article/ryTpn0orv#autoplay

NOTE ON THE CONTRIBUTOR

Raphael Cohen-Almagor, DPhil, St. Catherine's College, University of Oxford, is Professor and Chair of Politics and Founding Director of the Middle East Study Group, University of Hull. Raphael has taught, *inter alia*, at the universities of Oxford, Jerusalem, Haifa, UCLA, Johns Hopkins and Nirma, India. He was also Senior Fellow at the Woodrow Wilson International Center for

Scholars, Washington DC, and Distinguished Visiting Professor, Faculty of Laws, University College London. In 2022, he will be a Public Policy Fellow at the Woodrow Wilson International Center for Scholars, and in 2023 the Olof Palme Guest Professor, Lund University, Sweden. Raphael has published extensively in the fields of politics, philosophy, media ethics, medical ethics, law, sociology and history, including *The Boundaries of Liberty and Tolerance* (1994), *The Right to Die with Dignity* (2001), *Speech, Media and Ethics* (2005), *The Scope of Tolerance* (2006), *Confronting the Internet's Dark Side* (2015) and *Just, Reasonable Multiculturalism* (2021). He is now working on *Resolving the Israeli-Palestinian Conflict: A Critical Study of Peace Mediation, Facilitation and Negotiations between Israel and the PLO* (forthcoming 2023).

SECTION 3

Objections to Objectivity: Politics and Ethics of the Media

Chapter 8

Fake News, Double Spin and Strategic Lying in the Post-Truth Era

Ivor Gaber

Investigating the role of 'spin' in political communications is hardly a new undertaking. However, in this chapter a new variant of the practice – 'double spin' – is investigated and within that new variant, responding to the rise of a 'post-truth' environment the notion of 'strategic lying' is identified and developed. The chapter uses two British case studies – the referendum on whether the UK should leave the European Union and the subsequent victory of Boris Johnson's Conservative Party in the UK 2019 General Election. The chapter lays bare how the use of these spin techniques by the Leave side in the Brexit referendum, and the Conservatives in 2019, played a significant role in the final outcome of the two polls. In the tradition of Brian Winston, it is written by a broadcast journalist turned scholar and with a distinct argument and perspective.

Keywords: British politics, spin, Brexit, General Election, Boris Johnson

INTRODUCTION

There can be few academics who can claim to have identified the central role of fake news and falsehood (the currently fashionable term for lying) in modern mass communications as effectively, and as early, as Brian Winston. From *Lies, Damn Lies and Documentaries*, in 2000, to *The Roots of Fake News: Objecting to Objective Journalism* (with his son, Matthew) twenty years later, Brian has seen 'truth telling' (a term which neither Brian nor I would be comfortable with) as central to the business of communications. Of course, the sub-title of his latest book indicates that Brian is no starry-eyed romantic believing in the simple pursuit of truth, nor is he a wilfully myopic post-modernist arguing for the relativism of everything. In short, Brian is a paid-up member of the awkward squad (no, make that senior officer) made up of those who refuse to be pigeon-holed around this crucial topic – a squad to which I also claim membership.

Brian's refusal to be pigeon-holed, and his absolute commitment to factuality and the historical method, has never been more in evidence than in his trenchant contributions to sometimes heated (but always amicable) discussions on the editorial board of the *British Journalism Review* – an admirable publication that seeks to bring journalists and academics together to write, publish and argue. The academics nod sagely as Brian explains the centrality of Vlad the Impaler to the origins of fake news, whilst the journalists initially exchange cynical glances and eventually become entranced as Brian continues to weave his magical, but scholarly, tale.

In my own academic trajectory, I have long been a Winston fan. From his perceptive deconstruction and criticism of techno-determinism to his current mission to give the 'fake news' debate a more sophisticated analytical and historical context, Brian has been a force of nature both among academics and practitioners, ranging from the most esteemed documentary-makers to would-be journalists fresh out of university – all recognising their debt to Brian's copious contribution to the discipline.

From my own various academic resting places, I have also observed Brian enviously as an academic entrepreneur *par excellence* – a friendly but tough 'competitor' – at Westminster and Lincoln. And I have had the pleasure of witnessing Professor Winston's contributions at academic conferences where his papers have always been worth attending, not just for their invariably challenging, and frequently ground-breaking, content but also for his lively style of presentation.

Brian, like myself, came out of professional broadcast journalism and we found ourselves wandering in the unfamiliar groves of academe. Brian's background on Granada TV's *World in Action* led to him writing perceptively about the nature of the documentary genre and the broader history of mass communications, producing a number of landmark books in both areas. But it is his latest work, investigating the roots of fake news and the lying that goes with it, that I have found of particular interest at this historical juncture. Brian's understanding of the evolution of fake news has helped create new insights into the current state of political communications. In this chapter, using UK politics as my case study, I seek to analyse how fake news has been operationalised using two concepts – 'double spin' and 'strategic lying'.

DOUBLE SPIN AND STRATEGIC LYING

These concepts have become crucial components of the politician's armoury as they battle for control of election campaign agendas. There is little new to be said of political spin, as such; indeed, the concept, both in popular discourse and as a subject of academic investigation, has a somewhat dated feel about it. But double spin is of more recent vintage – indeed, is being theorised here for the first time. It can be characterised as an act of political communication that has an overt, above-the-line message – a traditional spun communication. But it also has below-the-line content designed to convey a broader positive message about the sender and/or a negative message about his or her opponent. In addition, it is designed to initiate or sustain a particular news agenda or to block or divert a damaging one. This is double spin but if the message itself contains palpably false, or substantially misleading, information then this brings us to the concept of strategic lying (Gaber and Fisher 2021).

The strategic lie is a form of double spin that aims to control the news agenda by means of either a straightforward lie or the distortion of factual information with the aim of misleading or deceiving its audience. It achieves its purpose in two ways. First, by making the lie as attention-grabbing as possible, thereby guaranteeing it wide exposure in both the mainstream media and the digital space. During the years of Trump's presidency, for example, US news organisations would usually delay their morning planning meetings until the president had tweeted, thus giving him a key role in determining that day's news priorities. Second, its impact is increased because the outrageous lie is invariably rapidly rebutted by opponents. But this act of rebuttal merely serves to ensure that its salience becomes further amplified by social media users and subsequently the mainstream media.

'Strategic lying' is not to be mistaken for 'fake news'. Admittedly, this term has become somewhat problematic due to its broad application, particularly when used as a form of abuse to attack the mainstream news media (Wardle and Derakhshan 2017) but for the purposes of this chapter it will suffice. For this context we will use the definition formulated by Waisbord (2018) which is that fake news usually refers to online content that appears to be from a conventional news source but, in fact, has been produced to deceive. In contrast, 'strategic lying' is a form of rhetorical spin in which the intention to deceive and mislead is more important than the appearance of veracity.

The rise of social media has been hugely significant in the genesis of 'strategic lying' as a campaigning tactic. While traditional campaigning methods, including the use of the mainstream media, continue to play a significant role in campaign messaging, social media networks enable the 'strategic lie' to have an impact far beyond its first iteration. Because of the affordances of social media, the strategic lie can spread rapidly and widely. A Labour Party report analysing the 2019 campaign characterised this practice as 'distributed spin':

> The Conservatives' core message 'Get Brexit Done' lent itself easily to the 'distributed spin' approach, whereby supporters can pick up and disseminate frames and messages and help to shape audiences' views of the campaign and related news stories (Labour Together 2020: 94).

Social media also ensures that statements of dubious factual accuracy are subject to less authoritative scrutiny than was the case when the mainstream media was the dominant political news gatekeeper. Given the sheer weight of social media postings it is almost impossible for experts or specialist journalists to check and challenge every statement of problematic veracity. A large-scale study of Twitter found that in all categories of information, but particularly political news, lies spread 'significantly farther, faster, deeper and more broadly than the truth' (Vosoughi et al. 2018: 1,146). Moreover, disseminating lies via social media also enables the sender to target messages at particular groups to a much greater extent than when using traditional media outlets.

There is a form of verification on social media – so-called 'citizen verifiers' – who seek to validate controversial claims and are authoritative, such as Full-Fact (https://fullfact.org/); some are of more dubious provenance – for instance, when the Conservatives launched their own phoney fact-checking party site during the 2019 election (Lee 2019). Nonetheless, even authoritative fact-checking is of limited utility. Nyhan et al. (2019), for example, found that correcting inaccurate statements online in real-time, by either journalists or a fact-checking organisation, had little impact on voting behaviour. Those who were sympathetic to the original message tend to reject the correction, discounting it as coming from a partisan source, or they barely notice it in the first place (Garrett and Weeks 2013). Even when the correction has been noted, Swire-Thompson et al. found that the correction faded rapidly from people's memories whilst a memory of the original lie remained. It is likely that this occurs because the original lie was seen as reinforcing existing political beliefs, or as Swire-Thompson et al. (2020: 21) put it: 'They might be a liar, but they are my liar.'

Accepting the lie enables people to avoid cognitive dissonance – described by Taddicken and Wolff (2020) as the emotion people feel when forced to confront information that contradicts their existing understandings and pre-dispositions. Avoiding cognitive dissonance is also a factor in what has become known as 'confirmation bias' which, according Nickerson (1998), is the bias that arises as a result of people only noticing and retaining information that reinforces their own worldview. Research in political psychology has also demonstrated the power of message repetition. This is partly as a result of a simple reinforcement effect but also because people tend to be 'cognitive misers' (Begg et al. 1992; Taraborelli 2008). In other words, people are more comfortable accepting information that they have previously processed instead of processing something entirely new. The profound emotional commitment evinced by supporters of President Trump in their belief that the election was 'stolen' is a vivid exemplar of all these phenomena.

THE CRISIS IN POLITICAL COMMUNICATIONS AND THE 'SELFISH POLITICAL GENE'

In *The End of History and the Last Man*, the American political scientist Francis Fukuyama asked: 'Is liberal democracy prey to serious internal contradictions, contradictions so serious that they will eventually undermine it as a political system?' (Fukuyama 1993: 21) The question this chapter poses is: Could one of these internal contradictions be attributed to the way our political communications system has evolved?

Fukuyama identifies a fundamental problem with liberal democratic systems in that they require citizens to be able not just to vote but to make that an informed vote; and that means citizens being enabled to monitor and evaluate the performance of governments (and other public bodies) between and during elections. This requires transparency and ultimately accountability throughout the governmental process. Thus, in theory, all political communications should be designed to increase transparency and enhance the electoral accountability of politicians – both those in government and opposition.

Most political messaging can be analysed in terms of its above and below-the-line content. For example, a simple public information announcement such as 'Wear Your Seat Belt' or, of late, 'Wear a Mask', does have an apparent and genuine public service content. But it also has the implicit message of 'We Care' – and, implicitly, those who criticise us don't care!

Thus, we have the paradox at the heart of modern political communications: that citizens want politicians – both those in government and opposition – to be trustworthy and accountable but, because their focus is, almost of necessity, on being re-elected, they cannot avoid the below-the-line agenda dominating their calculations when formulating political messages. This results in a substantial proportion of these messages being designed to achieve a positive impact rather than to increase public understanding. Over time this undermines the trust that is fundamental to the workings of democracy.

So why do politicians, consciously or otherwise, resort to such methods? Because they are required to seek re-election on a regular basis, this creates what I have termed elsewhere the 'selfish political gene' (Gaber 2007). The notion is based on the work of the biologist Richard Dawkins who coined the term the 'selfish gene' to help understand the process of evolution (Dawkins 1989). Dawkins suggested that all genes are, in essence, programmed to do just two things – survive and procreate. Politicians are essentially no different, regardless of the nature of the political system they operate in. Indeed, it could be argued that in a democracy, where the ballot box rather than the bullet determines who is in power, the selfish political gene kicks in with greater intensity. This is what is behind the concept of the 'permanent campaign'. First formulated by journalist and presidential adviser Sidney Blumenthal (1980), the permanent campaign requires politicians to be constantly calculating whether any particular speech, policy or press release will ultimately be electorally beneficial to him or her and their party – often characterised by the refrain 'How will it play'? This has two knock-on effects. First, governments make the communication of their messages, rather than delivering the content of their messages, their priority. Second, trust, not just in politicians but in the political system as a whole, wanes.

For example, an examination of the media releases sent out by the UK government's Department for Education in July 2021 suggested that all was going well in Britain's schools, colleges and universities. Of the 27 press releases issued in that month none suggested there were any problems, three had factual headlines and 24 had upbeat ones such as 'Thousands more children to benefit from free breakfast clubs', '£10 million scheme to help pupils boost core skills' and 'Thousands more students to learn ancient and modern languages'. In other words, the government, like all or most governments, was not only seeking to offer positive messages but also to convey the notion that there were no problems in the sector and that, in terms of education, it was doing a fantastic job – even though the education secretary at the time, Gavin Williamson, was widely seen as presiding over one of the worst periods in recent British educational policy-making.

A result of this type of communications debasement has meant we are facing a crisis in political communications. All contemporary measures of trust in both politicians and the media – old and new – validate this point. According to a Reuters Foundation report, only 36 per cent of British adults trust the media, one of the lowest figures in Europe; in the US it is even lower at 29 per cent. The Hansard Society's Audit of Political Engagement has found that 47 per cent of respondents felt 'they had no influence at all over national decision-making', the highest figure it has ever recorded. It is, I would contend, not coincidental that trust in the UK and US is most particularly steeply in decline – both have adversarial systems of it which reduces politics to a zero-sum game. In terms of political communications this means that politics is seen in terms of a simple relationship: 'If it's good for me it's bad for him/her' and vice versa. In such situations most, if not all, messages contain a double spin and promote the use of strategic lying.

CASE STUDY 1. – THE UK BREXIT REFERENDUM 2016

Strategic lying played a significant role in the 2016 Brexit referendum in persuading people to vote for Britain leaving the European Union. Boris Johnson, then out-of-office, was the main spokesperson for the Leave campaign but the mastermind was Dominic Cummings who went on to become, for a time, Johnson's chief advisor in Downing Street. Reflecting on the referendum campaign a year later, Cummings claimed that much of the campaign's success could be credited to two key slogans: 'We send the EU £350 million a week. Let's fund our NHS instead' (painted on the side of the Leave campaign bus) and 'Turkey (population 76 million) is joining the EU' (Cummings 2017). Both slogans were examples of effective campaign communications, but both were serious misrepresentations involving double spin and strategic lying. The above-the-line spin of both messages gave palpably false impressions of the factual reality surrounding the two issues but the below-the-line double spin was that these two pronouncements ensured that the dominating issues of the campaign were the cost to Britain of EU membership and the deep-seated fears about immigration.

The misleading claim that Britain sent £350 million a week to Brussels as part of its EU contribution – misleading because the figure was gross rather than net and earned a rebuke from the chair of the UK Statistics Authority as 'a clear misuse of official statistics' (Full Fact 2017) – ensured that even when the claim was effectively rebutted by Remain campaigners, audiences were simply reminded of the original claim. On almost the first day of campaigning, ITV News, the UK's leading commercial broadcaster, led with an interview with Boris Johnson almost exclusively devoted to the £350 million claim. Even though the interviewer effectively demolished the veracity of the figure, Johnson must have been very satisfied with the outcome – a full eight minutes of national airtime mainly focusing on the cost of UK's membership of the EU, and nothing about the benefits.

Cummings, in his blog about the campaign, sought neither to assert the truth of the claim nor admit that it was a falsehood. But what he did say amounted to a tacit admission that the claim was a piece of double spin, a strategic lie. He said it was designed to keep the news agenda focused on this issue, irrespective of its veracity. The fact that the claim was misleading and authoritatively rebutted was clearly beside the point – strategic lying is not about conveying information as such, even highly spun information, it is about making an impact. In his analysis, Cummings wrote: '… we said: "We send the EU £350m" to provoke people into argument. This worked much better than I thought it would.' He modestly describes the claim as 'a brilliant communications ploy'. In addition to the £350 million claim, Cummings also singled out the slogan 'Turkey (population 76 million) is joining the EU' as one that helped shift enough votes to secure victory. In 2019, after winning the General Election, Johnson was challenged about his use of this claim. He told a Channel 4 News reporter that he 'didn't say anything about Turkey during the referendum. Since I made no remarks … I can't disown them'. But the BBC's own fact-checking site – 'Reality Check' – reported that 'Boris Johnson talked about the issue of Turkey joining the EU several times in the lead-up to 23 June 2016 and was co-signatory of a letter to the prime minister warning about Turkish membership a week before the vote' (BBC 2019).

The potency of double-spun messages, as the Remain campaign discovered, is that in rebutting the messages they amplified and reinforced them by keeping them high up the news agenda. This has been described by Caroline Jack (2019: 441) as 'unintentional amplification' leading to 'inadvertent legitimisation' – the act of giving credibility to 'strategic lies' simply by repeating them. Inadvertent legitimisation also occurs when journalists accept these statements as factually, if inaccurately, based and, therefore, worthy of serious news coverage. Thus, they become responsible for allowing them to be considered as part of what Hallin (1984) has described as the 'sphere of legitimate controversy'.

In fact, throughout the Brexit campaign (and since), the BBC was criticised for allowing unsubstantiated claims, largely by the Leave campaign, into the sphere of legitimate controversy. The BBC's coverage is of particular significance since it has been for a long time, and remains, British adults' most used and most trusted source of news (Ofcom 2021) and is also, overwhelmingly, the largest source of news on social media (ibid). Their coverage of the referendum campaign was heavily criticised at the time, and since, for the 'phoney balance' they applied between authoritative and factually-based claims from acknowledged experts, official sources or legitimate fact-checking organisations (largely made by the Remain side) and the seriously misleading claims made by the Leave campaigners (Gaber 2018). For example, the fact that the head of the UK's national statistics agency said the £350 million figure was incorrect did not result in the BBC challenging the figure in any consistent way nor (better still) refusing to cover politicians repeating this canard; the same argument goes for the totally misleading claim that Turkey was about to join the EU. By not making these challenges, the BBC, in particular, given its pre-eminent role as the UK's leading news outlet, inadvertently increased the legitimacy of the false claims in the minds of voters.

Guardian columnist Catherine Bennett, writing at the time of the referendum, argued that the BBC '… allowed its obsession with balance to dictate that any carefully argued observation on Brexit, deserving of analysis, be promptly followed by its formal opponent's unsubstantiated bluster' (Bennett 2016). The *Financial Times* reported this author's referendum observations on the BBC's coverage:

> Professor Ivor Gaber points out that the BBC gave equal weight to the 1,280 business leaders who signed a letter to *The Times* backing UK membership of the EU and the (already oft reported) Leave view of Sir James Dyson. It did the same with the warnings of 10 Nobel Prize-winning economists and (frequently already cited) pro-Brexit Patrick Minford, and often referred unchecked to the discredited figure of £350 million UK savings from EU contributions. Gaber adds that much scepticism was bounced from news interviews to the BBC's (excellent but much less viewed) Reality Check service (Jack 2016).

CASE STUDY 2. – THE 2019 UK GENERAL ELECTION

Election campaigning in modern pluralist democracies requires parties to have strategies to ensure, or at least seek to ensure, that the mainstream news agenda (and, by extension, the agenda in the digital space) plays to their key campaign themes and imposes the news frames that suit their electoral strategies (Van Aelst and Walgrave 2017: 71). During the 2019 election campaign, the Labour Party was responsible for some misleading claims, but these were no more than the 'normal', *ad hoc* misleading statements that are an almost universal feature of election campaigns. The Conservatives – with Dominic Cummings at the helm – again turned to issuing 'strategic lying' statements that met the three criteria distinguishing 'strategic lying' from other forms of 'spin'. First, the repetition of falsehoods or seriously misleading statements despite knowing them to be so but being prepared to take any flak because in a 'post-truth' environment little long-term electoral damage ensues. Second, the statements were intended to maintain the campaign focus on news agenda items favourable to their side or enabled them to divert attention away from topics that they deemed unhelpful. Third, the statements were sufficiently attention-grabbing to ensure amplification by both the mainstream and social media.

The Conservatives wasted no time in setting out their spin strategy when they issued a doctored video clip showing Labour's EU spokesperson, Sir Keir Starmer, apparently unable to answer a question about his party's stance on Brexit, even though, in the actual interview, Starmer is seen confidently answering the question. There followed a furore about fake news and, defending the clip on *BBC Breakfast,* Tory Party chairman James Cleverly sought to laugh off the ruse by saying: 'Everyone could see the video was "obviously edited" … because of the music underneath' (Waterson and Syal 2019). Whether or not the joke was that obvious is unknowable but what is known is that the doctored clip had over a million views and the subsequent disavowal posts, many more – just one BBC report of the incident received 1.1 million hits on Twitter. And the rapid Labour rebuttal helped reinforce a key Tory campaign narrative – that Labour's policy on EU withdrawal was so confused that even the party's Brexit spokesperson appeared not to know what it was. Not content with the 'success' of the first doctored video clip, the Conservatives posted a second version of it later that day.

But, as frequently the case in British politics, it was the Irish question that caused the Conservatives, both during the campaign and subsequently, the most difficulty and hence the most need to engage with the strategic lie. Their key campaigning slogan – 'Get Brexit Done' – was sorely tested when they claimed that their nascent agreement to leave the EU was almost a formality. 'We're going to get Brexit done with a deal that is pre-cooked, ready to go, oven-ready,' Johnson said at the launch of the campaign (Wearmouth 2019). But it wasn't – as events after the election proved with the controversy over whether the trade border with the UK lay between Northern Ireland and the Irish Republic or between Northern Ireland and the British mainland. Five years after Brexit that issue remains unresolved and a source of continuing tension both between the UK and the EU and on the ground in Northern Ireland. But repeatedly during the campaign Johnson insisted there would be no border checks on either of the two potential borders despite this being directly contradicted in the UK/EU Withdrawal Agreement and even by the Prime Minister's own Brexit secretary and the UK Treasury. But the lie had the effect of dampening down any doubts about Brexit and reinforcing the 'Get Brexit Done' campaign theme.

Another example of a strategic lie centred on Conservative claims about Labour's spending plans. A frequent election refrain that has always played well for the Conservatives is that Labour cannot be trusted with the nation's finances. In the 2019 campaign, these claims were made even before Labour had published its plans with the Tories suggesting that Labour's spending commitments amounted to a £1.2 trillion – a vast sum, which the authoritative Institute for Fiscal Studies rebutted as a gross exaggeration, estimating the correct figure to be £80 billion. The claim was reinforced by another made-up figure released by the Conservatives about how much Labour's programme would supposedly cost the average taxpayer (Full-Fact 2019a). Both amounts were quickly challenged by public finance experts and fact-checking organisations, but the lies remained on the record and succeeded in achieving the Tories' main aim of establishing and reinforcing the narrative that Labour was a 'tax and spend' party.

Strategic lies were also mobilised to rebut the charge that Labour usually made that the National Health Service was 'not safe in Tory hands'. On numerous occasions Johnson asserted the Conservatives were on course to build 40 new hospitals, but the fact-checking organisations maintained only six had been approved while the others were mere aspirations (Boseley 2019). Also in the health field, the Prime Minister repeatedly said the government would be recruiting 50,000 additional nurses; but neutral fact-checkers pointed out this figure included 19,000 currently employed nurses who, the Tories hoped, would be dissuaded from leaving the NHS (Full-Fact 2019b).

These examples are significant because they focused on topics that were either central election campaigning planks for the Conservatives or central to their rebuttal priorities. The doctored video clip of Labour's Brexit spokesperson, apparently unable to explain his party's Brexit policy, was designed to contrast with the Tories' central slogan of 'Get Brexit Done' – the implication being only the Conservatives knew how to accomplish this; and Johnson's insistence that there would be no border checks between Great Britain and Northern Ireland was central to maintaining the key theme of 'Get Brexit Done'. The exaggerated claims about Labour's spending plans played to a long-used Tory campaigning theme that the Labour Party was financially irresponsible. The claims about the health service – new hospitals being built with extra nurses employed – were designed to counter Labour accusations that the Tories could not be trusted with the NHS.

By successfully employing the tactic of 'strategic lying' in the 2019 election campaign, the Conservatives kept the news agenda on their favoured ground. Just as the claims that the UK sent £350 million to the EU every week and that Turkey would shortly be joining the EU, certainly helped the Leave cause during the Brexit referendum, so the Conservatives' strategic lies in the 2019 election can be viewed in a similar light. Monitoring of radio and television coverage during the election campaign by the University of Loughborough revealed Brexit was the most covered topic, with the economy in second place (Deacon et al. 2019). And despite growing concern about the state of the National Health Service, the public continued to tell pollsters that Brexit was the most important issue facing the country (YouGov 2019).

The 'strategic lies' were made in the knowledge that the original false statements and their rebuttals would be widely disseminated by both mainstream and social media – particularly to those likely to be sympathetic to the Conservative or Leave cause. Just as importantly, the lies served to keep the national debate close to the Conservatives' agenda. Polling after the Brexit referendum (Prosser et al. 2016) showed the two major reasons people gave for voting to Leave the EU were concerns about sovereignty (which underpinned the notion of the £350 million figure) and immigration, which was underpinned by the prominence of the Turkey 'threat'.

CONCLUSION

The morphing of spin into double spin and strategic lying is clearly having a deleterious effect on the UK's democratic political culture. These techniques have been effectively utilised by political communication professionals who have understood and exploited social media to turbo-charge double-spin and its latest variant, strategic lying, in the setting, framing and priming of news agendas. To conclude, strategic lying was possibly best described, not by a scholar but by a radical journalist – the late Dawn Foster – who, during the 2019 election campaign, observed:

> … slash and burn and lie with impunity. Tell whatever falsehood you fancy, especially one that has a propensity to go viral. Get your smear heard as widely as possible, and if you're challenged, just lie. Far more people will see your initial lie than the follow-up correction, and few people will take the time to research any statistical embroidery or rewriting of the party's stance or record (Foster 2019).

In light of the events surrounding the 2020 US election and the subsequent invasion of the Capitol in Washington in January 2021, further research is urgently required not only to investigate the extent to which strategic lying is now a central feature in the political communications culture of liberal democracies but also to evaluate its impact on voter behaviour. On a practical level it is equally urgent that investigations are undertaken as to the extent to which media regulation (including online) and electoral regulation can be effectively mobilised to counter the negative impact that these techniques are clearly having on our democratic culture.

- This is an updated and revised version of 'Strategic lying': The case of Brexit and the 2019 UK Election, by Ivor Gaber and Caroline Fisher, the *International Journal of Press/Politics*, published online on 17 March 2021.

REFERENCES

BBC (2019) Reality check: Brexit: Did Boris Johnson talk Turkey during referendum campaign? 18 January. Available online at https://www.bbc.co.uk/news/uk-politics-46926119, accessed on 16 August 2021

Begg, Ian Maynard, Anas, Ann and Farinacci, Suzanne (1992) Dissociation of processes in belief: Source recollection, statement familiarity, and the illusion of truth, *Journal of Experimental Psychology: General*, Vol. 121, No. 4 pp 446-458. Available online at http://www.psychology.mcmaster.ca/bennett/psy720/readings/m4/BeggAnasFarinacci1992.pdf?origin=publication_detail, accessed on 18 August 2021

Bennett, Catherine (2016) The BBC's fixation on 'balance' skews the truth, *Guardian*, 4 September. Available online at https://www.theguardian.com/commentisfree/2016/sep/03/bbc-impartiality-skewers-evidence-based-facts, accessed on 16 August 2021

Blumenthal, Max (1980) *The Permanent Campaign*, New York: Beacon Books

Boseley, Sarah (2019) From 40 hospitals to six: How the Tories' NHS numbers don't add up, *Guardian*, 29 September, Available online at https://www.theguardian.com/society/2019/sep/29/from-40-hospitals-to-six-tories-nhs-numbers-dont-add-up, accessed on 16 August 2021

Cummings, Dominic (2017) On the referendum #21: Branching histories of the 2016 referendum and 'the frogs before the storm', *Dominic Cummings' Blog*, 9 January. Available online at https://dominiccummings.com/2017/01/09/on-the-referendum-21-branching-histories-of-the-2016-referendum-and-the-frogs-before-the-storm-2/, accessed on 16 August 2021

Dawkins, Richard (1989) *The Selfish Gene*, Oxford: Oxford University Press

Deacon, David, Goode Jackie and Smith, David (2020) What was all that about, then? The media agenda in the 2019 General Election, Jackson, D., Thorsen, E., Lilleker, D. and Weidhase, N. (eds) *UK Election Analysis 2019: Media, Voters and the Campaign*, Bournemouth: Centre for Comparative Politics and Media Research, Bournemouth University. Available online at https://duckduckgo.com/?q=UK+Election+Analysis+2019%3A+Media%2C+Voters+and+the+Campaign&atb=v172-1&ia=web , accessed on 16 August 2021

Foster, Dawn (2019) Something frightening is happening in British politics, *Jacobin*, 12 November. Available online at https://jacobinmag.com/2019/12/boris-johnson-tories-conservative-party-lies-uk-general-election, accessed on 16 August 2021

Fukuyama, Francis (1992) *The End of History and the Last Man*, London: Penguin Books

Full-Fact (2017) £350 million EU claim 'a clear misuse of official statistics', 20 September. Available online at https://fullfact.org/europe/350-million-week-boris-johnson-statistics-authority-misuse/, accessed on 16 August 2021

Full-Fact (2019a) Conservative Party manifesto 2019: Fact-checked, 24 November. Available online at https://fullfact.org/election-2019/conservative-manifesto-2019/?link_id=23&can_id=eb312ff746ffbf1a2d2e6d5fafc267e9&source=email-the-tories-nhs-lies&email_referrer=email_671294&email_subject=the-tories-nhs-lies, accessed on 16 August 2021

Full-Fact (2019b) Is the 50,000 more nurses claim from the Conservative manifesto accurate?, 10 December. Available online at https://fullfact.org/election-2019/50000-more-nurses-claim-conservative-manifestoaccurate/, accessed on 16 August 2021

Gaber, Ivor (2007) Too much of a good thing: The 'problem' of political communications in a mass media democracy, *Journal of Public Affairs*, Vol. 7, No. 3 pp 219-234

Gaber, Ivor (2018) New challenges in the coverage of politics for UK broadcasters and regulators in the 'post-truth' environment, *Journalism Practice*, Vol. 12, No. 8 pp 1,019-1,028

Gaber, Ivor and Fisher, Caroline (2021) 'Strategic lying': The case of Brexit and the 2019 UK Election, *The International Journal of Press/Politics*, published online on 17 March 2021. https://doi.org/10.1177/1940161221994100

Garrett, R. Kelly and Weeks, Brian E. (2013) The promise and peril of real-time corrections to political misperceptions, *Proceedings of the CSCW 2013 conference on computer-supported cooperative work* pp 1047-1058. Available online at https://vdocuments.mx/cscw2013-the-promise-and-peril-of-real-time-corrections-to-political-misperceptions.html, accessed on 17 August 2021

Hallin, Daniel C. (1984) The media, the war in Vietnam, and political support: A critique of the thesis of an oppositional media, *The Journal of Politics*, Vol. 46, No.1 pp 2-24

Institute for Fiscal Studies (2019) Labour manifesto: An initial reaction from IFS researchers, 19 November. Available online at https://election2019.ifs.org.uk/article/labour-manifesto-an-initial-reaction-from-ifs-researchers, accessed on 16 August 2021

Jack, Andrew (2016) Brexit briefing: Balance at the BBC, *Financial Times*, 11 August. Available online at https://www.ft.com/content/3236e982-5fb6-11e6-ae3f-77baadeb1c93, accessed on 16 August 2021

Jack, Caroline (2019) Wicked content, *Communication, Culture and Critique*, Vol. 12, No. 4 pp 435-454.

Labour Together (2019) Election review. Available online at https://docs.labourtogether.uk/Labour%20Together%202019%20Election%20Review.pdf, accessed on 16 August 2021

Lee, Dave (2019) Election debate: Conservatives criticised for renaming Twitter profile 'FactcheckUK', 20 November. Available online at https://www.bbc.co.uk/news/technology-50482637, accessed on 16 August 2019

Nickerson, Raymond S. (1998) Confirmation bias: A ubiquitous phenomenon in many guises, *Review of General Psychology*, Vol. 2, No. 2 pp 175-220

Nyhan, Brendan, Porter, Ethan, Reifler, Jason and Wood, Thomas J. (2019) Taking fact-checks literally but not seriously? The effects of journalistic fact-checking on factual beliefs and candidate favorability, *Political Behavior*, Vol. 42 pp 939-960

Ofcom (2021) News consumption in the UK, 27 July. Available online at https://www.ofcom.org.uk/research-and-data/tv-radio-and-on-demand/news-media/news-consumption

Prosser, Chris, Mellon, Jon and Green, Jane (2016) What mattered most to you when deciding how to vote in the EU Referendum?, *British Election Study*. Available online at https://www.britishelectionstudy.com/bes-findings/what-mattered-most-to-you-when-deciding-how-to-vote-in-the-eu-referendum, accessed on 16 August 2021

Swire-Thompson, Briony, Ecker, Ullrich K. H., Lewandowsky, Stephan and Berinsky, Adam (2020) They might be a liar, but they are my liar: Source evaluation and the prevalence of misinformation, *Political Psychology*, Vol. 41, No. 1 pp 21-34

Taddicken, Monika and Wolff, Laura (2020) Fake news in science communication: Emotions and strategies of coping with dissonance online, *Media and Communication*, Vol. 8, No. 1 pp 206-217

Taraborelli, Dario (2008) How the web is changing the way we trust, Waelbers, K., Briggle, A. and Brey, P. (eds) *Current Issues in Computing and Philosophy*, Amsterdam: IOS Press pp 194-204

Van Aelst, Peter and Walgrave, Stefaan (2017) *How Political Actors Use the Media: A Functional Analysis of the Media's Role in Politics*, Basingstoke: Macmillan

Vosoughi, Soroush, Deb, Roy and Aral, Sinan (2018) The spread of true and false news online, *Science*, Vol. 359 (6380) pp 1,146-1,151. Doi: 10.1126/science.aap9559

Waisbord, Silvio (2018) Truth is what happens to news: On journalism, fake news, and post-truth, *Journalism Studies*, Vol. 19, No. 13 pp 1,866-1,878

Wardle, Claire and Derakhshan, Hossein (2017) *Information Disorder: Toward an Interdisciplinary Framework for Research and Policy Making*, Strasbourg: Council of Europe. Available online at https://rm.coe.int/information-disorder-toward-an-interdisciplinary-framework-for-researc/168076277c, accessed on 16 August 2016

Waterson, Jim and Syal, Rajeev (2019) Keir Starmer: Tories' doctored TV footage is 'act of desperation', *Guardian*, 6 November. Available online at https://www.theguardian.com/media/2019/nov/05/tories-unrepentant-about-doctored-video-of-keir-starmer-tv-appearance, accessed on 16 August 2021

Wearmouth, Rachel (2019) No-deal Brexit threat as Tory manifesto rules out transition extension, *Huffington Post*, 24 November. Available online at https://www.huffingtonpost.co.uk/entry/no-deal-brexit-threat-as-tory-manifesto-rules-out-transition-extension_uk_5ddaa3d4e4b0913e6f6e03f7, accessed on 16 August 2021

YouGov (2019) YouGov tracker: Most important issues. Available online at https://yougov.co.uk/topics/political-trackers/survey-results, accessed on 16 August 2021

NOTE ON THE CONTRIBUTOR

Ivor Gaber is Professor of Political Journalism at the University of Sussex and a former radio and television producer and political correspondent for BBC TV and Radio, ITV, Channel Four and Sky News.

Chapter 9

The Media of the Past Determining the Politics of the Future?

Martin Conboy

31 January 2020 was a hugely important day for the UK both as a polity and as a national imaginary. The day the UK finally left the EU was also significant for the political representation of the UK in its national daily press. This chapter will consider the images and language deployed by British national newspapers on that day with a view to interpreting their continuing alignment to existing tropes of national identification. These representations and their political implications are compared with Ofcom statistics on readers' political preferences which indicate that these newspapers, still read predominantly by older, more conservative, anti-EU voters, are shaping the future for a younger demographic comprising more liberal, pro-EU voters.

Keywords: Brexit, newspaper demographics, style, image, narrative, nation

THE NATION BEYOND THE END OF HISTORY

Ernest Renan (1990 [1882]) first invited us to consider how nations exist through a dialectic: remembering and forgetting. The Brexit debate in Britain offers a prime example of how the style through which a nation is imagined plays a significant role in this exchange (Anderson 1983). Initial enthusiasm in the early 1990s at the end of the Cold War and German reunification drove commentators into print to proclaim a new post-nationalist era. On the neo-liberal right of the political spectrum, Francis Fukuyama saw the triumph of Western, market-based economics and global transactions. His prognostications were almost messianic in predicting the New World Order as 'the endpoint of mankind's ideological evolution' (1992: xi); a Manifest Destiny for the twenty first century. From the Marxist left, Eric Hobsbawm (1990) went so far as to foresee the end of nationalism as a meaningful political identity since it had ceased to be a vector facilitating historical development. Less benevolent analyses were also underway with Edward Luttwak's trenchant essay 'Why fascism is the wave of the future' (1994: 3-4).

The logic, then, seemed inexorably skewed towards a narrative that would see the victorious ideology and within it the associated economic model become the single prevalent mode of governance. Democracy's moral victory was taken as a template for universal progress. In a world dominated by a single, liberal, market economic model, it appeared that a global reach beckoned for this same economic order as a reinvigorated and more assertive global capitalism. Even China with its new economic model seemed to be on board. The Maastricht Treaty, signed in 1992, reinforced the onward post-Cold War momentum of the EU as an economic and political bloc even though, historically, the political assumption had always been that democracy could only thrive in individual nation states.

In an increasingly networked world, with overlapping interests and intersecting peoples, it was assumed that the nation state's appeal would quickly wane while cross-national, regional and global alliances would impose themselves even more strongly in the political sphere. The benefits of globalised trade and travel were not, however, universal. Groups of citizens were 'left behind' by outsourcing industries and services to cheaper overseas providers and international trade patterns appeared to bypass traditional working communities at the same pace as the technocratic and professional classes flourished. Parties of the left in much of Western Europe felt enabled to pitch towards the new demographics of affluence. Consequently, significant sections of the electorate felt ignored by politicians, had no voice to enable them to be heard, let alone listened to, and were neglected by the impersonal mechanisms of the economy. Beyond the East/West binaries, a new set of winners and losers became established both economically and politically. Cosmopolitanism, for those enjoying the fruits of globalised neo-liberalism, disempowered those left in more impoverished and parochial localities. The dispossessed, those 'left behind' by the onward march of global capitalism, were drawn back to the appeal of local solutions emphasising older images and narratives of the nation. Politicians who realised that harvested rich rewards – from Trump to Orbán, Bolsonaro to Erdoğan and, for our purposes, Farage, the Brexit Party leader, and Johnson.

Thirty years on from that turning point in history, far from being an irrelevance in an increasingly globalised world, the nation is, globally, enjoying a resurgence in both emotional and political appeal. Within this nationalist discourse, past narratives of national exceptionalism echo in the pseudo-historical analogies, images, characters and icons of the national story that all clamour for our attention. In Britain, we have our own small patch of parochialism that paradoxically builds upon notions of sovereignty which hark back to a Golden Era of ruling the waves, dominion 'East of Suez' and playing a leading role on the global stage (Bentley 2021).

Europe, embodied as the EU, became a convenient scapegoat as an external threat and was often presented to consumers of the right-wing press as the major alien outsider. The EU could seem a distant and elite set of discourses and practices unrelated to daily political life in the UK allowing British newspapers and other periodicals to provide regular representation of such a democratic deficit in exaggerated or plain false reports (Weymouth and Anderson 1999). Rejection of the EU was often articulated as a desire for more 'control', more democratic accountability. Readers were fed a news-media diet of a predominantly English nationalism laced with imperial nostalgia and boosted by partial memories of the war years. These nostalgia-tinged elements rooted in the reconstruction of a preferred narrative of past glories were complemented by explicit linkage of the EU as a source of threats, through immigration, to the British way of life and to jobs.

The deployment of imagery and narratives from an era when the UK was more or less England with a few exotic additions drawn from its Celtic neighbours is clearly not rationally coherent, yet national sentiments are rarely rational and it is the emotive nature of the vocabulary and imagery that the 'national' press exploits. This is the path to demographic success with their readers in recreating a shared sense of identity. This may exclude younger readers but, as we will see, as long as it provides for their base readership and their political preferences, that is enough. It may constitute a short-term strategy but if it maintains a commercial foothold in these challenging times for newspapers then it is obviously considered worthwhile. On these terms, national rhetoric whether in word or image is a highly pragmatic affair.

THE NATIONAL BASE OF NEWS VALUES: THE PATRIOTIC IMPERATIVE

It is generally agreed that news values are at once a commercial necessity and potentially a communal good. News media need to narrate the news from distinct communities as they depend on specific geo-political audiences for their relevance. This makes them attractive to advertisers and other investors who are reassured that the particular news media outlet that carries their interests has a ready and stable audience out of which profit can be extracted, wages paid, investments extended. This is hardly a new phenomenon and has been the case ever since the circulation of information for profit became a regular routine from the late Middle Ages. News values also create and maintain communities of readers/listeners/viewers who can feel bonded into an experience of sharing an information source with a set of relatively like-minded individuals (Conboy 2006). News media, therefore, work at a social as well as an economic level. Most analyses of news values (Galtung and Ruge 1965; Brighton and Foy 2007; Harcup and O'Neil 2017) highlight the national relevance of news as being of particular importance. There is a major difference, however, between news being of interest to a particular community and news being an existential support for a specific political position that has as its base the survival of a political position; that way lies propaganda. Yet one fundamental of nationalism lies in its potential activation for political positioning.

A nation should present itself ideally as being better or at least the best version for its participants/community. It draws, therefore, on all possible resources to amplify and thus reinforce such a position. This strategy includes news media that need to be sold to and consumed by national subjects already influenced by multiple sources of national ideology. As Billig (1995) highlights, some of these can be benign such as the stories told to children by their parents. Others can be more troublesome and include tales of superiority evidenced in war or demonisations of outsider groups who are presented as either rivals or inferior creatures.

THE STYLE OF IMAGINING THE NATION

The first point to stress is that the newspapers more or less aligned within their usual political preferences mapped on to cases for Leave or Remain. Conservative-supporting newspapers wholeheartedly backed Brexit while Labour/Liberal-Democrat/Unaligned went for at least a more sceptical reception if not outright critical rejection. All daily newspapers, unsurprisingly agreeing that the EU withdrawal was the most significant event of the day, marked it with special issues incorporating pull-out supplements, posters, memorial editions, extended analysis, free gifts, posters.

Daily Telegraph

The Conservative-supporting *Daily Telegraph* is probably as useful a place to start as any given the role that it and its political columnists, such as most notably Boris Johnson, played in fomenting attitudes to the EU from as far back as the 1980s. Contributing a strongly Eurosceptic line, he was the Brussels correspondent for the *Daily Telegraph* and later political columnist for the same newspaper from 1989. Often grotesquely exaggerating for effect, his line encouraged and fed into a broadly sceptical and sometimes hostile view of the European project. He continued his broadly hostile attitude to the EU between 1999 and 2005 as editor of the *Spectator*. The *Daily Telegraph*'s front page on 31 January 2020 (the day on which the withdrawal agreement came into force) has a large picture of Prime Minister Johnson extracted from his pre-recorded speech to the nation. He figures strongly in image and rhetoric as a personification of the successful outcome of the Brexit campaign, blending the group efforts of newspaper and, as presented here, nation. This is hardly surprising given the personal role Johnson had played in the long anti-EU campaign as mentioned above. The paper, like many on this day, marks the occasion with a special supplement. It has an eight-page supplement, 'TO MARK A CAMPAIGN THAT CHANGED HISTORY'. Significantly, this headline is printed in the national colours: red, white and blue. Below, the sub-heading reinforces the co-production of political event and editorial commitment: 'THE STORY OF THE TELEGRAPH AND BREXIT.'

To add a gloss to this self-promoting celebration, the newspaper produces a whole page back catalogue of cartoons from its cartoonist, Matt, that have charted the path towards this significant moment in British history. The paper claims that 'Euroscepticism was in our DNA', suggesting a familiar confluence between editorial preferences, readerships and national community (Conboy 2006).

Daily Express

In its front-page strapline, the *Daily Express* features a slogan, 'We're Backing Britain', as a retrospective rhetorical gesture to a brief campaign launched in the news media in 1968. This is an explicit nudge towards an older demographic, targeted by the newspaper, who alone would have direct memories of that campaign which aimed to encourage consumption of British-made goods to rectify imbalances in trade. This was several years before the UK's entry to the then-Common Market. Its opening salvo combines the collective pronoun 'we' with a highlighted prominence for Johnson as Prime Minister who is cited as if exclusively responsible for mapping out the contours of this new phase of national life. The slogan returns to the idea of a shared responsibility between nation, readership and editorial.

> At 11 pm tonight, we will leave the EU and on this momentous occasion the PM will herald a new era of 'renewal and change' for Britain

> YES, WE DID IT!

The oversize headline is accompanied by a map of the UK made up of dozens of pro-Brexit front pages of the *Daily Express* from the previous four years, displaying the consistency and prominence of the paper's support and adding credence to its claims for credit in securing this outcome on behalf of its readers. The special pull-out supplement celebrating the event has the paper's long-standing and emblematic Crusader on its front page – first used on 29 March 1930, to support the campaign of its owner, Lord Beaverbrook, for Empire Free Trade: the 'Imperial Crusade'. The Crusader is depicted standing on the iconic White Cliffs of Dover, with a cartoon speech bubble: 'We've got our country back' and highlighting the collective effort: 'YOU GOT BRITAIN OUT OF THE EU!.' Above this is the claim that this constitutes 'A NEW DAWN FOR BRITAIN'. At the bottom of the page is a reminder of their special edition from 8 January 2011 which launched the campaign as 'GET BRITAIN OUT OF THE EU' with the same Crusader in the same location saying: 'We demand our country back.' Using the Crusader as a prominent and consistent icon in the campaign stresses the continuity of its own tradition: 'Our 10-year fight to leave is greatest newspaper crusade.'

The Sun

The front page of the *Sun*, echoing the 'Get Brexit Done' electoral mantra of Johnson, leads with this statement:

> Tonight at 11 pm, after 30 years of resistance to the creeping danger of a European superstate, the great people of the United Kingdom have at last, finally … Got Brexit Done.

OUR TIME HAS COME

FAREWELL, AUF WIEDERSEHEN, ADIEU

Inside there is plenty more coverage and a characteristically tabloid competition (Bingham and Conboy 2015) offering readers the chance to win one of 100 souvenir 50p coins worth £10 each. Using a large image of the coin in question, symbolic of the UK's independent currency at the same time as it celebrates Brexit as a physical enactment of that new status, also forms part of the paper's virtuous self-association with the event.

Johnson features prominently in the supplement. A mock-up picture of a packet of breakfast cereal 'Special K' has been re-designed as 'EU Free Special UK' for the occasion and Johnson is seen in cartoonish representation with a bowl full of Union Jacks giving a delighted thumbs-up. The souvenir edition also makes claims for its crucial role in campaigning over 30 years with a selection of headlines and front-pages from the past. The supplement leads off with: 'AFTER A 30-YEAR BATTLE, A GREAT MOMENT FOR YOU, OUR READERS.' Its accompanying opinion piece starts with a statement of nationalistic exceptionalism bordering on bombast:

> The UK is a special nation. A great nation. We created the modern world.
>
> Over 10 centuries, the hard graft and ingenuity of these small islands in science, industry, music, art, sport, business and politics have enhanced the lives of billions. … There are many challenges ahead. But we'll rise to meet them. We're that kind of people.

It ends with a familiar reference to a war-time hero by echoing the famous words of Winston Churchill: 'Never in human history has so much been achieved by a nation of so few.' It then shifts for a moment looking to the future and predicting better days ahead for 'OUR' nation.

> For a greater Britain
>
> OUR TIME HAS COME
>
> (Photograph of Big Ben)

Tonight ... our nation's course changes for ever – and for the better

We will be finally be out of the EU

The free giant poster 'HOW THE SUN GOT BREXIT DONE' is a compilation of recognisable characters from Britain's past and present from Shakespeare to Queen Elizabeth II and sport and media celebrities figures such as Mo Farah and Holly Willoughby together with speech bubbles on variations of 'See EU'. All this is presided over by the larger figure of Johnson with his own 'See EU' bubble in large bold type. As with several other newspapers, the *Sun* is keen to illustrate just what a continuity of opinion and coverage it has provided on the relationship between the UK and the EU. On the reverse side, a poster lists famous milestones in the paper's self-proclaimed 30-year campaign with front pages reproduced to make its point that Brexit is the summation of its editorial campaigning over decades.

Daily Mail

On its front page, the *Daily Mail* opens with a militaristic but characteristically tabloid metaphor (Conboy and Eldridge 2021):

> At 11 pm our proud nation finally leaves the EU – still a friend of Europe, but free and independent once more after 47 years. Now, on this momentous day, we salute ...

> A NEW DAWN FOR BRITAIN

This is presented against a background of a Union Jack combined with an image of the White Cliffs of Dover. This visual metaphor of the last sight that troops saw on leaving for battle during World War II and the first aspect of Britain on their return was made famous by singer Vera Lynn. It is typical of the British media's tendency to focus on the country's history of engagement in world wars to bolster its contemporary sense of identity, feeding into the myth of Britain standing alone whereas, in fact, it was helped enormously in both world wars by soldiers from its colonies and by the strength of the US in both and the Soviet Union in the second. Although the paper does not have a special supplement it does devote ten inside pages to what it calls 'Brexit Day'. In keeping with tabloid tradition there is an offer on the next day's paper for a reproduction of the front page of this issue – as a free tea towel.

The Times

Its front page is the least wordy of all. It has a full-page image of Big Ben's clock face at a symbolically resonant 11 o'clock, the time when the UK officially leaves the EU, and simply the words: 'BREXIT – IT'S TIME.' In addition, there is a wrap-around section highlighting the stages in the relationship between Britain and the EU in pictures as well as key dates from 1951, when the precursor to the Common Market, the European Coal and Steel Community, was created.

Inside, the content is relatively low key in its series of retrospectives on negotiations and the PM's claims. As an exception to this, one of its comment pieces sets a very different tone from what one might expect from a newspaper of record in conflating history with bombast. Here, as often, English national history is seamlessly substituted for that of the UK as a whole.

> History tells us this is just the beginning
>
> … However, there is really only one event in Britain's past that compares in economic, ideological, cultural and political magnitude to today's departure from the EU and that is Henry VIII's spectacular withdrawal from Europe and England's rejection of foreign regulation between 1532 and 1534, the first great Brexit.

The Guardian

A newspaper firmly on the side of Remain, its main front-page headline sums up Brexit as the mistaken stance of a small and fading international player over-reaching itself:

> **Small island**
>
> After 47 years, Britain leaves the EU at 11 pm tonight – the biggest gamble in a generation

Yet even in its opposition to Brexit, the paper uses the iconic white cliffs but, in this interpretation, ironically as an image of a country in reduced circumstances with its national flag flying from a collapsing sandcastle in the foreground. Nevertheless, this illustrates the centrality of such imagery even across radically different political perspectives.

i

The *i* provides a further cautionary alternative to the celebratory tone of much of the right-wing press. Its front page announces:

> U.K.'s leap into the unknown
>
> At 11 pm tonight the UK leaves the European Union after 47 years of membership
>
> Questions over trade and future relations with Europe and America are unresolved

Boris Johnson urges national renewal, as Brussels mourns the loss of pragmatic friend

Bank of England cuts growth forecast – but still no interest rates rise

This is superimposed on a photograph of a night sky over Western Europe with illuminations from major conurbations subtly indicating where the weight of power in Europe actually resides.

Daily Mirror

Its front page is dominated presciently as it turns out by an emerging story from China: 'KILLER FLU: 150 BRITS IN QUARANTINE.' There is, however, a small insert on the top right of the page with a photomontage of a Union Jack fluttering in front of a Big Ben clock face on 11.00 and the following:

BREXIT DAY

Now it's time to bring the country back together

Daily Star

As if to damn all sides in the debate, the *Daily Star* chooses to present a sardonic, contrarian news item. While still utilising such terms as 'nation' and 'historic', it turns the reader's attention to the ending of the self-imposed month of abstinence after festive excess:

Tonight is a TRULY HISTORIC moment for our great nation … That's right, it's the end of Dry January!

Millions of people across the UK will be celebrating a landmark occasion today … As Dry January finally comes to an end and they can all go down the pub

DOES IT MATTER?

Certainly, newspapers are a medium in decline, an entertaining minority diversion for a residual base in an era of falling circulations that have been accelerated by the rise of digital platforms and the pervasiveness of socially mediated news. YouGov polling in 2016 (23-24 June), on the demographics and party affiliations of the recorded voting preferences from the referendum, indicated that Conservative voters split 61/39 in favour of Leave – a significantly large gap given that the difference in the final poll amounted to 4 per centage points of the votes cast. The reverse comparison with the largest opposition party, Labour, showed that their voters split in a similar fashion 35/65 in favour of Remain. Age was another aspect that showed divisions. Moving up the age range, the preference for Leave increased significantly to become the dominant choice in the over-60s. Among 18 to 24-year-olds 71/29 were in favour of Remain; 25 to 49-year-olds spilt 54/46 while a pivot then occurred with majorities for Leave at 60/40 and 64/36 among 50 to 64-year-olds and 65+ voters respectively.

Mediatique was commissioned to analyse long-term trends in the press market in the UK by the Department for Digital, Culture, Media and Sport. It published the review quoted here in February 2018 in summary with snapshots from 2007, 2012 and 2017. A mere 14 per cent of 16 to 24-year-olds reported reading newspapers for news, compared to 63 per cent using the internet. Total print reach by age-range showed that overall total usage of newspapers peaked among those aged 55 and over at 34 per cent whereas those aged between 18 and 34 were at 11 per cent (PAMCo 3 2019). Although based on different age categories, Mediatique also show trends within the consumption of individual print copies of legacy news brands: the *Sun* 5 per cent 15 to 34, 7.2 per cent 35+; *Daily Mail* 1.8 per cent 15 to 34, 7.4 per cent 35+; *Daily Mirror* 1.5 per cent 15 to 34, 3.6per cent 35+; *Daily Telegraph* 0.8 per cent 15 to 34, 2.7per cent 35+; *The Times,* 1.2 per cent 15 to 34, 2.4 per cent 35+; *Guardian* 1.4 per cent 15 to 34, 1.8; 0.5 per cent 35+; *i* 0.5 per cent 15 to 34, 1.1per cent 35+. Although not directly comparable in any statistically rigorous way, these figures confirm the trend for older Conservative voters who backed Leave to purchase newspapers that promote their views.

The question of sustainability is very important, given the contribution newspapers make to the creation of original journalism and the role they play in informing citizens. PAMCo, the audience measurement organisation, estimates that legacy news brands are responsible for around 50 per cent of all original news journalism in the UK, bigger than broadcasting and online put together (PAMCo 3 2019). In an era of declining sales there is still a significant role for newspapers as generators of news and most importantly opinion and in the digital era these views are transferred into the digital varieties of these news brands, forming a substantial part of people's daily media diet. Newspapers may be in decline in terms of hard-copy circulation but with two key caveats: first, their influence as news generators and digital repositories is still significant; second, an older demographic more inclined to vote, more inclined to vote conservatively and, for our purposes, more inclined to have voted Leave has been appreciating the anti-EU coverage of most of the British press for over 30 years and continues to do that into the present.

Newspapers know a lot about their readers and their political persuasions. They shape their editorial content to match these preferences. This has been the case since the nineteenth century when newspapers generally shifted from proselytising to matching readers' views in what Hampton (2004) highlights as a shift from an educational to a representational ideal. Furthermore, except in rare circumstances, newspapers in the UK have historically clung to fixed party-political allegiances with only minor deviations over time. News appears that can demonstrate – as in their celebratory issues on the day of Brexit – that they have devoted up to 30 years campaigning against the EU and, in that process, maintained their commitment to the political preferences of their readers.

CONCLUSION

Nationalism is essentially built upon symbols and narratives that attempt to unite a community while excluding anyone who does not belong within that group (Spencer and Wollman 2002). Intriguingly in the case of Brexit, the exclusion has drawn upon narratives and signs that have little or no relevance to a younger and more diverse generation of voters. Newspapers have driven a hard Brexit to the extent that they have, in the main, gambled on a set of representations that flatter the prejudices of an older and more conservative generation. As it is difficult to disinter nationalism in the British context from its many supporting imperial contexts and its overwhelmingly English character, independence for Britain means less the release from the burdensome weight of outside control and more a reassertion of the status of bygone days. British nationalism, therefore, in the media has continued to construct itself less in opposition to outside domination and threat and more as exercising power over outsiders in the service of British glory and profit.

A salutary commentary on the shifting demographics of conservative, anti-European attitudes that depend on the discourses of ancient glories was provided by the novelist and public intellectual, Ian McEwan:

> A gang of angry old men, irritable even in victory, are shaping the future of the country against the inclinations of its youth. ... By 2019, the country could be in a receptive mood: 2.5 million over-18-year-olds, freshly franchised and mostly Remainers; 1.5 million oldsters, mostly Brexiters, freshly in their graves (see Roberts 2017).

This sardonic yet eloquent view reinforces this chapter's claim that the political future of the UK has been hijacked by news media overly concerned with the resonance of images and narratives about the country's past.

REFERENCES

Anderson, Benedict (1983) *Imagined Communities: Reflectionson the Originsand Spread of Nationalism*, London: Verso

Bentley, Michael (2021) Populism and nationalism in recent British historiography, May, Niels, F. and Maissen, Thomas (eds) *National History and New Nationalism in the Twenty-First Century: A Global Comparison*, Abingdon, Oxon: Routledge

Billig, Michael (1995) *Banal Nationalism*, London: Routledge

Bingham, Adrian and Conboy, Martin (2015) *Tabloid Century: The Popular Pressin Britain, 1896 to the Present*, Oxford: Peter Lang

Brighton, Paul and Foy, Dennis (2007) *News Values*, London: Sage

Conboy, Martin (2006) *Tabloid Britain: Constructing a Community Through Language*, Abingdon, Oxon: Routledge

Conboy, Martin and Eldridge II, Scott A. (eds) (2021) *Global Tabloid: Culture and Technology*, Abingdon, Oxon: Routledge

Fukuyama, Francis (1992) *The End of History and the Last Man*, New York: Avon Books

Galtung, Johan and Ruge, Mari (1965) The structure of foreign news: The presentation of the Congo, Cuba and Cyprus crises in four Norwegian newspapers, *Journal of International Peace Research*, Vol. 1 pp 64-91

Hampton, Mark (2004) *Visions of the Press in Britain, 1850-1950*, Urbana and Chicago: University of Illinois Press

Harcup, Tony and O'Neill, Deidre (2017) What is news?: News values revisited (again), *Journalism Studies*, Vol. 18, No. 12 pp 1,470-1,488

Hobsbawm, Eric (1990) *Nations and Nationalism since 1780: Programme, Myth, Reality*, Cambridge: Cambridge University Press

Luttwak, Edward (1994) Why fascism is the wave of the future, *London Review of Books*, Vol. 16, No. 7, 7 April pp 3-4

Mediatique (2018) *Overview of Recent Dynamics in the UK Press Market*, Department for Digital, Culture, Media and Sport. Available online at https://assets.publishing.service.gov.uk/government/uploads/system/uploads/attachment_data/file/720400/180621_Mediatique_-_Overview_of_recent_dynamics_in_the_UK_press_market_-_Report_for_DCMS.pdf

PAMCo 3 (2019) Data for July 2018-June 2019. Available online at https://pamco.co.uk/news/newsletter-q3-2019/index.html

Renan, Ernest (1990 [1882]) What is a nation? Bhabha, Homi K. (ed.) *Nation and Narration*, London: Routledge pp 8-22

Roberts, Dan (2017) Death of '1.5m. oldsters' could swing second EU vote, says Ian McEwan, *Guardian*, 12 May. Available online at https://www.theguardian.com/politics/2017/may/12/15m-oldsters-in-their-graves-could-swing-second-eu-vote-says-ian-mcewan, accessed on 15 July 2021

Spencer, Phillip and Wollman, Howard (2002) *Nationalism: A Critical Introduction*, London: Sage

Weymouth, Peter, J. and Anderson, Tim (1999) *Insulting the Public? The British Press and the European Union*, London: Routledge

NOTE ON THE CONTRIBUTOR

Martin Conboy is Emeritus Professor of Journalism History and co-director (with Professor Adrian Bingham) of the Centre for the Study of Journalism and History, at the University of Sheffield. He has produced fourteen books on the language and history of journalism as well as numerous contributions to scholarly journals and edited volumes. His most recent publications are the *Edinburgh History of the British and Irish Press*, Vol.3 (with Bingham, 2020) and *Global Tabloid* (with Eldridge, 2021). His research has been funded by the AHRC, the Dutch NWO and Marsh's Library, Dublin.

Chapter 10

Towards Restorative Narrative

Pratāp Rughani

This chapter argues for an experiment in bringing together moving image and mediation practices to create a more relational media – socially designed and biased enough to nurture the connective tissue between communities, drawing on practices from restorative justice including deep listening and searching for shades of grey. Meanwhile, swathes of social and mass media are increasingly polarised. Key production processes and financial structures feed this trend, magnifying the attitudes and algorithms that lean towards conflict. This trend hollows out the quality or sometimes the prospect of dialogue in the public sphere and threatens to break the connective tissue that forms the habitus of UK multi-cultures. In response to these issues, the chapter suggests some strategies to refuse and reverse toxic polarisation. It argues that the need for participatory and community media is stronger than ever and asks: what is needed to create meetings and media to build creative explorations that nurture empathic understanding, especially when we disagree? Finally, can the processes of restorative justice offer a model for 'restorative narrative' that could frame a new media genre of storytelling designed to build mutual understanding and connection that obtains on either side of emotive issues whether or not we agree?

Keywords: restorative narrative, polarisation, mass media, ethics

Mass media journalism typically presents words, images, rushes and stories by grasping, heightening and juxtaposing tension and differences. This suits (and is shaped by) a news storytelling culture that privileges black-and-white clashes of current or coming conflict. The bias leans towards the dramatic, serving audiences that mostly expect and reliably consume this dynamic to 'make sense' of a far more complex world.

These dynamics are recently joined, supported and extended by swathes of social media that blur distinctions between fact and editorial comment, further enabled by the now commonplace rendering of disinformation in the texture of communications. Today, far too much of our mixed media landscape can be characterised by 'toxic polarisation' (Coleman 2021). Whilst liberal democracies are familiar with articulating threats to 'free speech', they are less practised in reflecting on and counteracting the insidious effects of speech untethered from community values or a connecting vision. This primes the landscape for a culture of polarisation to flourish.

In 'old media', this dynamic was already problematic. I quickly found in my work in print, radio and television current affairs that the compression necessary for short sound-bites and 'punchy' headlines meant that shades of grey were better explored elsewhere, some distance from the news agenda. I settled on longer-form documentary practices.

Across thirty years, in many places and with people facing conflict or its aftermath, I have listened closely to and reported on the aftermath of atrocity, sometimes engaging disparate arguments on different sides of an event, idea or issue. In South Africa, Rwanda, Aboriginal Australia, the UK and elsewhere I have tried to explore counter-arguments with each side in the search for understandings for diverse audiences, conceiving documentary film as a kind of arena in which many experiences can unfold, with enough open space for an audience to make sense of competing perceptions and experiences and settle on their own view. Today I wonder if this is enough. Rather than mirroring reality, too much media risks further damaging the situations it purports to describe, leaving a more polarised trail for audiences and uncomfortable but necessary questions for practitioners (Rughani 2010: 169).

I'm about to make an argument for an experiment in bringing together film and mediation practices to rethink the information architecture for a more relational media – socially designed to be biased enough to nurture the connective tissue *between* communities, drawing on practices from restorative justice including deep listening and searching for shades of grey. In making the case, it's important to underline the essential work of robust and rigorous reporting and its significance, for example in exposing crime, corruption and holding officials to account. Errol Morris's film *The Thin Blue Line* (1988) was both a stylistic innovation in documentary practice and is widely credited with securing the release from prison of Randall Adams who had been convicted for a murder he did not commit. Morris urges that documentary innovation should not be marked by a retreat into partiality and implicitly cautions against the solipsistic dangers of relativism:

> To those who argue that there's no such thing as objective truth, I say ask a man strapped in an electric chair who says 'I didn't do it' ... forgive me there is such a thing as truth – the truth (Morris 2011).

The argument here is not about 'objectivity' or the importance of investigative journalism or the inevitable 'black-and-white' aspects of the fourth estate. Rather it is a response to the reflex polarisation of media cultures and the risk of public scepticism turning further towards cynicism, with consequences for social cohesion in diverse communities where the work of creating and recreating dialogue in UK multi-cultures is fragile and, by turns, contested.

TIPPING POINTS

It is widely documented how voting is fuelled by playing on fear of the 'outsider', stereotypes and bigotry, often seeded by Russian bots. Their pivotal effect in fuelling the 'alt right' has already tipped many elections. In 2018, the UK Electoral Commission found the Vote Leave Campaign guilty of breaking electoral law, referring them to the National Crime Agency for investigation. In May 2020, police confirmed that no action would be taken. Pro-Brexit campaigns paid £3.5 million to AggregateIQ (AIQ) to collect and analyse people's data in order to personalise fake political slogans – for example, to spread the lie that Turkey was about to join the EU, to whip up and channel racialised fear. Dominic Cummings, Vote Leave's director, boasted on AIQ's website: 'Without a doubt, the Vote Leave campaign owes a great deal of its success to the work of AggregateIQ. We couldn't have done it without them.'

How can storytelling travel a wiser route to enable open discussion that might withstand visceral prejudices? Just ten years ago, Wael Ghonim's Facebook page was widely credited as a catalyst for the Tahrir Square demonstrations that marked the brief Arab Spring in Cairo in 2011. The web enabled freer speech but that season, in Egypt, ended in military intervention, a coup and the return to dictatorship in all but name. Ghonim later re-evaluated social media, disturbed by its reckless use by populists, activists and dictators. He fled Egypt and later co-founded a new social media platform, Parlio, that included a civility pledge and used real names. 'We're here to learn new perspectives; not to win arguments,' the platform said. Trolling was forbidden and 'expanding horizons' privileged.

Parlio developed from Ghonim's question: how to design social media experiences to nurture thoughtfulness, civility or quality of engagement? Assessment of such aspirations is overdue (especially since Parlio was bought by Quora in March 2016). Are my 'likes' the reward for agreement with a view floating on the surface that suits another's preconception rather than a deeper engagement with ideas? Where are the algorithms and metrics that reward us rethinking, changing our minds even, rather than approving our own echo?

For all their benefits, the deep shadows of social media platforms are increasingly apparent, yet it's taking far too long for Twitter and Facebook, especially, to deliver or enforce a robust ethical framework or act meaningfully on existing policies to quickly and reliably screen out abuse or disinformation. National governments appear at a loss to apply the norms expected of broadcast media, despite these channels' significant experience of navigating the tensions between 'free speech' and 'hate speech'.

Meanwhile, the profits of online vitriol are not properly taxed and the platform's income generation model rewards a lucrative trade in the heat and friction of polarisation, weakening and even denaturing the very tissue that holds a culture together.

DOCUMENTARY: PROMOTING A MORE RELATIONAL, PARTICIPATORY APPROACH

The flourishing of an easy trade in bigotry-fuelled conflict online reminds me of Leni Riefenstahl's riposte fifty years after making *Triumph of The Will* (1935), her striking documentary, commissioned by Hitler, introducing him to film audiences and featuring the Nazi Nuremberg rallies of 1934. Riefenstahl maintained that it did not matter what the Nazi speeches she featured were about: 'Whether it was about politics or vegetables or fruit, I couldn't give a damn. ... To me the film was not about politics, it was an event. ...' What does political responsibility mean? And to whom is one responsible? Riefenstahl wanted to make a 'great' film, to hell with the consequences.

Ray Müller's flirtatious rapport and the careful documentary interview technique he used in the making of *The Wonderful, Horrible Life of Leni Riefenstahl* (1993) encouraged Riefenstahl to speak out on these issues. In Müller's admirable and long documentary (188 mins), his relational approach revealed more of Riefenstahl than his subject intended. In shorter works, too, the directed camera can 'see', revealing to audiences things that are easily overlooked when *a priori* ideas stand in the way of what is in front of our eyes. The ability to be alive to nuance is essential here, flourishing in documentary's observational modes, if a space can be configured to loosen pre-conceived story structures and open out on other ways of looking.

When shooting *Justine* (Lotus Films, 2013),[1] about a young woman who rarely speaks, I made an 'anti-journalistic' choice to avoid naming the principal character's neurological condition, as I was concerned that if she were introduced in terms of her medical history, it might keep her sealed in a box (an audience's idea of 'neurological disorder' for example) from which she might not escape. This was arguably a strange choice but I was concerned that when most media engages with people with disabilities, the disability or 'condition' is the 'news-worthy' fact. The risk is that such reportage collapses the individual into her diagnosis and eclipses the person herself.

Is a different kind of communication possible through a more relational, participatory approach where stories emerge 'with' and 'alongside' rather than simply 'about' the other? Pioneering Vietnamese video artist Trinh T. Minh-ha describes her aspiration in moving image practice as restoring proximity of the subject and recognising the place of subjectivity:

> In the context of power relations, speaking for, about, and on behalf of is very different from speaking with and nearby ... what has to be given up first and foremost is the voice of omniscient knowledge (Hohenberger 2008: 118-119).

Close listening when making *Justine* helped my direction and camerawork be led by shifts in her emotional temperature and small happenings. Configuring this space brought changes that re-formed the narrative so that a new visual journey emerged, that is more led by Justine's experience and decisions. The 'advanced neurological disorder' and 'autism' labels typically led to a pathology of Justine suggesting that it would be very difficult for her to show empathy – either cognitive or affective. Yet close attention to Justine revealed (and possibly facilitated) her clearly empathic responses recorded on camera in several situations.

Freed of the medical labels, it was easier to observe and film, and on showing a fine-cut to her family, her mother paused to say: 'God. I never thought she would do that,' when observing a sequence in which Justine was able to anticipate other children's needs and take initiative to help them by opening a gate.

Likewise, audiences started to hear and see aspects of Justine that undercut conventional expectations. Justine could start to emerge (I speculate) more on her own terms, rather than those of conventional media interest, that typically frames and reduces her to her 'disabilities'.[2]

Justine opening a gate: A still from the film, Justine *(photograph by Pratāp Rughani)*

When storytelling, it's essential to ask: how do the subjects of these stories benefit from their involvement and who else benefits? Despite *Justine*'s micro-budget, interest in the film on the educational and film festival screenings circuit generated income. That money went to Justine and supported some leisure interests, so she has seen direct benefits in her life. Payments should be carefully agreed to avoid the dangers of 'cheque-book journalism' but it is also time to offer a new transparency in the financial flows of productions and ensure that the main participants see real rewards.

FINDING AN AUDIENCE

Films such as *Justine* found audiences at film festivals, community screenings and galleries. Leading UK gallery spaces, so recently uninterested in promoting documentaries, are now replete with them as audiences respond to socially-engaged art. Here, the storytelling can be less circumscribed and offer a more open encounter. Media in gallery spaces can experiment with other ways of seeing. A retreat from broadcast and mass media, however, risks reducing work to bourgeois entertainment, ultimately decorative in its setting, whilst mainstream and social media bifurcate into mutually enforcing bubbles.

Even the making of mainstream broadcast documentary still struggles to resist the gravitational pull to exaggerate and heighten differences and to keep attention through ad-breaks – sometimes seriously distorting information in the search for the most 'compelling' narrative. Some documentaries tip into becoming more openly partisan and adversarial media. Yet this adversarial posture undermines the potential to find a common ground that can nurture the kind of trust to renew connection through an exploration of difference. That connection can be within tantalising reach since, underneath the culture clashes of 'identity politics', groups professing mutual loathing often find that there is much more that they agree on.[3]

In today's age of Trumpian tweets, racism (among other hatreds) is brazen and normalised. But Hannah Arendt reminds us that the totalitarian impulse is not the property of a single political complexion (Arendt 1958).

ATTRACTORS

Views are triggered and easily congeal. Why? Professor Peter Coleman, of Columbia University's Center for Cooperation and Conflict Resolution, leads a research centre whose studies conclude that the neurology of intractable polarisation is producing a hard-wired response through 'attractors' that are hard to shift. Our brain's amygdala is activated by fear and much of social media's platform engineering triggers these responses. As Coleman et al. argue (2005):

> Attractors, in short, channel mental and behavioural experience into a narrow range of malignant (but coherent) states. Attempting to move the system out of its attractor promotes forces that reinstate the system at its attractor. This means that attempts to change the state of conflict without changing the mechanisms that continually reinstate the conflict are likely to be futile, resulting only in short-term changes. To promote lasting change, it is necessary to change the attractor states of the system. This is no easy feat, since it is tantamount to changing the mechanisms responsible for the system's dynamics.

Is it possible, however, that with the right support, attractors could be supported to drive virtuous, rather than just vicious circles?

DESIGN FOR DIALOGUE

Journalism's production and editorial guidelines have arguably a bigger sector-wide role to play at this juncture, when under-regulated media grows a culture of advanced polarisation and hate speech flourishes. Facebook's tilt towards 'neo-Nazi shopfronts' is tracked in the Center for Countering Digital Hate's publication *Hatebook* (see counterhate.com/hatebook). Moreover, enforcement of the National Union of Journalists' Code of Conduct[4] and ethics guidelines, broadcasters' editorial guidelines and regulatory frameworks to map out responsible media spaces is needed (Rughani 2013: 101-105).

Significantly, some small alternatives are emerging from grass-roots local groups such as the community-owned Bristol Cable,[5] founded in 2014, that re-centres the social context stories live in and return to. Initiatives such as Tortoise Media[6] embrace 'slow news' as an approach to distil depth from the continuing flow of superficial news updates. Both invite more participatory news values.

Dialogue and listening that privilege the space to reflect and reconsider could lead us to change our minds and escape the 'gravitational pull' of attractors. In my documentary practice, I have been fortunate to be present when people determined to pursue a vision or ideal of reconnection decide to make something better from our divisions. I have seen this unfold in entrenched conflicts, such as at the Truth and Reconciliation Commission hearings of the new South Africa for Channel 4 in 1998; the evolution of a new police service in Northern Ireland in 2004, and among London students from many diverse ethnic backgrounds decrying Islamophobia (2001 to the present).

I have also seen it fail when the conditions for good faith in listening on each side were not developed, for example at the Aboriginal Reconciliation Convention, in Australia, in 1997, when the then-Prime Minister, John Howard, reduced the history of Indigenous genocide to a 'blemish' and hectored his Aboriginal audience with the pride settler Australians feel in their nation-building. There followed an extraordinary moment. With an invisible signal, the bulk of the Aboriginal audience quietly stood, remained listening, then slowly turned their backs on Howard. It was a moment that called for statesmanship with a Prime Minister standing for the wider community beyond their own partisan interests. Instead, Howard became yet more shrill, rattled through his notes and left without discussing or listening to any Aboriginal speakers.[8]

It was a profoundly disappointing and shocking moment but it did not surprise many Indigenous survivors whose dignity in attending remained an unseen, unwanted gift. A recent report indicates that as many as 500 Aboriginal and Torres Strait Islander people have died in custody in Australia in the thirty years since a royal commission gave recommendations aimed at preventing Indigenous deaths in the justice system, disfiguring an Australia where black lives have yet to really matter (Allam 2021).

A culture is clearly needed to reinforce a different form of communication that privileges empathy, connection and the development of a deeper confidence to make space for another's experience. In that space of listening, compassion can grow, even in extreme situations.

How to curate spaces and discussions that enable such journeys? What in our communication privileges the softening of conviction and the quieter confidence to doubt and enable another's experience to influence us? Can documentary makers be struck by how the 'storifying' of life can be richer and more interesting than the *a priori* narratives that often deliver journalists and filmmakers to a place of difficulty or conflict? How can the door to the dialogic be opened?

Modelling this approach is key. A recent BBC project, built on research into 'humanbecoming', suggests this useful, tested methodology (Kasriel 2020):

- Ask your speaker to explain their perspective and why they feel so strongly. Listen, without interruption, putting aside judgements, counter-arguments and solutions.

- Summarise the core of what you have heard and check you have understood correctly, including the emotions and texture of their story. This does not mean you have to agree.

- Ask whether they agree with your summary. If not, ask them to explain more.

- Continue with this process till the speaker gives a resounding 'Yes.' They should at this point be likely to listen to your side of the story.

The spirit of this is receptivity rather than agreement. Agreement may not follow. The point is not to agree or persuade through duress but to experience relatedness that may unsettle each other's convictions and open new channels of communication and affect. If receptivity suffuses our listening, answers may emerge, perfumed with similar qualities. NPR broadcaster Krista Tippett, in *The Art of Generous Listening* (2019), explains how her radio series, *On Being*, strives to create understanding for how another thinks. Tippett suggests we look more to 'how' and 'why', rather than 'what' and 'when' as keys to developing dialogue. By shifting our attention we expand the foundations of relatedness to focus on what truly matters, she says, and we can develop 'discernment'. 'The point is not to agree but to come into relationship. What we have in common are our questions.'

Designing for dialogue may begin as a response to political polarisation, but its effects are joyfully unpredictable. Exploring such questions will likely be profoundly inter-disciplinary. For all the advances of the West's Enlightenment, our scholarship risks being imprisoned in its own specialisms. In the face of complex challenges, the weakness of trying to tackle big questions in separate compartments is clear.

Preparing the ground by learning to listen and the creativity of dialogic encounters should lead us to rethink not just why we got here but to imagine something finer.

RESTORATIVE NARRATIVE

Reflecting on many years of documentary practice with an emphasis on production ethics, the central question for me is now: how can the dynamic affordances of interactive and social media be harnessed for a different kind of storytelling, rooted in production practices of deeper listening and a rigorous search for what connects us – what we have in common, rather than the easy reflex of reacting to opposing views? With that commitment to shared community, how can documentary and other media practices engage difference better? Instead of feeding the easy heat of triggering reflex reactions, can storytellers invent media that aims to restore relationship, understanding and connection – a media that truly mediates between us?

What might success look like in this context? As with restorative justice approaches and some forms of mediation, a key focus is on creating the conditions for deeper attention, rather than attempting to cajole others into a surface agreement that may prove counterproductive. A key to unlocking polarised and apparently intractable conflict is a shift towards acceptance of the other. The work of philosopher Emmanuel Lévinas is useful here, especially his insistence on meeting the gaze of the other and the foundational ethics of cultivating this kind of attention (Hand 1989).

Some remarkable examples of the journalism that embodies this approach are collected from the edges of human endurance in the work of the Forgiveness Project[7] and the work of its founder Marina Cantacuzino. Her essay 'As mysterious as love' emphasises the cross-currents of feeling and insight where polarisation and hatred can give way to release (not necessarily forgiveness) in a jagged journey that is ultimately about reconciliation with experience and with oneself: 'Making peace with a painful event is what allows people to live with hurt and catastrophe, find resolution and move on' (Cantacuzino 2015: 12). Reconciliatory stories are hard to surface – in situations of trauma even the questions can be very hard to approach. Marian Partington, whose younger sister Lucy was a victim of the serial killers Fred and Rosemary West, eventually came to ask how she could help perpetrators to become free of the pain that led them to cause harm in the first place. Her insight gave direction and the journey of her grief unfolds just the kind of delicate journey whose deeper strength is hard to recognise – or sometimes even to understand – in cultures of oppositional storytelling (Partington 2016).

The fragile beginnings of structured support for a change in approach from media makers may be emerging. In 2013, Images and Voices of Hope developed the genre of restorative narrative 'proposing that by following the arc of recovery instead of focusing exclusively on traumatizing events, victims and the helplessness that follows, they could help build capacity in the communities they serve'.[8] Now merged with the Peace Studio, the initiative offers space for 'reflective practice' to support a shift in awareness to help practitioners configure this newer trajectory in storytelling. The resulting stories can open audiences to our own (sometimes small) restorations with things we may find 'unforgivable'. Stories of reconnected communities become tangible by tilting production ethics to seek narratives that privilege listening, exchange and shared concerns. Stories that chart and document collective commitment to a dynamic of exchange might then lead to reconnection or 'restorative narrative' as a recognised strand of media production. The prize here is not necessarily agreement on an issue between formally polarised people but enough of a convergence of experience for mutual understanding of the other. Indeed, stories of restoration of connection can model that possibility to others. If we see such stories regularly in our media, they become a more tangible possibility.

CONCLUSION: RE-CONCEIVING MEDIA AS ETHICALLY RESPONSIBLE

Can a story production process now emerge that re-conceives media as ethically responsible 'connective tissue' to configure a public space to enable storytellers, subjects and audiences to understand and come into relationship with others' diverging perspectives? Achieving this means letting go of the pretence of *a priori* pseudo-objectivity. In their article 'Racism, hate speech, and social media: A systematic review and critique', Matamoros-Fernández and Farkas (2020: 218) note: 'There is a preponderance of research on racism, hate speech, and social media done by white scholars that rarely acknowledges the positionality of the authors, which risks reinforcing colour-blind ideologies within the field.'

Recognising our 'positionality' by developing a reflexive awareness is a significant move in creating an environment that can reach beyond a single perspective towards a deeper pluralism. This paradox remains a challenge for many media practitioners. Many of us like to think that we are 'impartial' or that we have already escaped the gravitational pull of our own conditioning, when the idea that we are already free of our biases can be the very blinkers that reduce our ability to recognise how our limitations may invisibly structure our thinking and storytelling. The humbling recognition of our limitations and the work that flows in building teams to research broader perspectives can map out a new alchemy in storytelling.

Just as some natural history programming features a 'making of' section that unpacks the technical triumphs and hardships, could a 'story lab' sidebar or section of a restorative article or programme reveal the restorative work that enables the prospect of reconnection and community forged from diverse perspectives? If the medium can become the message, what if the process of creating that media is dedicated to restoring relationships through the light of understanding difference – inventing an avowedly restorative media. What new visions may then flow from these new narratives and the ethics of such a media practice?

NOTES

[1] Film (and debate) available online at https://ethics.arts.ac.uk/

[2] For an exploration of the approach to storytelling taken here and the foundational ethical questions that underpin this trajectory, see Ethics for making, by Pratāp Rughani and Wakulenko (2020). Available online at https://screenworks.org.uk/archive/volume-10-2/ethics-for-making

[3] See https://www.theguardian.com/politics/2021/nov/17/voters-in-west-divided-more-by-identity-than-issues-survey-finds, accessed on 26 November 2021

[4] https://www.nuj.org.uk/about-us/rules-and-guidance/code-of-conduct.html, accessed on 21 November 2021

[5] https://thebristolcable.org/, accessed on 20 November 2021

[6] https://www.tortoisemedia.com/, accessed on 25 November 2021

[7] https://www.theforgivenessproject.com/, accessed on 29 November 2021

[8] https://thepeacestudio.org/, accessed on 27 November 2021

REFERENCES

Allam, L. (2021) 'Beyond heartbreaking': 500 Indigenous deaths in custody since 1991 royal commission, *Guardian*, 6 December. Available online at https://www.theguardian.com/australia-news/2021/dec/06/beyond-heartbreaking-500-indigenous-deaths-in-custody-since-1991-royal-commission, accessed on 7 December 2021

Arendt, H. (1958) *The Origins of Totalitarianism*, New York: Meridian Books

Cantacuzino, M. (2015) *The Forgiveness Project: Stories for a Vengeful Age*, London: Jessica Kingsley, second edition

Coleman, P., Vallacher, R. R., Nowak, A. and Ngoc, L. B. (2005) Intractable conflict as an attractor: Presenting a dynamical model of conflict, escalation, and intractability, *SSRN Electronic Journal*, Vol. 50. Available online at DOI: 10.2139/ssrn.734963

Coleman, P. (2021) *The Way Out: How to Overcome Toxic Polarisation*, New York: Columbia University Press

Hand, S. (ed.) (1989) *The Lévinas Reader*, Oxford: Basil Blackwell

Hohenberger, E. (2008) Vietnam/USA: Trinh T. Minh-ha in an interview, Pearce, G. and McLaughlin, C. (eds) *Truth or Dare: Art and Documentary*, Bristol: Intellect Books pp 104-121

Kasriel, E. (2020) Deep listening: Finding common ground with opponents, BBC News, 4 March. Available online at https://www.bbc.co.uk/news/health-51705369

Morris, E. (2011) Annual BAFTA David Lean lecture: Investigating with the camera. Available online at https://www.bafta.org/media-centre/press-releases/errol-morris-delivers-the-2011-bafta-david-lean-lecture, accessed on 8 December 2021

Matamoros-Fernández, A. and Farkas, J. (2021) Racism, hate speech, and social media: A systematic review and critique, *Television & New Media*, Vol. 22, No. 2. Available online at https://doi.org/10.1177/1527476420982230, accessed on 7 December 2021

Müller, R. (1993) *The Wonderful, Horrible Life of Leni Riefenstahl*. Available online at https://learningonscreen.ac.uk/ondemand/index.php/prog/004ACA50?bcast=2766017, accessed on 24 May 2020

Partington, M. (2016) *If You Sit Very Still*, London: Jessica Kingsley

Rughani, P. (2010) Are you a vulture? Reflecting on the ethics and aesthetics of atrocity coverage and its aftermath, Keeble, R. L., Tulloch, J. and Zollmann, F. (eds) (2010) *Peace Journalism, War and Conflict Resolution*, New York: Peter Lang pp 157-172

Rughani, P. (2013) The dance of documentary ethics, Winston, B. (ed.) *The BFI Documentary Film Book*, London: Palgrave Macmillan pp 98-109

Tippett, K. (2019) *The Art of Generous Living*. Available online at https://www.youtube.com/watch?v=J5W36VWNd9E, accessed on 30 November 2021

NOTE ON THE CONTRIBUTOR

Dr Pratāp Rughani is Director of Lotus Films and Professor of Documentary Practices at the University of the Arts London, where he is Head of Research at the London College of Communications. He is a documentary-maker with a particular interest in how film can help create the conditions for inter-cultural communication. He is a trustee of Pragya and the Karuna Trust, NGOs working in the UK and India for social and environmental justice. He feels a debt of gratitude and appreciation for Professor Brian Winston and would like to thank him for his thoughtful leadership and academic insight over decades. The path to deeper reflection is ever-inspired by Thea Ellora. See https://www.arts.ac.uk/research/ual-staff-researchers/pratap-rughani and http://www.lotusfilms.co.uk.

Appendix 1

Beyond the Bog-Standard Grammar School: In Conversation with Brian Winston

Richard Lance Keeble discusses with Brian Winston his career and ideas in depth, the people who influenced him so deeply – and his family and schooling background.

Richard Keeble: You studied law at Oxford, Brian. How come?

Brian Winston: You have to understand that it's all to do with one's background. In my case, coming from an immigrant background, the ambition of aspirant immigrant families was towards established professional careers. So there's a profound hostility. I think culturally, or there was half a century ago or more, towards people who were talented artists or whatever. I remember my mother actually saying to me when I expressed a real interest in history: 'Be a schoolteacher?!' That was not deemed to be sufficiently prestigious. So I was sort of conned into law as an available profession, if you like. You could do what you liked as long as it was medicine or law or accountancy: it had to be a recognisable professional qualification. Otherwise, it didn't give the family the status they wanted. OK, so my drift towards the law was entirely conditioned by the social situation of the immigrant Jewish community in London in the 50s.

My friend Frank Usher, whose dad was a cockney taxi driver, was also a beneficiary of this. Walter Isaacson was our history teacher who had escaped from Nazi Germany clutching a newly-minted PhD from Frankfurt. He had a profound influence on us and he made it his business to take a bunch of us from a bog-standard grammar school, in Kilburn, north west London, with lower middle class/upper working class kids, and get two or three to Oxbridge every year. He told us that was how he was repaying his debt for asylum. So Isaacson had a profound effect on us, and that was why I was thinking about taking history at university, obviously. Anyway, my friend Frank Usher was also involved in this. I remember very distinctly a moment in the fifth form. I was sitting in front of Frank and he said: 'This is quite a different picture of Parnell to the one given by James Joyce' or something like that. Isaacson looked down at him (he was a pacer) and said simply: 'So Usher, you understand.' I swear to God that was the moment when Frank got to Oxford.

There was also an English teacher. He was a former Fleet Air pilot, a terrific guy called Vic Callaghan, who told us we didn't need to read any of the set books for A level. So these were the two people who were really influencing me at this point.

Anyway, Frank was head boy and he noticed that outside the career master's office an advert had fallen off the notice board for open scholarship exams. He picked it up and it said: 'Merton College Oxford Open Exam: Three guineas.' Because Merton was so rich, it didn't charge five guineas like everybody else. So Frank took the exams for Merton on the very sound academic basis that they were cheaper than anywhere else. Frank, indeed, did very well and got to read PPE. In that year, when he was doing this, I was messing about in the third year of sixth form waiting to take my Oxford open scholarship.

I then decided to read for law because obviously that meshed with family aspirations and everything else. But I must confess, I do think there was a certain cultural aptitude. After all, my intellectual tradition was very much one of inquiry, argument, contradiction, et cetera. Somebody once said that Judaism was a 4,000-year-old argument with God. So I felt attracted and still do to the notion that there's no argument which should not be confronted and dealt with rationally and that the Jewish tradition in some very fundamental sense was a rational tradition. I mean, there's obviously a more spiritual side to the faith. But the dominant tradition we're dealing with is one of the endless arguments. It's a tradition of rationalism which is summed up for me by the mediaeval rabbi Maimonides. His secular role was as Saladin's doctor so he wrote a great deal about medicine. But he also commented on the holy texts where he took a rational view. His masterwork is called *A Guide to the Perplexed* and it's to do with questions rather than answers. It's about reaching rational decisions about what you do and what you don't do. That approach has come to influence me a great deal.

Richard Keeble: So in what way do you think that studying law has influenced you both as an academic and as a broadcaster and journalist?

'Real Sense of Social Injustice'

Brian Winston: I think there are a couple of things in play here – and on quite different registers. Firstly, I was moved towards journalism because I had a real sense of social injustice.

Richard Keeble: Right.

Brian Winston: Which obviously has to do with the law, and the notion that the law can be used to establish and maintain social justice – that was extremely important.

Secondly, there was the question of methodology. How do you win arguments? Lawyers paint their opponents into corners so that their argument cannot be sustained. You don't win arguments by shouting and you don't win arguments by appeals to externals so much as by logical application, which slowly limits the range of argument your opponent can put forward until they are forced to admit their case cannot be sustained. Couple that with the notion of social justice, which I think is very much bound up with my vision of what journalism is. And there you have it, really.

Richard Keeble: Fascinating. So did you do any journalism at Oxford?

Brian Winston: Sure. I edited a few editions of *Isis*. But the first piece I ever wrote was for an up-market magazine called the *Elizabethan*. It was to do with an experience I had during my third year in the sixth form. It was quite weird because I hung around in order to take the Oxford exams around Christmas. And having gone home and having got a place, I then had the rest of the year off until September. In that time, I messed about and did lots of things. For instance, I was, for a time, a supply teacher – and the experience further confirmed my passion for social justice. One of the things that I most remember was this: I was an 18-year-old given the lowest Blue stream of the 11-year-olds (the other streams above were Red and White). I remember saying to this 11-year-old lad: 'You're very good at arithmetic. I think you could do your maths with the Red kids. Or the White kids.' I remember this lad looked at me and said: 'We're Blue, Sir. We ain't never gonna be White.' I thought to myself: 'This is a tragedy. This is an outrage.' And I wrote a piece about it which was published. It was about educational dead-ends and ambition and all of those distorting, outrageous elements that ensure our society doesn't live to its full potential.

Richard Keeble: Was that school, Brian, in London?

Brian Winston: Yeah. The primary school I went to and then the secondary modern I taught at, which was adjacent to it, was called Wykeham and it was on the North Circular Road in Neasden. So it's scarcely fancy.

Richard Keeble: Did you do any film reviewing at Oxford?

Brian Winston: Sure. I remember writing up an essay on Eisenstein, the Russian revolutionary director, and his 1944 film *Ivan the Terrible*. I wrote that up as a sort of fairly serious piece of work – conscious of the fact that writing about film wasn't exactly respectable. So I position myself at the end of Oxford by nailing my flag to a media mast.

Richard Keeble: After Oxford, your first job is with *World in Action*. How did that come about?

Brian Winston: The whole situation is ridiculous. On the one hand, I've got this family tradition with my mother wanting me to enter a business with far more respectability than journalism. On the other hand, the BBC and Granada visited Oxbridge looking for talent. As I recall it, the BBC had 12 production traineeships and Granada half a dozen. Outside of these 18 jobs, what you really needed was a family connection: an uncle, say. Now, I did have a family connection. Another profound influence on me, whom I haven't mentioned yet, was my cousin. Charlie Cooper was a distributor of contemporary films. He was a communist and responsible for distributing the Russian revolutionary classics and the works of great filmmakers like the Indian Satyajit Ray and so on. Charlie was a butcher originally and got involved with the distribution of radical films as part of his political work. And he turned it into a business. As a result, I saw these films in his front room in Wembley Park – I was extraordinarily privileged. Charlie obviously was interested in us all becoming communist, but somehow I didn't quite. I became obsessed with film. I could see upon reflection that I actually took away a great deal of politics as well, although not formally. In fact, what I took away formally was the notion that as a journalist, the job was essentially to offer correctives to social injustice – and the way to do that was by maintaining an apparent neutrality. You didn't belong to anything. And so, I have never been a member of a political party nor, indeed, even a campaign. I've always been an independent person on the grounds that journalists have to be that if they're going to function. Now, I can see that upon reflection as being rather naïve. But that was the bottom line.

Richard Keeble: We were talking about those Oxford interviews for entry into journalism.

Brian Winston: I certainly didn't get a job at the BBC. I was already out of step because I thought you had to get people's attention and take a position that would illuminate them, et cetera. And all the things that I felt went with the social function and purpose of journalism was sort of anathema to the BBC, which was then, and indeed still is, addicted to the spurious notion of objectivity. All that went down like a lead balloon. I seem to remember a somewhat uneasy interview which didn't get me very far. The Granada meeting was slightly different. I didn't get one of the jobs; it turned out they were looking for directors for *Coronation Street*. And I would say by way of a joke: who do they appoint instead of me? Well, it was Mike Newell (of *Four Weddings and a Funeral* fame). And Michael Apted (of

Coal Miner's Daughter and *Seven-Up* fame). But they gave me a job as a researcher on the newly-launched *World in Action*.

The Crucial Question: 'Why is this Lying Bastard Lying to Me?'

Richard Keeble: Tell me about some of the colleagues you worked with there.

Brian Winston: I was presented there with strong models of journalistic practice, specifically tabloid journalistic practice. There was an effing and blinding ex-editor of the northern edition of the *Daily Express*, a role he filled when he was 27. He was the Beaverbrook protégé, an Australian called Tim Hewat, and he was looking for researchers because he had just started this current affairs programme called *World in Action*. Tim was really interesting. He had a reputation for radicalism which he didn't deserve. He was a right-wing Tory who never saw a piece of news or information that he didn't want to question. Thus, his underlying approach was to ask this question: 'Why is this lying bastard lying to me?' It has nothing with objectivity or anything else. Tim was just interested in gaining attention and illuminating situations and not following through on received opinions. That was his basic position, and he took a view, which remains to this day somewhat outré – that the whole idea of objectivity was actually wrong. You gave people information and you allow them to come to conclusions. But you didn't spuriously claim you were being objective. I'll give you an example: he was obsessed with the notion of people killing each other on the roads through drunk driving. So to illustrate a story about this he got actors to appear as dead bodies on a given suburban stretch of road. And then he drove the camera through them with the voice-over talking about how, in the last six months, 15 people or so have died on the road. He caused endless trouble with the Independent Television Authority.

Tim's successor, who has sadly died, was a Scottish hack journalist called Alex Valentine. He was a Reuters man and for him, there was no point to journalism if you fail to communicate. Therefore, the first thing you had to do was get people's attention. And that needed visualisation. For instance, we did a show about the evils of bronchitis, which was still a real killer. We opened with a high angle shot of Coronation Street and out of every doorway emerged a coffin and pallbearers. A driving Australian voice-over gave the death statistics for bronchitis. You'd never ever forget that.

I remember we spent hours and hours trying to think of gimmicks. The British Army was stretched around the remains of the empire, so I was charged with finding, I seem to remember, 16,000 toy soldiers, then hiring the main stage of the British Pathé and putting these soldiers out to represent the army. How could we show the evil tentacles of the Daily Mirror Media Group? I remember we had a long discussion about that. They had just opened the Daily Mirror Tower in Holborn. So we thought of getting a huge scroll of newsprint and unravel it down the side of the building. You started with the evils of media ownership and concentrations but anything abstract had to be concretised in the name of illumination. And that's my training as a journalist.

Richard Keeble: Your books very often include graphs and visuals. I guess that was partly inspired by your time on *World in Action*.

Brian Winston: Oh yes. There was no question that I was influenced in that way. But I hadn't been contaminated effectively. There was, in fact, an inherent tension which has conditioned my entire life: between this desire to lay things out for people and get their attention and leave them to their own devices – and this awareness that there would inevitably come a measure of interpretation.

Richard Keeble: As Nietzsche said: 'There are no facts. There's only interpretation.'

Brian Winston: Sure. And that stress is very difficult to live with. Stuart Hood, who finished up as the highest-placed communist in the history of the BBC thus far and who controlled BBC2, wrote somewhere the stress just got to be too much. I could see that was true of me in a lesser way. I was acutely conscious of not telling the truth in some way, but I'm not quite sure what the truth was. I was caught between those two stances: of having a view and of being a neutral journalist. There was a tension.

As you know, I was obviously involved with radical media politics. There were groups around, interestingly enough, involving people who became very famous and important like Tony Garnett. I remember we created the Free Communications Group. And one of the things the group did was to leak all of the big documents relating to the Independent Television licence fee awards. Just to cause trouble, really.

In the end I was sort of forced out. I couldn't maintain the illusion of neutrality. Why weren't we telling the truth? By which I meant why weren't we revealing everything that we knew, rather than pretending simply to be laying out the 'facts'? The tension between being a journalist and a commentator didn't go away and I became sort of unemployable.

There's a story which comes from a slightly later period when I was at the BBC, I moved from Granada to the BBC and I worked for a lovely man called Tony Smith, who was the editor of *24 Hours*. He was a very laid-back, quiet, polite gentleman who finished up as the president of Magdalen College, Oxford. I remember we were having an argument at one point and he looked at me in exasperation and said: 'I must say, Brian, my attitude to the BBC is quixotic. But your attitude, if I may say so, is bloody quixotic.'

There was clearly no space for being 'bloody quixotic' so I started scribbling. Because there were obviously scribbling opportunities around. And I walked off the job, went to work for the government! I worked for the Central Office of Information making propaganda films and, at the same time, writing incendiary pieces for the radical press. I mean, I was elected the emergency media editor of the underground newspaper, *Ink*, following the contentious publication of the *Schoolkids Edition* of the radical magazine, *Oz* – which ended up with Richard Neville and others being sent to prison – a notorious event in media history.

The edition of *Ink* had a libellous cover on it provided by Gerald Scarfe, which I ran gleefully. I then get a letter from a lawyer for Mary Whitehouse, the notorious blue-stocking, who is seen fornicating with Rupert Bear on the cover, saying that she was going to sue. And of course, in those halcyon days, you couldn't sue for cartoons. So it was quite an interesting time. I'm in this weird position whereby on the one hand, I've got a bevy of indigenous beauties whom I'm wandering around Welsh tin mines with, recording upbeat pieces to cameras about the wonders of Britain for the Central Office of Information. On the other hand, I'm producing libellous pieces for radical mags. I'm a confused bear, obviously.

First Move into the Academy

Richard Keeble: Your first move into the academy was somewhere obscure in Oxfordshire. How did how did that come about?

Brian Winston: Well, friends and I knew John Tilley. He was an American without a trace of an American accent and he was very very wealthy. He had a huge house in remotest Oxfordshire, which he decided to convert into a school. So in 1971, I become media course director at Alvescot College. As a teacher I began to put my ideas into writing. It seemed to me that there was a serious misunderstanding of the nature of technological media change – which was absolutely central to the political agenda. If it's making an argument about the inevitability of the technological advances of capital, about the unstoppable movement of technological developments, et cetera, this is all obviously extremely ideological. I didn't quite see it that clearly at that point. My only thought was to look at the history of the development of the technology as a way, of course, of casting doubt on the conventional histories. That is really where the first book comes from: I was saying that the nature of technological change is not as you think it is. The history is not the progress of great men or, obviously, great women. It's not unstoppable. It's conditioned not by the needs of society as a whole, but by the needs of the industry exploiting the media. I emerge eventually with a revisionist history of media technology which is designed to dispute, at a fundamental level, the validity of technological determinism. None of the people credited with the invention of these devices actually did anything of the kind. Virtually none of them were 'invented'. They were all just knocking around one way or another. And secondly, chaps were seeking to establish markets and they were looking for opportunities which were conditioned by the market. Those were the essential ideas I was exploring in my first 'Dangling Conversations' books.

Richard Keeble: Let's talk about your work with the Glasgow University Media Group.

Brian Winston: In 1974, I was appointed research director of the Glasgow University Media Group under Professor John Eldridge – and became particularly concerned with the political implications of the news and its ideological underpinnings. An opportunity presented itself to explore this at a scale that had never been attempted before. Curiously, Richard, this was determined technologically by the introduction of home video recording. Now you could record the news and you didn't have to take the journalists' word for it. You could say there were other accounts available. We got a huge sum of money from the Social Science Research Council to study television coverage of industrial relations – in effect, the misrepresentation of trade unions.

Richard Keeble: Looking at *Bad News* and *More Bad News*, which the group produced, each chapter doesn't have the name of the writer because I presume they were all written collaboratively. How did you manage that?

Brian Winston: I think it happened more or less by happenstance. We tended to write things from our own perspective and brought them together. So it was a collaborative work from that point of view. There were people who were primarily involved in coding and getting down 'the facts' as it were that we could work with. And then they could be processed either by me and others who understood how you put them together in news stories. Jean Oddie, the wife of the comedian Bill Oddie, was a sociologist, a glamorous figure who talked her way into newsrooms. They told her everything and then got very embarrassed when she wrote it all up.

Richard Keeble: Richard Hoggart's Foreword to *Bad News* is surprisingly defensive. He's essentially saying: 'OK, people in the business, we've got these critics around, don't respond over-sensitively to them. Listen to what they're saying.' So, Brian, what did you think about that and the extraordinary reaction of the BBC to your findings?

Brian Winston: Actually, none of it was surprising. Richard Hoggart was close to the sociologists who were aware that our kind of research had never been done before and that the BBC wouldn't know how to cope with it. The BBC's hysterical response was actually to attempt to destroy the reputations of all the people involved. They tried to say we were all communists – which was marginally true but ridiculous because it said nothing about the actual findings.

Richard Keeble: I remember reading the Glasgow University Media Group's books when they first came out and they were really inspirational for me because they were so different: they were saying things I believed but hadn't seen in print before. I'm sure for many other people, too, they were really inspirational. It's the depth of the study, the range, the clarity and the journalistic liveliness of the text this is so excellent.

Brian Winston: Thank you. But let me stress, the purpose of the exercise was certainly not to uncover the ideology of the news. We actually adopted in some curious way the same rhetoric of objectivity. The BBC reports this story. We had an objective analysis of the same data to get to a quite different story. So we constantly question the BBC's ability to present us with an account that is, indeed, objective. The BBC simply cannot claim political neutrality for its journalism.

Richard Keeble: Returning to your own writing on the media, Brian, tell us about your *Misunderstanding Media*.

Brian Winston: Well, after Glasgow I fled to the States and, in 1979, because it became clear to me that I had become unemployable in Britain. I became chair of the Department of Cinema Studies at New York University. In *Misunderstanding Media* (1986), I stressed that unless the social need for media change was present in the society, the technology did not develop. This illustrated the fact that histories which highlighted the eureka moments of all these great 'inventors' were complete nonsense. Instead, I wrote a history of the technology which privileged external social factors and forces encouraging or delaying the development and application of any particular technique. In this way, I presented a sort of revisionist history of media technology which hypothesises that there has to be a 'social necessity' causing the adoption of change. All this led me to posit a virtual law, if you will, which states that new technologies are introduced insofar as they serve a social purpose. So every one of these technologies has a pre-history of equipment and insight and fundamental science and all sorts of other factors.

Richard Keeble: What kind of reception did the book get?

Brian Winston: The publication was really the beginning of my reputation but, at the time, nobody took any notice of it at all. Now it has hundreds of citations and its own article in Wikipedia.

George Stoney: 'The Most Amazing Human Being I Have Encountered'

Richard Keeble: Could you talk about any other person who has deeply influenced you.

Brian Winston: Well, I was really influenced by George Stoney, who died in his 90s – still, by the way, teaching at NYU. He was the most amazing human being I have encountered. It's George who is responsible for stripping away for me all the residual notions of objectivity and providing me with a clear understanding that what we're dealing with, essentially, is ideology. He was a deeply fascinating character. His great great grandfather was a Protestant doctor on the Aran Islands of Galway in the 19th century and he had emigrated to the south of the United States, to Georgia – so George was a Southerner. I think there's an element of the Southern Baptist interventionism in George. It forges his fundamental approach, not that he was remotely religious. But he was sure as hell ready to mess with people's lives and improve their situations (as he saw them) at the drop of a hat in the name of some agenda of his own.

Becoming entangled with George was to have your life affected extremely. We all have stories of how George would fix things. And in my case, he simply decided he was going to make a movie about the Aran island where his ancestors had worked. He needed somebody to look after his class at New York University while he worked on the movie and I was, apparently, to do this. So I did it. And for the time it took him to film *Man of Aran: How the Myth was Filmed*, I taught his documentary film study class at NYU. This meant that for the next 14 years, the effect of this man on my life was immeasurable. It was amazing.

So here he is, a Southerner, a radical, an activist. And he is interested in the media insofar as they effect social change and correct the inequities of the world. He starts his career working for the Rooseveltian agency, the Farm Settlement Administration, the FSA. And his work at the FSA includes things like trying to bring agriculturalists, farmers of colour and Caucasians together to make them see their commonalities of interest. That's what he's interested in. How do you do it? Well, what have you got available? You've got bits of paper, you can produce documentation and there's this thing called film. He doesn't really care about the media as such. He's coming from an ideologically conditioned position which in some ways doesn't mesh with European assumptions about socialism. You have to understand: it's Rooseveltian. He's a Southerner dedicated to trying to find ways of making the world a better place, which includes using the media if they become viable. So he works for the FSA and he starts making little bits of film. He happens to be a very, very good old-fashioned filmmaker. So for George you have to talk about the underlying factors that are involved but not in a negative way. No Big Ideas or Marxist theory. Rather you settle on a little thing that you can actually fix. So he was proudest at the end of the day of a campaign, which included making films, to bring the salmon back to the Hudson. And he won a major award for a documentary – which was actually a training film – for *All My Babies* made in 1953 at the behest of a mid-wives' organisation in Georgia, dedicated to improving the hygiene conditions under which children of colour were being born.

When he is asked to produce another film about the Aran islands, *Man of Aran: How the Myth is Filmed*, and being in his nineties, he simply tells the filmmakers that I will write the script. Behind all of this is his career with the National Film Board of Canada just when the portable video app is being introduced which could allow for the first time a diffusion of editorial control. Previously you couldn't actually do that in practice because the technology was so complicated. Now they started sharing directorial control of radical, community-based films which coalesced into a programme at the National Film Board of Canada called *Challenge for Change/ Pour un société nouvelle*. One of the most important groups that he shares the equipment with are Indigenous filmmakers. There are also women, Bonnie Klein and others, who held out the new equipment to community groups in French-speaking Quebec.

George realises that to make things work you can't have Marxist-Leninist analysts explaining in a highfalutin fashion what is going on with the ideological creation of the media. What you need is a bunch of people whose primary function is to create 'little films' that can then be inserted into public debate on issues that matter – like people being mistreated by social services – but not as an expression of the evils of capital or whatever, but simply as a fact that if you went to the social services, you were given a hard time. George made it possible for their voice to be heard. Of course, he slowly fell out with the Canadian Film Board because giving out cameras was for them far too radical an approach.

He next decides he'd like to apply his ideas to filming in America. So George comes up with a perfectly viable scheme to implement his ideas – through the development of training opportunities. The logic of his argument would appear to have been that the exploitation of new equipment required the training of people who could enable its utilisation. This he set about doing in a programme at NYU called the Alternate Media Center. So George gets it into his head that in parallel with the Alternate Media Center, he needs to pressure the emerging cable industry into providing platforms for their subscribers to produce their own programming under the guidance of his graduates. Thus George's filming has nothing to do with truth, fiction, fact. It was about what people wanted to say. He gets into bed with the Federal Communications Commission suggesting to them they make it a requirement of their licensees who are exploiting this new platform of cable television, that they provide a channel or two free for people to programme. And it's agreed!

For many years George is not recognised for being what he was – a really key figure in the development of the media.

Meanwhile, there's a revolution going on in the making of mainstream documentaries, which he's really not interested in at all. There's a group of filmmakers at the National Film Board who are exploiting the arrival of 16mm format. That becomes a whole new school of filmmaking initially called Cinéma Verité since the French are heavily involved. But it's now also known as Direct Cinema.

What do I take away from my time with George? Well, it seems to me that what you're dealing with are fundamental assumptions about how change occurs and what you need to understand to make change happen. Now it occurs to me that you have to understand the underlying ideological underpinnings but at the same time *the only thing that matters is how is this going to work?*

Political Economy – and Salmon in the Hudson

Richard Keeble: So your notion of ideology emerges from a notion of the political economy, essentially?

Brian Winston: Yes, it does. But that kind of rhetoric can be obscuring because it's too broad and cannot be translated into effective interventions. The political economy approach is not going to bring salmon back to the Hudson, right?

Richard Keeble: Tell us about your winning the Emmy in 1985 for scripting episodes of the WNET series, *Civilization and the Jews*.

Brian Winston: At the time I'm still working, as is George, at NYU and I'm a pretty traditional filmmaker. And I win an Emmy for an absolutely classically-organised. historical documentary predicated on the business of: 'let's explain something that isn't properly explained'. So it's journalism essentially. It doesn't explain why the Nazis were the Nazis. It doesn't get into any of the socio-economic circumstances that cause the rise of fascism. Rather, it intervenes in the historical argument about the nature of the Holocaust. Was it planned or was it an accident? There are two historical schools. The dominant school believes it was all planned. I am interested in the other view – promoted by the historian, Professor Yehuda Bauer, who says the Holocaust was an accident, an opportunity, a masturbatory fantasy of the fascists that they could murder all the Jews. They had spoken about wanting to murder all the Jews for decades but they didn't think they could accomplish it necessarily. Then the circumstances of the war were sufficiently confused to allow for this opportunity to be exploited. So we made a film for popular consumption which simply presented another point of view of that history.

Richard Keeble: You are developing all the time your knowledge of high theory, right?

Brian Winston: Sure: the film studies department at NYU is a bastion of high theory and the appointment of a grubby television producer such as me is seen as complete anathema. Indeed, I become the head of cinema studies at NYU having produced a couple of books, but nothing really very serious. While doing this job, I actually do catch up with a lot of high theory. For instance, Peter Wollen shows up for a semester and gives the students a series of talks on the importance of semiotics in film studies. I just sit in on the process. So I have this sort of very privileged, idiosyncratic introduction to high theory which, of course, then starts to condition what I'm working on, especially given the context of George Stoney's practical approach.

Subsequently, I become dean at Pennsylvania State University and although I continue to write, building the largest communications unit in an American university distracts me. Also I now have American children so we decide to come back to Britain. And in 1992 I get a job as Director of Journalism Studies at Cardiff University. I remember the professors at the other two major journalism schools at that time, Hugh Stephenson, at City University, London, and Peter Cole, at Sheffield, sent me a letter saying: 'Welcome to this infamous club of journalism professors.' From Cardiff I go to Westminster where I wasn't particularly happy: it was just a complex situation and very bureaucratic.

Then I got this job at Lincoln which gave me the freedom to explore the general processes of information – to try to understand them in general terms but still grounded, as it were, in practicalities. So my work increasingly became a critique of the simple-minded approach to the idea of impact of media and the influence that it has. People have a view of the impact of technology – media technology – which is monolithic and doesn't acknowledge the fact that different people respond to messages in different ways. This was a level of sophistication which had previously escaped me.

Richard Keeble: When you came to Lincoln in 2002 it was very low in the league tables. What were your thoughts on joining such a new, young university?

Lincoln: The Opportunity to Build a 'University of Distinction'

Brian Winston: The fact that the institution is brand new is of no concern to me whatsoever. It's an opportunity to build something, right? Which brings me back to the story I told you about when I was a supply teacher: I'm still concerned to help the Blue students join the White students.

I was also lucky to work alongside the founding Vice-Chancellor, David Chiddick. He was a town planner by trade and had been a deputy vice-chancellor at Leicester. He really was something of a genius in terms of his own discipline. I can remember reading his first mission statement for the university (of Lincolnshire and Humberside, as it was then) – and it was that it become the university of just Lincoln. I remember David saying: 'Look, it's simple. If you do a study of the population and you ask people "What do you think about the University of Lincolnshire and Humberside?" they don't have a clue what you're talking about. They all do believe there is already a University of Lincoln.' Obviously, it was like falling off a log to rename it. So he re-named it and in 2002 the mission statement says: 'Our ambition is to be a university of distinction in five years.' Again, I remember a conversation with him when I said: 'Surely you jest?' He looked at me and replied: 'OK, ten years!' I was really impressed by that. I thought here was a 'can-do guy' whose heart was in the right place as regards broadening educational opportunity. It was a sort of marriage made in heaven. After all, I'm hopeless with bureaucracy. I'm noisy and I've got a terrible temper: I'm constantly breaking eggs left, right and centre in order to make an omelette. And we have a very large media enterprise. David gives me my head and I think I made 14 new appointments quite quickly (including you, Richard, as Professor of Journalism) so we're rolling.

Richard Keeble: In 2007, David Chiddick bestowed on you the highest academic honour at the university making you The Lincoln Professor. What did you feel about that?

Brian Winston: Well, I got into real trouble both bureaucratically and in various other ways, and was given the title by David as a sort of consolation prize. Nobody quite knows what it means but I'm very pleased. I'm happy to be The Lincoln Professor.

Richard Keeble: In what ways have your writings and thinking evolved since the appointment?

Brian Winston: In recent years I have finally come to understanding that my journalistic/more theoretical mode could not co-exist. I have primarily been thinking about the media's impact and our failure to understand how the media actually work. People too often see direct causation when, in fact, causation operates very indirectly. So my work over the last decade or so has been to rewrite the history of the communications industry in terms of fundamentals. Take the Facebook nonsense. Currently, I cannot believe the situation we're in: millions of words about Facebook and freedom of expression. But it's simple: Zuckerberg's a publisher and we've known what to do with publishers for five centuries. If he publishes it, then he's responsible for it. You know, there's a 237-word section in the current telecommunications legislation in America, which says, by the way, these new platforms are not publishers. Bullshit, of course, they are publishers and they should be regarded by the law as such. All this endless argument about the infringement of his freedom or whatever. It's got nothing to do with it. He's a publisher, right? And he should be bound by the rules relating to publishers throughout the history of print. What with Zuckerberg and these fellows regarding themselves as being above the law and setting up their own commissions: it's all absolute nonsense in terms of the history that I have been looking at for 40 or 50 years. The bottom line is that we are talking about publishing. We know about that: we have been doing it for half a millennium. I am simply uninterested in spurious debates about freedom of expression etc. There is no such thing as free speech. There is only free speech under the law and we have spent the last half century ignoring that simple truth at our peril. I see no reason for a debate about freedom of expression. Close it down. Subject it to our traditions of publishing.

Richard Keeble: I see that in recent years you've been working very collaboratively with a number of folk – for instance, your Chinese PhD student Wang Chi, Gail Vanstone, of York University, Toronto, and your son, Matthew. It's clearly a deliberate move on your part.

Brian Winston: You get to a point in life, I think, when if you have established any sort of reputation with publishers that gives you an advantage in terms of producing books, you are sort of duty-bound to share that. Also, you don't know everything. I knew nothing about feminism. I've had to learn about feminism from Gail. I mean, look at who I am and what my social background is. I have areas to catch up on. The notion of the universality of media is obviously something that I need to deal with and cannot very easily write about it. My son, Matthew, for instance, having worked on the gonzo journalist, Hunter S. Thompson, for his PhD at Cardiff, was aware of the critiques of objectivity and so provided crucial input into the theoretical chapters in the 'fake news' book we wrote together.

On Living in a World of Uncertainty

Richard Keeble: So Brian, you have collaborated with your Chinese student for your book *The Act of Documenting* (2017). But some academics refuse to work in China given their appalling record on human rights. How do you respond to that line?

Brian Winston: Well, first of all, I'm not knee-jerk about any of that stuff. Because it seems to me that forcing people into isolation is not an unmitigated good. On the contrary, my sense is that people need support but this can lead you into awkward political situations on the ground. For instance, I am an anti-Zionist. I was brought up in a Zionist family. I am interested in the Middle East in some detail and I've written about it, obviously. But I've been firmly an anti-Zionist ever since the election of the right-wing Likud. Still, I'm an optimist. Israel was founded as a socialist state and the Socialist Party – with Ben-Gurion, Golda Meir, all those people – was originally running the country. OK, they behaved at times very badly the way colonial powers behave, but they weren't themselves ideologically capitalists; they were compromise capitalists. The right-wing were always marginalised. Now they've been in charge for 40 years. Would I want to be supportive of them? No chance. But I am still close to a number of very fine Israeli scholars and filmmakers who need support.

Richard Keeble: You wouldn't boycott Israel even though you don't support the Israeli state. You're saying the same thing applies to China.

Brian Winston: Yes, but you still all the time have to make political judgements. For instance, you could get to the point where if you get off the plane, they're going to arrest you, and that's a situation that could well exist in countries like China. I've worried endlessly about teaching documentary in summer schools to young Chinese students because if they take notice of what I'm saying they could put themselves in danger. I'm constantly grappling with those sorts of issues. But the people who are boycotting Israel, worrying about the naked aggressions against the Palestinians, live in a black and white world. I suppose if you want to summarise what I've been saying from the outset it's this: I live in a world in which complex issues need to be disinterred, evaluated and carefully considered. And that's quite hard to do at the moment. If I went to China I could well be in personal danger. I remember the police knocked us out of a series of independent documentary festivals one night in 2012 at 11 o'clock. The only time in my life I'm confronted by three policemen – at 3am. What are you doing here? they ask. And they continue to ask me questions. The following morning a young lady at the British Embassy, in tears, rings me, asks if I was arrested and when I say not tells me to forget it. The bottom line is that people are always doing things you don't expect. I don't live in a black and white world: I live in a universe of complete uncertainty and always have.

Appendix 2

Professor Brian Winston: The Range and Depth of his Academic Achievements

Academic Roles

1971-72	Media Course Director, Alvescot College, Alvescot, Oxfordshire
1972-73	Video Course Director, Department of Film, Theatre and Television, Bradford College of Art, Bradford
1973-79	Head of General Studies Department, National Film School of Great Britain, Beaconsfield, Buckinghamshire
1974-76	Research Director, Media Project, Department of Sociology, University of Glasgow, Glasgow (concurrent with National Film School appointment) (SSRC funded)
1976-77	Visiting Adjunct Professor, Undergraduate Film and Television Department, School of the Arts, New York University, New York, USA (on leave from National Film School).
1979-86	Professor, Undergraduate Film and Television, Professor and Chair, Department of Cinema Studies, Tisch School of the Arts, New York University, New York, USA
1986-92	Dean, College of Communications, Pennsylvania State University, University Park, PA
1992-97	Director, Centre for Journalism Studies, Head of Mass Communications, University of Wales College of Cardiff
1997-2002	Head of School of Communication, Design and Media, University of Westminster
2002-2005	Dean, Faculty of Media and Humanities, University of Lincoln
2005-2007	Pro-Vice Chancellor, University of Lincoln
2007-	The Lincoln Professor, University of Lincoln

2013-2017 Visiting Professor, Beijing Normal University; Research Fellow, Academy for International Communication of Chinese Culture

2017-2019 Visiting Professor, North-East Normal University, Changchun

2017-2019 Visiting Professor of Media, Technology and Society, Digital Cultures Research Centre, University of the West of England, Bristol

Published Papers, Refereed Papers and Review Articles

1975 Intervention, *L'Attualità in TV/ News and Current Events on TV*, XXVII Prix Italia, Turin: Edizioni RAI

1977 How visual is television news?, *Journalism Studies Review*, Vol. 1, No. 2, Cardiff: Centre for Journalism Studies, Cardiff College, University of Wales

1980 Disingenuousness and television news reports, *The Journal of the National Academy of Television Arts and Sciences*, New York: NATAS, Vol. XVII, No.1, Spring

1981 Review article: *Future Developments Telecommunications. The Wired Society and Communication Satellite Systems*, by James Martin, *Journal of Broadcasting*, Vol, 25, No. 1 Winter

1983 The interview as an unnatural act, *The Independent*, New York: Foundation for Independent Video and Film, Vol. 6, No. 3 March

1983 Play it again, Sam (article on American TV) for special edition of *The Literary Review* in connection with New York Art Exhibit 'Brand New York' at the Institute of Contemporary Arts, London, October/November

1984 What took so long? – Re-examining the technical history of television, *Intermedia*, London, International Institute of Communications, Autumn

1985 Review article: *Visible Fictions*, by John Ellis, *Quarterly Review of Film Studies*, Los Angeles, University of Southern California

1985 A whole technology of dyeing – Ideology and technology in the development of colour film, *Daedalus*, Boston, The American Academy of Arts and Sciences, Vol. 114, No. 4, Fall

1986 Survival of national networks in an age of abundance, *Intermedia*, London, International Institute of Communications, Vol. 4, No. 6 p. 30

1987 A mirror for Brunelleschi, *Daedalus*, Boston, The American Academy of Arts and Sciences, Summer, Vol. 116, No. 3

1989 HDTV in Hollywood: Lights, camera, inaction, *Gannett Centre Journal*, New York, Columbia University, Summer

1990 Review article: *News in the Regions: Plymouth Sound to Moray Firth*, by Alistair Hetherington, *Journalism Quarterly*, Vol. 67, Vol. 2, Fall

1990 Rejecting the Jehovah's Witness gambit, *Intermedia*, International Institute of Communications, London, October/November

1993 Review article: *Contested Culture*, by Jane Gaines, *Journal of Media Law*, Vol. 14, No. 2

1993 Review article: *Future Visions*, Tanya Wollen (ed.), *Journal of Media Law*, Vol. 14, No. 3.

1994 Review article: *Ethical Issues in Journalism and the Media*, Ruth Chadwick and Andrew Belsey (eds) *Journal of Media Law*, Vol. 15, No.2

1994 Review article: *New Vocabularies in Film Semiotics*, by Robert Burgoyne et al., *Textual Practice*, Vol. 8, No. 3, Winter

1994 The licence fee, stupid!: The BBC's Charter renewal, *Media Information Australia*, No. 74, November

1996 Myth of the internet (with Paul Walton), *Index on Censorship*, Vol. 25, No. 168, January

1996 There's no such thing as cheap speech, *The Communications Review*, Vol. 1, No. 3

1997 Review article: *Fractal Dreams: New Media in Social Context,* Jon Dovey (ed.) *European Journal of Communication*, Vol. 12, No. 1

1997 The journalist's perspective, *Health Scares: Conflicting Agendas,* School of Postgraduate Studies in Medical and Health Care, University of Wales, Swansea, May

1998 The camera never lies: The partiality of photographic evidence, *TMG, Tijdschrift Voor Mediageschiedenis*, Netherlands Association for Sound and Image

1998 Review article: *Parchment, Printing, and Hypermedia* , by Ronald Deibert, *European Journal of Communication*, Summer, Vol 13

1999 Lying in public: British television regulators invent a new offence, *Screening the Past* (refereed electronic journal), Australia, La Trobe University (November)

2001 Documentary: How the myth was deconstructed, *Wide Angle*, Vol. 21, No. 2

2002 Towards tabloidization?: Glasgow revisited 1975-2001, *Journalism Studies*, Vol. 3, No.1

2002 Review article: *John Grierson: Life, Contributions, Influence,* by Jack C. Ellis, *Journal of Visual Anthropology*

2008 Contributions to *International Journal of Communications,* University of Southern California

2008 Hula hoop or contraceptive pill?: The social impact of technology, *Navigationen – Internet: öffienlichtkeit(en) im umbruch,* Vol. 2 pp 1,619-1,641

2009 Let them eat laptops, *International Journal of Communications* (e-journal)

2009 *Messages* Round-Table (with Adrian Bingham, Megan Mullen, Stephen J. A. Ward), *Media History,* Vol. 15, No. 1

2009 The subject and the indexicality of the photograph (with Hing Tsang), *Semiotica*

2009 A riddle wrapped in a mystery inside an enigma: Wiseman and public television, *Studies in Documentary Film,* Vol. 3, No. 2. Winter

2012 Editor, *fusion,* Lincoln, Charles Sturt and New South Wales Universities (e-journal)

2014 Current debates: The Griersonian tradition post-war – Decline or transition? *British Journal of Film and Television,* Vol 11, No. 1

2014 A handshake or a kiss: The legacy of George Stoney (1916-2012), *Film Quarterly,* Vol. 67, No. 3 pp 35-49

2014 The greatest documentaries of all time: *The Sight and Sound* 2014 poll, *Studies in Documentary Film,* Vol. 8, No. 3 pp 267-272

2015 An English approach to national identity and cultural image discourse system: From Shakespeare to the 20th century, *International Communication of Chinese Culture,* March

2015 The documentary script as an oxymoron, *Journal of Screenwriting,* September

2016 Time for a cover-up, *British Journalism Review,* Vol. 27, No. 2

2016 Pumping in oxygen, *British Journalism Review,* Vol. 27, No. 4

2018 *Review* article: *The Conscience of Cinema: The Works of Joris Ivens 1912-1989,* by Thomas Waugh, Amsterdam University Press, 2016, *Studies in Documentary Film,* Vol. 12, No. 1

2018 'Le rapport de face à face' in digital documentary, *Post Script,* Vol. 36, Nos 2 and 3

2020 The danger of state subsidy, *British Journalism Review,* Vol. 28, No. 1 (with Matthew Winston)

Chapters in Books

1973 The end of the book, *Education Without Schools*, Buckman, P. (ed.) London: Souvenir

1983 On counting the wrong things, Mosco, Vincent and Wasko, Janet (eds) *Critical Communications Review: Vol. I*, Norwood, N. J.: Ablex

1986 Escapist realism, Brown, Les and Walker, Savannah Waring (eds) *Fast Forward: The New Television and American Society*, Kansas City: Andrews & McMeel

1988 The tradition of the victim in Griersonian documentary, *Image Ethics*, Gross, Larry, Katz, John and Ruby, Jay (eds) New York: Oxford University Press

1988 Great artist or fly on the wall, *Visual Exploration of the World*, Ruby, Jay and Taureg, Martin (eds) Aachen: Rader Verlag

1988 Documentary: I think we are in trouble, *New Challenges for Documentary*, Rosenthal, Alan (ed.) Berkeley: University of California Press

1988 Direct cinema: The third decade, *New Challenges for Documentary*, Rosenthal, Alan (ed.) Berkeley: University of California Press

1988 The fault in ourselves, *Communications Research: The Challenge of the Information Age*, Sharp, Nancy Weatherly (ed.) Syracuse, N.Y.: Syracuse University Press

1989 What information revolution?, *Perspectives on Culture and Society*, Gibby, Patricia Martin (ed.) Muncie: Ball State University

1989 Marshall McLuhan, *Encyclopaedia of Communications*, Barnouw, Eric (ed.) Oxford University Press, New York

1990 How media are born, *Questioning the Media*, Downing, John et al. (eds) Newbury Park, California: Sage; reprinted, second edition, 1995

1993 HTDV in Hollywood: Lights, camera, inaction, *Demystifying Media Technology*, Everette, Dennis and Pavlik, John (eds) Mountain View, California: Mayfield

1993 Documentary film as scientific inscription, *Theorizing Documentary*, Renov, Michael (ed.) New York: Routledge/American Film Institute

1993 The CBS Evening News, April 7, 1949, *Getting the Message*, Eldridge, J. E. T. (ed.) London: Routledge

1994 Public service broadcasting, *Behind the Screen*, Hood, Stuart (ed.) London: Lawrence & Wishart

1995 Tyrell's Owl: The limits of the technological imagination in an epoch of hyperbolic discourse, *Theorizing Culture*, Adams, Barbara and Allan, Stuart (eds), London: University College London Press

1996 Jean Rouch, *Oxford History of the Cinema*, Nowell-Smith, Geoffrey (ed.) Oxford: Oxford University Press

1998 Tony Garnett, *Encyclopaedia of Television*, Newcombe, Horace (ed.) Chicago: Fitzroy Dearborn

1998 The camera never lies: The partiality of photographic evidence, *Image-Based Research: A Sourcebook for Qualitative Researchers*, Prosser, John (ed.) Falmer: Psychology Press

1998 Not a lot of laughs: Documentary as a popular form, *Dissident Voices, Moving Lives: Television Culture and Political Change*, Wayne, Mike (ed.) London: Pluto Press

1998 Theatrical and television documentary: The sound of one hand clapping, *Cinema Futures: Cain, Abel or Cable?: The Screen Arts in the Digital Age*, Elsaesser, Thomas and Hoffmann, Kay (eds) Amsterdam, University of Amsterdam Press

1999 Honest, straightforward re-enactment, *Joris Ivens and the Documentary Context*, Bakker, Kees (ed.) Amsterdam: Amsterdam University Press

2000 Triumph of the will, *Movies as History*, Ellwood, David W. (ed.) London: Sutton Publishing

2000 Breakages limited, *Electronic Media and Technoculture*, Caldwell, John Thornton (ed.) New Brunswick, New Jersey: Rutgers University Press

2000 Making Connections: The ECHR, the ITC and the documentary, *From Grierson to the Docusoap: Breaking Boundaries*, Izod, John and Kilborn, Richard (eds) Luton: University of Luton Press

2001 Smell the tulips: The internet, neoliberalism and millenarian hype, *Access Denied in the Information Age*, Lax, Stephen (ed.) London: Palgrave Macmillan

2001 The coming of 16mm sound film, *Weltwunder der Kinematographie*, Polzer, Jochim (ed.) Potsdam: Polzer Media Group

2002 Media technology, *International Dictionary of Social & Behavioral Sciences Section*, Schudson, Michael (ed.) Amsterdam: Pergamon

2002 Technical history of television, *The Television History Book*, Hilmes, Michele (ed.) London: BFI

2003 Paying the piper: The realist film in the service of the British State and a little touch of Harry in the night: British documentary film in World War II, *Kulturfilm*, Zimmermann, Peter (ed.) Konstanz: UVK Medien

2006 North American documentary in the 1960s, *Contemporary American Cinema*, Williams, Linda and Hammond, Michael (eds) Maidenhead, Berkshire: Open University Press

2007 Rouch's 'Second Legacy': *Chronique d'un été* as reality TV's totemic, *Building Bridges: The Cinema of Jean Rouch*, Brink, Joram ten (ed.) London: Wallflower

2008 Freedom of communication, *The Blackwell International Encyclopaedia of Communication*, Donsbach, Wolfgang (ed.) Massachusetts: Wiley-Blackwell

2009 English roots of the free press, *The Encyclopaedia of Journalism*, Sterling, Christopher H. (ed.) Los Angeles: Sage

2010 Combating 'a message without a code': Writing the 'history' documentary, *Televising History: The Pasts on the Small Screen*, Bell, Erin and Gray, Ann (eds) Basingstoke: Palgrave Macmillan

2011 Documentary, *The Routledge Companion to Film History*, Guynn, William (ed.) Abingdon: Routledge

2012 Theory for practice, *Critical Cinema*, Myer, Clive (ed.) London: Wallflower

2012 'Ça va de soi': The visual representation of violence in the holocaust documentary, *Killer Images: Documentary Film, Memory and the Performance of Violence*, Brink, Joram ten and Oppenheimer, Joshua (eds) New York: Wallflower/Columbia University Press

2012 Foreword, *Rewind: British Artists' Video in the 1970s & 1980s*, Cubitt, Sean and Partridge, Stephen (eds) New Barnet, Hertfordshire: John Libbey

2014 The conventions of the BBC, *Is the BBC in Crisis?*, Mair, John, Tait, Richard and Keeble, Richard Lance (eds) Bury St Edmunds: Abramis

2014 To play a role that was in fact his (her) own, *The Grierson Effect*, Williams, Deane and Druick, Zoë (eds) London: British Film Institute/Palgrave Macmillan

2014 Foreword, *Documentary in Changing State*, MacKeogh, Carol and O'Connell, Diog (eds) Cork: Cork University Press

2015 Peirce's better triad, *A Critique of Judgment in Film and Television*, Panse, Silke and Rothermel, Dennis (eds) London: Palgrave

2015 Surveillance in the service of narrative, *Blackwell Companion to Contemporary Documentary*, Lebow, Alisa and Jahusz, Alex (eds) Boston: Blackwell

2015 Impact of new media: A corrective, *Communication and Technology*, Cantoni, Lorenzo and Danowski, James A. (eds) Berlin: De Gruyter

2015 No broadcaster is an island, *The BBC Today: Future Uncertain*, Mair, John, Tait, Richard and Keeble, Richard Lance (eds) Bury St Edmunds: Abramis

Keynotes and Presentations

Manchester University, Florence, Italy, Edinburgh Television Festival, Edinburgh, UK, British Film Institute, London, Los Angeles, USA., Annenberg School of Communications East, University of Pennsylvania, USA, Society of Cinema Studies, University of Wisconsin, Madison, USA, National Humanities Centre, University of North Carolina at Chapel Hill, Rockefeller University, New York, Annenberg School of Communications East, University of Pennsylvania, Philadelphia, International Institute of Communications, annual meeting, Edinburgh, Ball State University, Muncie, Indiana, Northeastern University, Boston, University of Strathclyde, Glasgow, the Capital College, Harrisburg, Pennsylvania, Columbia University, New York, Minneapolis College of Art and Design, Minneapolis, Marywood College, Scranton, Pennsylvania, The Society of Professional Journalists, Pittsburgh, Whitney Museum, New York, Dublin, Eire, Economics Club of Greater Orlando, Florida, Ohio University Film Conference, Society of Cinema Studies.

University of Southern California, Los Angeles, British Film Institute, London, International Symposium on Film, Television and Video, Fu Jen Catholic University, Tapie, Taiwan, Université Robert Schuman, Strasbourg, Institute of Contemporary Arts, London, North Carolina, The Hague, Netherlands, Universities Film and Video Council, London, International Animation Festival, Cardiff, University of Southern California, Los Angeles, Centre for Journalism Studies, College of Cardiff, University of Wales, Cardiff, University of the West of England/Brunel University, Australian National University, Canberra, Film Festival, Sheffield, Harvard University, Boston, Media Education Forum For Wales, Coleg Glan Hafran, Cardiff, Stuttgart, Germany, Yvyskaala University, Yvyskaala, Finland, Prix Italia Seminar, Naples, Italy, University of Auckland, NZ, Stockholm University, Sweden, University of Trondheim, Norway, Film History Symposium, Netherlands Filmmuseum, Amsterdam, Intercultural Institute of Timisoara, Baine Herculane, Romania, Nottingham, Southampton Institute, Association for Journalism Education, City University, London, International Documentary Film Festival, Amsterdam, Joris Ivens Foundation, Nijmegen, Netherlands, Sterling University, All Party Parliamentary Parenting Group, Westminster, American Association for History and Computing, Baylor University, Texas.

Danish Film Institute, Copenhagen, University of Bergen, University of Utrecht, Imperial College of Science, London, Haus des Dukumentarfilms, Berlin, Saõ

Paolo Film Festival, Vienna, University of Gottingen, São Paulo, Brazil, University of the Algarve, Faro, ASJMC International Conference, London, Byron Bay, NSW, Australia, University of Luton, University of Udine, Italy, Reuters Institute, University of Oxford, Birkbeck College, University of London, University of Westminster, Netherlands Institute for Sound and Vision, Hilversum, University of East London, Jerusalem Film Festival, New York University, Hong Kong Baptist University, University of the West of England, Cody International Center, St Francis Xavier University, Nova Scotia, Canada, University College London, Independent Documentary Film Festival, Beijing, University of Lund, Queen's University, Belfast, University of Melbourne, MECCSA, University of Ulster, Derry, University of Lund, Sweden, Huston Film School, University of Ireland, Galway, University of Stockholm, Yamagata International Film Festival, University of Ulster, Derry, University College, London, Tel Aviv University, CUNY, New York, American University, Washington, Nehru University, New Delhi, Charles University, Prague, Ryerson and University of Toronto, University of Glasgow, Chengdu University, Beijing Film Academy, University of Haifa

Honours and Awards

1974 Recipient (with Department of Sociology, University of Glasgow), Social Science Research Council major grant to investigate 'Television Coverage of Industrial Relations'

1985 Recipient, US National Emmy – 'Outstanding Individual Achievement, writing for an information series' for Episode 8 of *Heritage*

1985 Recipient, US Christopher Award for *Heritage* script

1986 Recipient, the Joss Award, Communications Institute, Hebrew University, Jerusalem

1986 Recipient, New York State Council on the Arts grant to prepare report 'Brunelleschi's Mirror: Art & Technology' (with Whitney Museum, Department of Film & Video)

1999 Recipient, Best Book of 1998: *Media Technology and Society: A History from the Telegraph to the Internet*, American Association for History and Computing

2012 Recipient, Special Jury Award, Learning on Screen Awards: *A Boatload of Wild Irishmen*, British University Film and Video Council

2014 Recipient, Special Award for 'increasing understanding of human rights': International Press Institute (Vienna) Book Awards

2014 Short-Listed: *The Documentary Film Book*, Kraszna-Krausz Book Awards

Index

Alvescot College 169

American Society of Newspaper Editors 13

Andrew, Dudley 39, 40, 50

Atget, Jean-Eugène-Auguste 40-43, 50

Audience engagement 19, 65-74

BBC 4, 6, 7, 11, 58, 105, 107, 120, 131, 132, 133, 136, 137, 138, 158, 161, 166, 168, 170, 171, 181, 185, 186

Brexit Referendum 2016 21, 125, 130-132, 134, 135, 136, 147

British Journalism Review 4, 21, 109, 126, 182

Broadcasting Code 104, 108

Cahiers du Cinéma 39

Charlie Hebdo 20, 110-144

Chi, Wang 16, 19, 23, 37, 74, 177

Chiddick, David 1-2, 22n, 23, 175-176

Christians, Clifford 19-20, 77-93, 114, 119

Cinéma Vérité 11, 28, 173

Cohen-Almagor, Raphael 20-21, 110-122

Cole, Peter 175

Communications Act 2003 13, 96, 104, 105, 106

Communist/s 166, 168, 170

Conboy, Martin 22, 139-150

Conservative Party/Conservatives 21, 125, 133, 134, 135, 136, 137

Conspiracy documentary 19, 52-64

Critical inquiry 20, 84-87, 89, 90n

Cummings, Dominic 21, 130, 131, 132, 136, 153

Daily Express 143, 167

Daily Mail 145, 148

Daily Mirror 147, 148

Daily Star 147

Daily Telegraph 142-143

Danish cartoons see *Jyllands-Posten*

Dawkins, Richard 129, 136

Direct Cinema 11, 13, 27, 28, 173, 183

Documentary audiences 65, 66-74

'Double spin' 21, 125, 126, 127, 130, 131, 135

Dworkin, Ronald 110, 111, 120

Eldridge, John 170

Elizabethan 165

Enlightenment 54, 80, 86, 90n, 92, 94, 95, 158

Epistemology 17, 52, 54, 81, 85

Ethics 12, 18, 19, 21-22, 27, 28, 35, 63, 65, 69, 74, 77, 82, 89, 91, 93, 119, 122, 151, 157, 159, 160, 161, 162, 183

European Union (EU) 21, 22, 125, 130, 131, 132, 133, 134, 135, 136, 137, 139-150, 153

'Fake news' 18, 21, 23, 52, 64, 125-138, 177

Financial Times 132, 137

Frankfurt School 85, 90n

Free Communications Group 168

Free speech 15, 101, 110, 114, 116, 118, 119, 120, 121, 151, 153, 177

Fukuyama, Francis 128-129, 136, 139, 150

Gaber, Ivor 21, 109, 125-138

General Election 2019, UK 21, 125, 131, 132, 136

Glasgow University Media Group (GUMG) 5, 6-8, 22n, 23n, 170-171

Granada 4, 126, 166, 168

Grierson, John 11, 12, 13, 23, 28, 31, 51, 53, 162, 182, 183, 184, 185

Guardian 10, 15, 108, 132, 136, 138, 146, 148, 150, 161

Guardian Journal, Nottingham 17

Habermas, Jürgen 20, 85-86, 89, 90n, 91

Hate speech 86, 153, 157, 160, 161

Hewat, Tim 167

Hill, Annette 19, 65-74

Hoggart, Richard 170

Hood, Stuart 168, 183

Horkheimer, Max 85, 86, 90n, 92

i 146-147, 148

Ideology 13, 20, 47, 80, 86, 88, 89, 140, 142, 171, 172, 174, 180

Index on Censorship 100, 108

'Information revolution' 8, 10

Ink 169

Instrumentalism 20, 86-87, 89

Internet 4, 9, 10, 23, 38, 87, 98, 99, 100, 103, 105, 107, 120, 122, 148, 181, 182, 184, 187

Isaacson, Walter 163

Isacsson, Magnus 18, 27-37

Ivan the Terrible 165

Johnson, Boris 125, 130, 131, 133, 134, 136, 140, 142, 143, 144, 145, 147

Jyllands-Posten 15, 110, 112, 115, 120

Kracauer, Siegfried 19, 39-51

Labour Party 127, 134

Leave campaign 21, 125, 130, 131, 132, 134, 135, 142, 147, 148, 153

Marxist-Leninist 173

Menne, Jeff 39, 40, 51

Merton College 4, 164

Mill, John Stuart 18, 20, 80, 92, 94, 96-97, 108

Myth 88, 145, 150, 172, 173, 181

Naïve realism 39-51

Nash, Kate 19, 52-64

National Union of Journalists 157

News 88, 90, 104, 107, 119, 120, 121, 127, 128, 131, 132, 133, 134, 137, 138, 141, 142, 143, 145, 147, 148, 149, 150, 151, 152, 154, 157, 161, 167, 170, 171, 180, 181, 183

Ofcom (Office of Communications) 22, 94, 96, 98, 103, 104, 105, 108, 132, 137, 139

Offence 12, 16, 19, 20, 94, 97, 100, 101, 103, 104, 105, 106, 107, 108, 110, 111, 112, 113-114, 116, 119, 120, 121

Online Safety Bill 20, 94, 100, 101, 105, 107, 108

Oppenheimer, Joshua 19, 68, 69, 185

Perspectivism 20, 87-88

Petley, Julian 16, 20, 94-109

Philosophy-of-the-human 19, 77-79, 81, 84, 89

Photography 9, 12, 19, 23, 39, 40-42, 43, 45, 50, 51

Pornography 95, 99, 111

'Post-truth' 18, 21, 64, 133, 136, 138

Propaganda 90, 91, 141, 169

Remain campaign 131, 132, 142, 146, 147, 148, 149

Restorative narrative 22, 151, 159-160

Ricouer, Paul 83-84, 92

Ridicule 20, 21, 110, 111, 112, 114, 115, 117, 118, 120

Rughani, Prātap 22, 151-162

Rupert Bear 169

Rushdie, Salman 4, 14, 15, 23, 96, 97, 108, 115, 120

Saussure, Ferdinand de 9, 85

'Slow news' 157

Spin see 'Double spin'

Stephenson, Hugh 175

Stoney, George 171-174, 175, 182

'Strategic lying' 21, 125, 126, 127, 130, 131, 132, 134, 135, 137

Sun 144-145, 148

Sunday Times 2

Technology 4, 8, 9, 10, 23, 27, 46, 48, 49, 51, 54, 58, 62, 64, 86, 87, 88, 91, 92, 96, 150, 169, 171, 173, 175, 180, 182, 183, 184, 186, 187

The Act of Killing 19, 68-72, 74

The Satanic Verses 14, 15, 110, 112, 115, 120, 121

The Times 132, 145-146, 148

Tilley, John 169

Tory Party see Conservative Party

Tulloch, John 22n, 162

University of Lincoln 1, 2, 5, 12, 16, 22n, 175, 179

Usher, Frank 163

Vanstone, Gail 16, 19, 23, 36n, 65, 66, 67, 68, 73, 74, 177

Waugh, Thomas 18, 27-38. 182, 185

Whitehouse, Mary 95

Williams, Deane 19, 39-51

Winston, Brian 1-2, 3-23, 27, 35, 36, 37, 53, 64, 65, 66, 67, 68, 73, 74, 77, 89, 94, 95, 96, 97, 98, 99, 102, 105, 107, 108, 110, 111, 121, 125, 126, 162, 163-178, 179-187. *The Image of the Media* 3, 5, 23; *Bad News* 5, 6, 23, 170; *More Bad News* 5, 7, 23, 170; *Media Technology and Society* 4, 10, 23, 187; *A Boatload of Wild Irishmen* 4, 187; *A Right to Offend* 4, 14, 23, 110, 121; *Misunderstanding Media* 8, 23, 171; *Technologies of Seeing* 9, 23; *Media Technology and Society* 4, 10, 23, 187; *Lies, Damn Lies and Documentaries* 10, 11, 23, 125; *Claiming the Real II* 11, 13, 23, 64; *The Documentary Film Book* 12, 23, 28, 37, 74, 162, 187; *The Rushdie Fatwa and After* 4, 15, 23, 96, 108; *The Act of Documenting* 16, 23, 37, 65, 66, 67, 74, 177; *The Roots of Fake News* 17, 23, 64, 125; *Messages: Free Expression, Media and the West form Gutenberg to Google* 23, 95, 108, 182

Winston, Matthew 17, 21, 23, 64, 125, 177, 182

World in Action 4, 126, 166-167, 168

Zhangke, Jia 19, 39, 47-49, 50

Ingram Content Group UK Ltd.
Milton Keynes UK
UKHW021816130423
420127UK00009B/839